Contents

D1394199

Introduction

This new edition of *English Vocabulary in Use: pre-intermediate & intermediate* still retains the features that made the first edition so popular:
- The format of presentation on the left-hand page and practice on the right-hand page.
- Approaching vocabulary in a variety of ways: topics (e.g. Food), word formation (e.g. Prefixes), words and grammar (e.g. Uncountable and plural nouns), collocation and phrases (e.g. Make, do and take), functions (e.g. Apologies, excuses and thanks), concepts (e.g. Time), varieties of English (e.g. Formal and informal English), etc.
- A student-friendly Answer key, including not only correct answers to right/wrong exercises, but also possible answers for more open-ended exercises.
- Usage notes that are ideal for self-study learners.
- A complete Index at the back of the book, listing all the target words and phrases with a phonemic transcription to help you with pronunciation.

What is different about the new edition?

Colour

The first thing you will notice is that the new edition is in colour. This makes the text and the artwork more attractive, and it also makes the book easier for you to use: the different sections and headings are now clearer, and the usage notes are shown against their own colour background, so you can find them and read them more easily.

Use of the *Cambridge International Corpus*

This new edition has made extensive use of the *Cambridge International Corpus* of written and spoken English. This has been important in two ways:
- the frequency information in the *Corpus* has helped to guide the selection of words and phrases in the book and ensure that the vocabulary will be suitable for pre-intermediate and intermediate learners of English;
- example sentences are the same or similar to those in the *Corpus*. In other words, the examples show you words and phrases being used in their most typical contexts.

Collocation and phrases

The new edition concentrates even more on showing words in common collocations and phrases. For example, when you study different meanings of *see* (Unit 27), you will learn that it often appears in these phrases: *I see*, *I see what you mean*, *I'll see what (he says)*, etc. In a unit on physical appearance (Unit 48), you will meet these common collocations: *blonde hair*, *tall and slim*, *medium height*, etc.

New units

In response to suggestions from teachers and students, there are now six completely new units in the book:

Likes, preferences and interests (Unit 19)   Have and have got (Unit 25)
Frequently asked questions (Unit 20)   Leave, catch and let (Unit 28)
Common responses (Unit 21)   Global problems (Unit 88)

Many other units have been significantly revised, e.g. The place where you live (Unit 54), City life (Unit 65), Life in the country (Unit 66), In the office (Unit 72), Music (Unit 77), Computers and the Internet (Unit 81).

The usage notes are shown against a colour background and most have been placed in the left-hand margin; this makes them easier to see and read, and creates more space on the page. As a result, there are now more pictures in the new edition, more example sentences, and more new words and phrases to learn.

I very much hope you will enjoy working with this new edition of *English Vocabulary in Use: pre-intermediate and intermediate*.

Stuart Redman (London, 2002)

Using this book

Who is this book for?

English Vocabulary in Use: pre-intermediate and intermediate has been written to help learners at this level to improve their English. It has been designed for students who are studying on their own, but it can also be used by a teacher in the classroom with a group of students.

How is the book organised?

The book has 100 two-page units. The left-hand page explains the new words and phrases chosen for that unit. They are all highlighted in **bold** and most units contain approximately 25 new words or phrases. The right-hand page gives you a chance to check your understanding through a series of exercises which practise the new vocabulary.

There is an Answer key at the back of the book. This gives *correct* answers to exercises with 'right' or 'wrong' solutions, and also *possible answers* for exercises which do not have 'right' or 'wrong' solutions.

There is an Index at the back of the book. This lists all the words and phrases introduced in the book and refers you to the unit or units where these words/phrases appear. The Index also includes a phonemic transcription for most of the words, and on page 243 you are given special help with the pronunciation of approximately 200 words which present particular problems for many learners of English.

The left-hand page

This is the page that introduces the new vocabulary for each topic or area of language. First of all, the vocabulary is divided into a number of sections (A, B, C, etc.) with simple clear titles. Then, within each section, new words/phrases are explained using a number of different techniques:

1 A short definition.
   e.g. **unemployed** (= without a job); **hang on** (= wait); **feel like** (= want or desire *infml*)
   The abbreviations *fml* or *infml* tell you if a word is either 'formal' or 'informal'.

2 A short explanation.
   e.g. He **admitted** steal**ing** her money, but **denied** tak**ing** the computer (= he said 'yes' he took the money, but 'no' he didn't take the computer).

3 A synonym or opposite.
   e.g. **dreadful** (= terrible); **dirty** (*opp* clean)

4 In a situation. With some words and phrases it is easier to see their meaning when they are in context, e.g. [This is from a text about a motoring accident] '... The driver of the Mercedes was OK, but the other driver was **badly injured**, and both cars were **badly damaged**.'

5 A picture or diagram. This seems the obvious way to explain a large number of concrete nouns and verbs.

   e.g. **carrot** 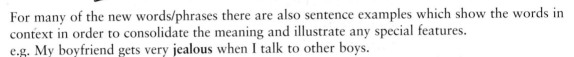   Go along here and **turn left**.

For many of the new words/phrases there are also sentence examples which show the words in context in order to consolidate the meaning and illustrate any special features.
e.g. My boyfriend gets very **jealous** when I talk to other boys.
   The plane **appeared** in the sky, then suddenly **disappeared** behind a cloud.
   Some people **can't stand** (= hate) work**ing** at the weekend. [can't stand + *-ing* form]

Finally, a big effort has been made to introduce new words alongside other words that often appear with them (this is called 'collocation').
e.g. **miss the bus; a strong accent; the car broke down; it's vitally important; fasten your seat belt; go on holiday; give someone a hand; to a certain extent; a terrible pain**, etc. There are many more examples of collocation in this new edition, and with the support of the Cambridge International Corpus you can now be sure that the examples included are some of the most important ones.

The right-hand page

This page contains the exercises to practise the new vocabulary presented on the left-hand page. In general, the first exercise practises the form of some of the new words, and then there are further exercises which focus on the meaning. In most units there is at least one exercise which gives learners a chance to think about and practise new vocabulary in relation to their own lives, and/or a task which invites learners to do something with the vocabulary outside of the book. In every unit there is a range of exercise types to help to maintain your interest.

How should I use the book?

The first four units teach you some important words and phrases, but they also give you information about vocabulary, plus ideas and techniques to help you learn vocabulary. Do these units first, then work through the book studying the units which interest you.

If you go to English lessons, you may also want to study Unit 5. This introduces vocabulary that is often used by teachers or needed by students in the classroom, e.g. *cassette recorder*, *clean the board*, *Could I borrow a pen?*, *What does that mean?*, etc.

Everything you need is in the book. The new vocabulary is explained on the left-hand page, and the exercises have an Answer key at the back of the book. But it is still important to have your own dictionary. A good bilingual dictionary will give you support in your first language, and a monolingual dictionary produced for intermediate learners will give you added practice in English. Use these to help you. (See Unit 3 for more information and ideas.)

Finally, you can visit the 'in Use' website at http://www.cambridge.org/elt/inuse/.

Good luck.

Summary of abbreviations used in the book

n	noun
v	verb
adj	adjective
opp	opposite
infml	informal word or expression
fml	formal word or expression
(U)	uncountable word
(C)	countable word
sb	somebody
sth	something

(NOT ~~I lost the bus~~)   indicates that a word or expression is wrong

Learning and revising with this book

Look at Exercise 1.1 on the next page before you read this page.

A Have a routine

A **routine** means doing certain things often and in the same way. If you are using this book for **self-study** (= to study alone), it helps to have a routine. So, **how much time can you spend** on the book each day or each week? Here are some ideas:
- if you are studying a new unit, spend **at least** (= a minimum of) half an hour or 45 minutes
- if you are **revising** (= studying a unit for a second or third time), five or ten minutes is very useful.

So, plan longer periods for new units and shorter periods for **revision**.

B Using the book

Do different things to **maintain your interest.** (= keep your interest high) For example:
1 Don't study the units in the same order as the book. **Choose** (= select) units that **interest you** (= are interesting for you).
2 When you do a unit, you can read **the whole** (= all) of the **left-hand page** (= page on the left), then **do the exercises**. Or, do the exercises first, then read the left-hand page if there is a problem.
3 Be <u>active</u> when you are learning. For example:
   - when you are reading the left-hand page, use a highlighter pen to mark new or interesting vocabulary;
   - practise **saying the words aloud** (= speaking them), so you can **pronounce them** (= say the pronunciation), and also **silently** (= without a noise) in your head to help you to remember them;
   - put new words in your own notebook using some of the ideas from Unit 2.

C Revision

It's easy to forget words that you learn, but if you revise for short periods, it helps you to remember words and make them part of your active vocabulary. Here are some ideas.

1 Do exercises in pencil. Check your answers when you finish, then **rub them out** (= remove them using a rubber). Later, come back and do the exercises again. Use the left-hand page if you have a problem.

rubber

2 When you read a left-hand page for a second time, have a **blank piece of paper** (= paper with no writing on it) with you. When you come to a new word **in bold** with a definition in (**brackets**), **cover** the definition (= put the paper over it) and try to **define** it (= give the meaning/definition).
3 Revise for short periods but do it often. **Five minutes a day** (NOT five minutes ~~per~~ day) is probably better than half an hour a week; but half an hour a week is probably better than two hours a month.
4 Be <u>active</u> when you revise, e.g. test yourself, practise the pronunciation, write down important words and phrases in your notebook with example sentences.

Exercises

1.1   **Read these questions. What do you think? (Answers are on the opposite page.)**

1 Is it better to plan regular self-study, or just study when you've got some free time?
2 Is it a good idea to study the units in the same order as they appear in the book?
3 Is it a good idea to write down new words in a notebook when you are studying a unit?
4 Is it necessary to revise vocabulary (= study it again for a second or third time)?
5 Is it better to revise vocabulary occasionally for long periods of time, or is it better to revise regularly for short periods of time?

1.2   **Find your way round the book.**

- Turn to the Topic units in the Contents on pages iv–v.
- Take a blank piece of paper and cover the right-hand side of the page with the examples.
- Read the list of unit titles, and write down your own examples – one or two for each unit.
- Are there any unit titles you don't understand? Are there any units where you can't think of examples? If so, turn to that unit and find out what it is about.

You could use similar titles in your own vocabulary notebook (see Unit 2).

1.3   **Complete the table.**

noun	verb
definition	...define...............
revision	....
pronunciation	....
choice	....
interest	....

1.4   **There is a mistake with the <u>underlined</u> words. Can you correct each one?**

1 Did you <u>make</u> all of the exercises?
2 I studied for <u>one half hour</u>.
3 Do you always read the <u>left page</u> first?
4 I <u>passed</u> twenty minutes on the first exercise.
5 I read the <u>all</u> page.

1.5   **True or False? If the sentence is false, rewrite it to make it true. Write in pencil.**

1 In this book, most of the important new vocabulary is shown in **bold** print.   True
2 Definitions/explanations of new words are often in **brackets** after the word.
3 A **routine** means doing certain things in a different way each time.
4 If you **maintain** something at a level, it means you keep it at the same level.
5 **At least** 50 people means a maximum of 50 people.
6 If you write something then **rub it out**, you remove it from the page.
7 If you do something **silently**, you do it without a noise.
8 **Revision** means studying something for the first time.
9 If you read a **whole** book, you read all of it.
10 A **blank** piece of paper is full of writing.

Check your answers. Look at any wrong answers carefully, then rub them out. Do the exercise again tomorrow.

2 Keeping a vocabulary notebook

A Organising your notebook

Give each page a title, e.g. sport, education, verbs followed by an *-ing* form, etc. When you learn new words and phrases, write them on a suitable page.

B What do I need to record?

what?	how?	example
Meaning	a translation	remember = lembrar [in Portuguese]
	b definition/explanation	A **pond** is an area of water smaller than a lake.
	c synonym or opposite	**awful** (= terrible); **ugly** (*opp* beautiful)
	d picture	**saucepan**
	e example sentence	My hands were cold, so I **put on** my **gloves**.
Pronunciation	phonemic symbols	**ache** /eɪk/
	or your own system	ache [like 'make']
Part of speech	noun (n), verb (v)	gloves (n); remember (v); careful (adj)
Grammar	make a note +	**enjoy** + *-ing* form; I **enjoy going** to parties.
	example sentence	**weather** (uncountable); We had **lovely weather** in Italy.
Common partners	phrase or sentence	**make** a **mistake**; **on the phone**; (a) **black coffee** (= coffee without milk)
Special style	make a note	**purchase** (= buy: *formal*) **kids** (= children: *informal*)

You don't need to record all of these things for every word or phrase. **The most important thing** is to show the words in typical examples. Leave space in your notebook as well, then you can come back and add more information later if you learn something new.

C Organising words on the page

Don't just write lists of individual words. Put words together that appear together, e.g. **blonde hair** (*opp* black hair), **get off the bus** (= go out of the bus). Make the pages interesting with pictures, diagrams and example sentences.

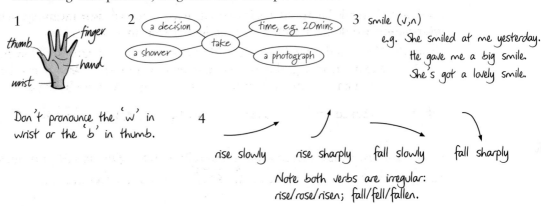

1 thumb finger hand wrist

Don't pronounce the 'w' in wrist or the 'b' in thumb.

2 a decision — take — time, e.g. 20mins
a shower — take — a photograph

3 smile (v,n)
e.g. She smiled at me yesterday.
He gave me a big smile.
She's got a lovely smile.

4 rise slowly   rise sharply   fall slowly   fall sharply
Note both verbs are irregular:
rise/rose/risen; fall/fell/fallen.

Exercises

2.1 Organise this list of words into three groups and give each one a title.

unfriendly	put on	platform	gloves	unhappy
train	get on	unable	size	jumper
wear	late	unkind	tie	passenger

Find the units in this book which may include these words. Add more to each group.

2.2 Fill the gaps with suitable words to form common partners with the nouns in bold.
1 She's _get on_ **the phone** at the moment.
2 A: Do you want milk and sugar? B: No, just a .... **coffee**, please.
3 If you're cold, why don't you ...... _were jumper_ your **coat**?
4 I don't usually .... that **mistake**.
5 She .... me a big **smile** this morning.
6 It was the third ...... _passenger_ of my **left hand**.

2.3 <u>Underline</u> the correct answer.
1 A pond is:
   a bigger than a lake   b <u>smaller than a lake</u>   c the same size
2 I really enjoy:
   a play tennis   b to play tennis   c <u>playing tennis</u>
3 When we were on holiday we had:
   a lovely weathers   b lovely weather   c <u>a lovely weather</u>
4 The underlined letters in **a<u>ch</u>e** are pronounced the same as in:
   a ma<u>ch</u>ine   b cat<u>ch</u>   c <u>ch</u>emist
5 The past tense of 'fall' is:
   a fell   b felt   c <u>falled</u>
6 You can 'get off':
   a <u>a bus</u>   b a kitchen   c a noise
7 'Rise sharply' means:

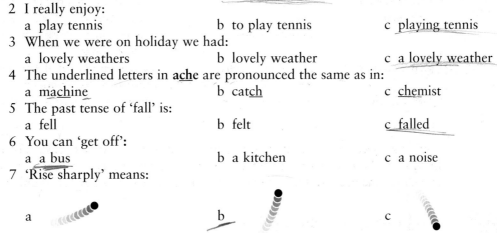

   a   b   c

8 'Purchase' is:
   a an informal word for 'buy'   b a formal word for 'buy'   c a formal word for 'child'

2.4 Look at the words below. What is the best way to record their meaning? What other information would be useful? Use a dictionary to help you.

Example You could record 'dream' with a translation, a picture (see Unit 9), or an explanation, e.g. things you imagine in your sleep. 'Dream' can be a verb or noun and is often followed by 'about', e.g. I dreamt about you.

dream	concentrate	beard	nearly	empty	rescue	knife

2.5 Write down three more nouns that often follow 'take'. Do the same for 'make' and 'do'.

take ... _a shower_ .... make _taken_ .... do _thock_ ....

3 Using a dictionary

A What dictionaries do I need?

Buy a good **bilingual** dictionary <u>and</u> a good **English–English** dictionary. The bilingual dictionary is easier for you to understand; but it's also good for you to work in English as much as possible.

large dictionaries	*medium-sized dictionaries*
Cambridge Advanced Learner's Dictionary	Cambridge Learner's Dictionary
Longman Dictionary of Contemporary English	Longman Active Study Dictionary
Oxford Advanced Learner's Dictionary	Oxford Wordpower Dictionary

B What information does a dictionary give me?

Look up a word (= find a word in a dictionary) and you will get this information.
- the meaning, e.g. **homesick** = unhappy because you are away from home for a long period
- the pronunciation (using phonemic symbols), e.g. **island** /aɪlənd/, **lose** /luːz/, **tiny** /taɪni/
- the part of speech, e.g. **dirty** *adj* (= adjective), **choose** *v* (= verb), **law** *n* (= noun)
- word grammar, e.g. **advice** (U) (= uncountable noun), **begin** (**began, begun**) (= the past tense and past participle)
- common collocations (see Unit 12), e.g. **do homework** (NOT ~~make~~); It **depends on** you (NOT ~~of~~)
- example phrases or sentences, e.g. The train leaves from **platform** seven.
- sometimes synonyms or opposites, e.g. **polite** (*syn* = **courteous**; *opp* = **impolite**)

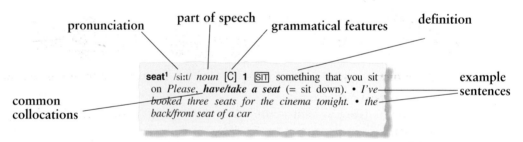

C How can I use my dictionary?

When you look up a word, put a **tick** (✓) next to it. Each time you return to a page with a tick, look at it quickly to check you remember the word.

When you see a new word or phrase in a text, first try to **guess the meaning** (= try to think of the meaning from the context), then **carry on** (= continue) reading to **see** (= find out) if your **guess** is correct. Use your dictionary to **check the meaning.** (= find out if the meaning is correct)

Don't just read definitions. The example phrases and sentences show you how a word or phrase is used, and they often help you to understand the meaning more clearly.

If you look up a word in a bilingual dictionary and get several different translations, check in a monolingual dictionary to see which translation is the best one in the context.

Remember that many words have more than one meaning. The first meaning in the dictionary is not always the one you want. Read through the different meanings.

Exercises

3.1 Complete these sentences about dictionary use.

1 It's important to have a good English–English dictionary and also a .... dictionary, which is easier to understand.
2 Dictionaries show the .....w.or.d.s....... using phonemic symbols.
3 Dictionaries will tell you if a noun is countable or ....
4 Dictionaries show synonyms and .... where they exist.
5 If you meet a word you don't know, you can try to .... the meaning from the context, or you can .... it .... in a dictionary.

3.2 Right or wrong? If the answer is wrong, correct it.

1 **Advice** is a countable noun.   _Wrong (advice is an uncountable noun)_
2 **Homesick** means you are unhappy living at home and you want to leave.
3 You don't **make homework**, you **do homework**.
4 **Carry on** means the same as **continue**.
5 The opposite of **polite** is **unpolite**.
6 The past tense of **begin** is **begun**.
7 **Dirty** is an adjective.
8 If you **look up** a word, you find the meaning in a dictionary.
9 Trains arrive at and leave from **platforms**.
10 **Depend** is followed by the preposition **of**.

3.3 In the word 'island' /aɪlənd/, the letter 's' is silent (= not pronounced). Use your dictionary to find the silent letters in these words. (Do not include the letter 'e' at the end of a word.)

knife   comb   castle   salmon   receipt

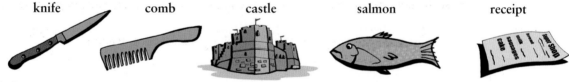

3.4 Use a dictionary to find the answers to these questions about words on the left-hand page.

1 What does **tiny** mean?
2 How do you pronounce **lose**? (Is it the same as 'ch<u>oo</u>se' or 'ch<u>o</u>se'?)
3 What is the opposite of **lose a game**?
4 What are the past tense and past participle of the verb **choose**?
5 What noun is formed from the verb **choose**?
6 What part of speech is **homesick**?
7 What two verbs often go before **homesick**?
8 Can you complete this common phrase? **law and** ....

3.5 Match the sentences on the left with the different meanings of 'bar' on the right.

1 They've put bars in front of the window for extra security.
2 We went to a bar in the centre of town.
3 Could you get me a bar of chocolate?
4 You have to order drinks at the bar.

> **bar**[1] /bɑːʳ/ *noun* [C] **1** DRINKING a place where alcoholic drinks are sold and drunk, or the area behind the person serving the drinks *I met him in a bar in Soho.* **2** BLOCK a small block of something solid *a chocolate bar • gold bars* **3** LONG PIECE a long, thin piece of metal or wood *There were bars on the downstairs windows.*

4 English language words

A Parts of speech

nouns	e.g. chair, information, happiness
verbs	e.g. choose, tell, complain
adjectives	e.g. happy, tall, dangerous
adverbs	e.g. slowly, carefully, often
prepositions	e.g. in, at, on
articles	e.g. definite article (the); indefinite article (a/an)

B Special terms

Uncountable noun: (U) a noun which has no plural form and isn't used with the indefinite article, e.g. Can you send me some information? (NOT ~~an information~~ or ~~informations~~)

Plural noun: (pl) a noun which only has a plural form and isn't used with the indefinite article, e.g. He was wearing blue trousers and a white shirt. (NOT ~~a blue trouser~~)

Infinitive: the base form of a verb, e.g. We decided *to stop* for lunch.

Phrasal verb: a verb + adverb or preposition, e.g. wake up, turn sth on, look after sth/sb.

Idiom: a group of words with a meaning that is different from the individual words, e.g. never mind, keep an eye on sth, etc.

Transitive verb: a verb which needs a **direct object**, e.g. The police caught the man ['the man' is the direct object of the verb 'caught']. A verb which doesn't need a direct object is **intransitive**, e.g. Tim and his brother are always *arguing*.

Informal: a word or phrase which is informal is used mostly in spoken English. Formal English is more common in writing or with people you don't know very well.

Many words also have **synonyms**, which are words with the same meaning, e.g. 'big' and 'large' are synonyms in many contexts. The **opposite** is 'small'.

C Word building

In the word *uncomfortable*, *un-* is a **prefix**, *comfort* is a **root**, and *-able* is a **suffix**. Other common prefixes include: *re-, in-* and *dis-*. Suffixes include: *-ity, -ment* and *-ive*.

D Pronunciation

NOTE

Dictionaries usually show stress with a ' before the main syllable, e.g. re'turn.

Dictionaries show the pronunciation of a word using **phonemic symbols**, e.g. book /bʊk/, before /bɪfɔː/, cinema /sɪnəmə/, and so on.

Every word has one or more **syllables**, e.g. 'book' has one syllable, 'before' has two syllables, 'cinema' has three syllables, and so on.

For pronunciation, it is important to know which syllable has the **main stress**, e.g. on 'before' it is the second syllable (be<u>fore</u>), and on 'cinema' it is the first syllable (<u>ci</u>nema), and so on.

E Punctuation

full stop **.**   comma **,**   brackets **( )**   hyphen **–**   question mark **?**

Hyphens are used to connect certain words or parts of a word together, e.g. a ten-year-old child.

Exercises

4.1 There is one word missing in each line of the text. Where does the missing word go? What could it be? What part of speech is it?

Last year I went to → for my holiday. I spent the
first week Seville staying with a couple of friends,
and then I a train to Barcelona, where I spent
another ten days. It is beautiful city and I had a
marvellous time. I stayed in a very hotel right in the
centre, but I didn't mind spending a lot money
because it is a wonderful and very convenient. My
brother recommended it; he goes Spain a lot and
he stays anywhere else.

1 Spain (noun) ....
2 ....
3 ....
4 ....
5 ....
6 ....
7 ....
8 ....
9 ....

4.2 In the dialogue below, find at least one example of the following: an uncountable noun, a plural noun, a phrasal verb, and an idiom.

A: It's 8 o'clock. We'd better get a move on if we're going to meet Sue at the airport.
B: That's OK. Her flight doesn't get in until 8.50.
A: Yes, but it'll take us an hour to get to the airport – you know what the traffic is like.
B: OK. I'll just go and get changed.
A: What's wrong with your shorts?
B: I don't like driving in shorts. I'm going to put some jeans on.

4.3 Look at the <u>underlined</u> verbs in these sentences. Which are transitive? Which are intransitive?

1 She <u>broke</u> her leg.
2 <u>Take off</u> your jacket.
3 I <u>got up</u> at 7.30.
4 She <u>doesn't like</u> Chinese food.
5 We <u>arrived</u> late.
6 He told me to <u>sit down</u>.

4.4 How many syllables are there in each of these words?

English (2)	noun	decide	informal
before	adjective	education	opposite
preposition	adverb	understand	pronunciation

Now mark the main stress on each of the words.

4.5 Look at these words and answer the questions below.

| happy | lucky | dangerous | cheap |

1 What part of speech are these words?
2 Change each one into an adverb.
3 Write down a synonym for the first two words.
4 Which prefix do you need to form the opposite of the first two words?
5 Write down the opposite of the last two words.

5 Classroom language

A Equipment

These are some of the things you may use in your classroom or school.

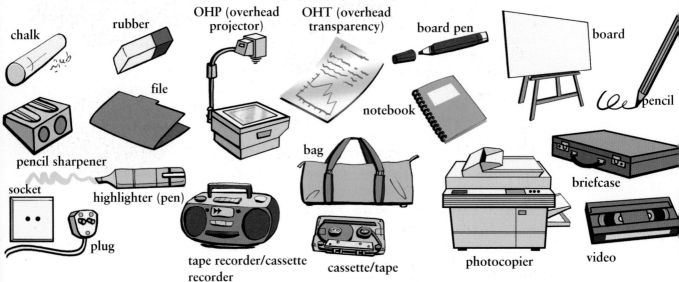

chalk · rubber · OHP (overhead projector) · OHT (overhead transparency) · board pen · board · file · notebook · pencil · bag · pencil sharpener · briefcase · socket · highlighter (pen) · plug · tape recorder/cassette recorder · cassette/tape · photocopier · video

We can use some of these nouns as verbs: **video a programme** (= record it on video); **photocopy an exercise**; **highlight new words**; **file some papers** (= put them in a file).

B Classroom activities

Things students or teachers do in the classroom:
Look up a word (= find the meaning of a word in a dictionary)
Borrow someone's dictionary or rubber (= use it and then return it)
Rub out mistakes in a notebook (= remove mistakes using a rubber)
Plug in the tape recorder (= put the plug in the electric socket)
Turn up the tape recorder if you can't hear it (= increase the volume) (*opp* **turn down**)
Rub things **off** the board (= remove writing from the board)
Correct students' English (= give the correct English if students make mistakes)

Things a teacher may ask students to do in the classroom:
Could you **clean** the board, Carlos? (= remove all the writing from the board)
Write these words **down**. (= write these words on a piece of paper/in a notebook)
Enrique, could you **swap places** (= change places) with Lorena?
Kim, could you **share** your book with Petra? (= use it together at the same time)
Repeat this sentence after me. (= say it again)

C Questions about vocabulary

What does 'plug' mean? (NOT ~~what means plug~~?)
How do you **pronounce** it?
How do you spell 'bicycle'?
How do you use 'anyway' **in a sentence?**
What's the difference between 'lend' **and** 'borrow'?

Exercises

5.1 Label these pictures, then check your answers on the opposite page.

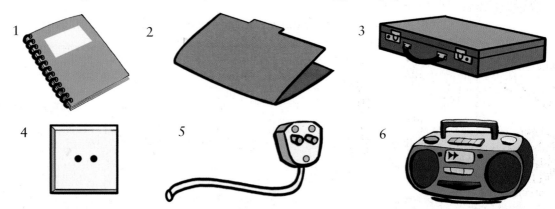

1
2
3
4
5
6

5.2 Answer these questions.

1 What do you rub off the board? writing
2 What do you put in a tape recorder? listening
3 What do you put on an OHP?
4 What do you keep in a file?
5 What do you put in a briefcase?
6 What do you put in a socket?
7 What do you use a rubber for?
8 What do you use a photocopier for?
9 Why do you turn up a tape recorder?
10 Why do you share a book with someone?

5.3 Match the verbs on the left with the nouns on the right.

1 correct   a places
2 clean   b a word
3 borrow   c someone's mistakes
4 swap   d the board
5 video   e a dictionary
6 do   f a programme
7 turn up   g an exercise
8 look up   h the tape recorder

5.4 Here are some answers. What are the possible questions?

1 A: .... ?   B: It means to exchange places.
2 A: .... ?   B: /swɒp/ Like 'shop' or 'stop'.
3 A: .... ?   B: S-W-A-P.

5.5 Think about your last lesson (in English or any other subject). Did you do any of these things?

Did you   clean the board?   share a book with anyone?
          use a rubber?   look up any words?
          borrow anything?   make any mistakes?
          watch a video?   write anything down in a notebook?

6 Prefixes

A With the meaning 'not'

Prefixes can be added to some words to give them a negative meaning.

happy	unhappy	like (v)	dislike (v)
possible	impossible	legal	illegal (= against the law/wrong)
correct	incorrect	regular	irregular, e.g. irregular verbs

NOTE

Word stress doesn't usually change, e.g. happy/unhappy; but it can to emphasise the negative:

A: Was he <u>happy</u> about the change?

B: No, he was very <u>un</u>happy about it.

un- is the most common, e.g. **unfriendly, unable, unusual, unnecessary, unemployed** (= without a job), **untidy** (= not in order; also, **in a mess**), **unkind, unpleasant** (= horrible).

in- is often used before words with a Latin origin, e.g. **invisible** (= cannot be seen), **informal, inadequate** (= not good enough, e.g. The car park is inadequate for a big supermarket like that).

im- is used before some words beginning with 'm' or 'p', e.g. **impolite, impossible, impatient** (someone who is 'impatient' wants things to happen now; they cannot wait for things), **immoral.**

il- can be used before 'l', e.g. **illegible** (= impossible to read because the writing is bad).

ir- is only used before a few words beginning with 'r', e.g. **irresponsible.**

dis- is used before some adjectives, e.g. **dishonest** (a 'dishonest' person is someone you cannot trust, and often does not tell the truth), and a few verbs, e.g. **dislike, disagree.**

B Verb prefixes: *un-* and *dis-*

With some verbs, these prefixes can also mean 'the opposite of an action'.

The plane **appeared** in the sky, then suddenly **disappeared behind** a cloud.
I **locked** the door when I left, but then I lost the key and couldn't **unlock** it when I got back.
I **got dressed** (= put on my clothes) and had my breakfast.
I **got undressed** (= took off my clothes) and got into bed.
I had to **pack my suitcase/do my packing** (= put everything in it) very quickly, so when I **unpacked** (= took things out) at the hotel, most of my clothes looked terrible.

C Other verb prefixes with specific meanings

re- (= again)   The shop **closed down** but it'll **reopen** next month.
                  I failed my **exam** but I can **retake/redo** it next year.

over- (= too much) My boss is **overdoing** it at the moment. (= working too hard)
                  I went to bed very late and I **overslept** (= slept too long) **this morning.**
                  The shop assistant **overcharged** me.
                  (= asked me for too much money)

mis- (= badly or incorrectly) I'm afraid I **misunderstood what he said.**
                  Two of the students **misread** the first question.

Maybe I overate.

Exercises

6.1 What's the opposite of these words? (The words in the last column are verbs, the rest are adjectives.)

1 _un_.happy	5 _im_.patient	9 _im_.polite	13 _un_.lock
2 _in_.correct	6 _ir_.regular	10 _in_.visible	14 _un_.pack
3 _il_.legible	7 _un_.friendly	11 _un_.employed	15 _dis_.agree
4 _im_.possible	8 _in_.formal	12 _dis_.honest	16 _dis_.like

6.2 What's the reverse of these actions?

1 do one's packing   _unpack_
2 lock the door
3 appear
4 get dressed

6.3 Agree with these sentences, using a synonym from the left-hand page for the <u>underlined</u> words.

1 It's <u>against the law</u>, isn't it?
   Oh yes, it's _illegal_.
2 His room is always <u>in a mess</u>, isn't it?
   Yes, it's very _unkind_
3 He <u>took off his clothes</u>!
   Yes, he got _unpacked_
4 This handwriting is <u>impossible to read</u>.
   Yes I know, it's completely ....
5 She <u>can never wait for five minutes, can she</u>?
   No, she's very ....
6 The conference centre <u>wasn't good enough</u> for 500 people, was it?
   No, it was completely .... for that number.
7 She's <u>horrible</u> sometimes.
   Yes, she can be very ....
8 I'm afraid they <u>sometimes steal things and tell lies</u>.
   I know. They're both ....

6.4 Complete the verbs in these sentences.

1 I completely dis_agree_.......................... with him on this subject.
2 I'm sorry, I mis.......................... her message.
3 We un.......................... as soon as we got to the hotel, then went out for a walk.
4 She was here a minute ago, then she dis.......................... . I don't know where she is now.
5 My homework was so bad that I'll have to re.......................... it.
6 Her alarm clock didn't go off and she over..........................
7 She finally managed to un.......................... the door and we were able to go inside.
8 I dis.......................... the film, but the others enjoyed it.
9 I don't think I'll pass the exam, but I can always re.......................... it in September.
10 She's over.......................... things at the moment. She needs a complete break from her job.
11 The post office shuts for lunch but it should re.......................... at 2.00 pm.
12 I was very angry because they over.......................... me by about £5 in that shop.

6.5 Keep several pages in your notebook for verbs or adjectives which combine with these prefixes. You can add new words to your lists and test yourself at the same time.

7 Noun suffixes

A Verb + noun suffix

verb	suffix	noun
improve (= get better)	-ment	**improvement**
govern (= control affairs of a city or country)		**government**
manage (= direct or control a business)		**management**
elect (= choose somebody by voting)	-ion	**election**
discuss (= talk about something seriously)		**discussion**
inform (= tell someone something)	-ation	**information**
jog (= running to keep fit or for pleasure)	-ing	**jogging**
spell (e.g. S-P-E-L-L)		**spelling**

There has been a **big improvement** in the economy. Who do you think will **win the election**?
The problems are due to **bad management**. I'm not very **good at spelling**.

B Adjective + noun suffix

adjective	suffix	noun
weak (*opp* strong)	-ness	**weakness**
happy		**happiness**
ill (= sick/not well)		**illness**
stupid (*opp* intelligent, clever)	-ity	**stupidity**
active		**activity**
similar (= almost the same; *opp* different)		**similarity**

We have a **weak government**. What's her **main weakness** as a manager?
She was **ill** for a long time. Hepatitis is a very **serious illness**.
The two boys are **quite similar**. There is a **similarity between** all three sons.

C Pronunciation

Adding a suffix to a verb or adjective may change the pronunciation.

verb	noun
educate	education
advertise	advertisement

adjective	noun
similar	similarity
stupid	stupidity

D -er/-or and -ist

These suffixes can be added to nouns or verbs. They often describe people and jobs.

-er	-er	-or	-ist
ballet **dancer**	bus **driver**	television **actor**	**artist**, e.g. Picasso
pop **singer**	shop **manager**	film **director**	economist
murderer (= person)	professional **footballer**	translator	psychologist
who kills someone)	**employer**	computer **operator**	journalist

Exercises

7.1 Complete the tables and mark the stress on each word. The last two in each column are not on the opposite page, but do you know or can you guess the noun formed from them?

verb	noun	adjective	noun
educate	*theacher*	stupid	*dorm*
improve	*improver*	happy	*happer*
jog	*juggler*	weak	*weikest*
govern	*govrner*	similar	*triid*
spell	*spwizired*	active	*exsporty*
hesitate	*failer*	sad	*sader*
arrange	*oareganiser*	popular	*famas*

7.2 Combine words on the left with the correct suffix on the right to complete the text.

improve	televise	weak	govern
elect	educate	manage	stupid

-ment	-ity	-ness
-ion	-ation	

In his first broadcast on (1) ...*television*... since he won the (2) ...*manager*... last month, the Prime Minister promised to make health and (3) ...*educate*... his top two priorities.

And in a strong attack on the previous (4) ...*govern*... , he said that the present (5) ...*improve*... of the British economy was caused by their (6) ...*welweak*... and bad (7) ...*telewnn*... . He said things were going to change, and he hoped the British people would be able to see a big (8) ...*elect*... in the economy by the end of the year.

7.3 Write down the name of the person who does these things as a job.

1 drive ...*driver*...   3 act ...*acter*...   5 economics ...*economer*... *en*
2 translate ...*tarunlater*...   4 psychology ...*psycholger*... 6 football ...*footballer*...

7.4 Match words from left and right to find the names of eight jobs.

pop	bus
shop	child
film	ballet
computer	professional

psychologist	dancer
singer	manager
operator	driver
footballer	director

7.5 Complete the definitions below.

1 An employer is a person or company that ...*employs people*...
2 A murderer is a person who ...*potanal football*...
3 A bank manager is a person who ...*ballet daner*...
4 A television actor is a person who ...*child manger*...
5 A translator is a person who ...*operter computer*...
6 A lorry driver is a person who ...*bus driver*...
7 A journalist is a person who ...*pop singer*...
8 An artist such as Picasso is a person who ...*film diracketer*...

8 Adjective suffixes

A Noun or verb + suffix

noun or verb	suffix	adjectives
danger, fame	-ous	**dangerous, famous** (= known by lots of people)
music, politics, emotion, economics, industry	-al	**musical, political, emotional** (= have or show strong feelings), **economical** (= saves you money), **industrial** (= connected with industry and factories)
cloud, sun, fog, dirt	-y	**cloudy, sunny, foggy, dirty** (*opp* clean)
attract, create	-ive	**attractive** (= pretty, good-looking); **creative** (= ability to produce new ideas; with imagination)

The roads were **dangerous** this morning: it was **foggy** and I couldn't see far.
He was very **emotional** when he said 'goodbye'.
Did you buy a diesel car because it's more **economical** than petrol?
I'm afraid you'll have to clean the floor – it's very **dirty**.

B -able

This common suffix creates adjectives from nouns <u>and</u> verbs:
an **enjoyable** evening   a **comfortable** chair   Jeans are still **fashionable**.
suitable (= right/correct for a situation), e.g. A grey suit is very **suitable for** a wedding.

Sometimes **-able** means 'can be done':
washable (= can be washed), e.g. Is this jacket **washable**?
reliable (= can be trusted), e.g. I've never had a problem with the car – it's very **reliable**.

Words ending **-able** quite often express the opposite meaning with the prefix **un-**:
unsuitable (= not right/correct for a situation), e.g. Jeans are **unsuitable** for weddings.
unbreakable (= cannot be broken), e.g. The glass in the shop window is **unbreakable**.

Words ending **-ible** sometimes add the prefix **in-** to form an opposite:
incomprehensible (= cannot be understood), e.g. This street map is **incomprehensible**.
invisible (= cannot be seen), e.g. Trees surround the house, so it's **invisible** from the road.

C -ful and -less

-**ful** often means 'full of' or 'having the quality of the noun':
careful (= doing sth with care and attention), e.g. **careful driver**
helpful (= able to help), e.g. Her **advice** was very **helpful**.
painful (= giving pain), e.g. It was **painful** when I hit my hand.
useful (= has a lot of use), e.g. I found it a **useful book**.
thoughtful (= kind and thinks of others)

painful   thoughtful

-**less** often means 'without':
careless (= without care, and causing mistakes), e.g. His work is full of **careless mistakes**.
useless (= without use and often terrible), e.g. This knife is **useless** – it won't cut anything.
homeless (= with nowhere to live), e.g. Many families are **homeless** because of the war.

Exercises

8.1 Write an adjective (or adjectives) formed from these nouns or verbs. Cover the opposite page first.

1 danger *dangerous*
2 attract ~~famous~~
3 create ~~carater~~
4 cloud ~~cdiones~~
5 suit ~~suiter~~
6 use ~~user~~

7 care ~~carer~~
8 thought ~~thouther~~
9 politics ~~poliecen~~
10 enjoy ~~enjaer~~
11 pain ~~pains~~
12 dirt ~~dirter~~

13 sun ~~suny~~
14 music ~~murcie~~
15 comfort ~~comfertebel~~
16 fame ~~fames~~
17 rely ~~rely~~
18 emotion ~~emiptica~~

8.2 Fill the gaps with suitable adjectives from the opposite page.

1 You must be very ...*careful*... when you drive in wet weather.
2 Everyone in my country has heard of her; she's very ...*smart*...
3 The tourist information office was very ...*strong*... , and told us everything we needed to know.
4 This is a very ...*long*... road, you know. There were three serious accidents on it last year.
5 It was very ...*tired*... when I hit my leg against the corner of that table.
6 This bag is very ...*big*... : I take it to work and when I go on holiday.
7 We've never had problems with our TV in ten years; it's been very ...*old*...
8 The factory is in the ...*nebound*... part of the city, and it's not very attractive.
9 A 100 gram bag is 80 pence, but the 200 gram bag is only £1.20, so it's more ...*havey*... to buy the larger bag.
10 It's terrible that there are so many ...*people*... people in a country that is so rich.
11 Teenagers want to be ...*capered*..., and wear all the latest styles.
12 I can't understand a word of these instructions – they're ...*dad*...

8.3 How many of these words can form opposites with the suffix *-less*?

1 wonderful   2 useful   3 awful   4 careful   5 beautiful

What are the opposites of the other words (the ones without *-less*)?

8.4 Match adjectives from the left with the most suitable nouns from the right.

homeless	famous		actor	bed
careless	useful		party	mistake
comfortable	cloudy		advice	area
industrial	enjoyable		family	morning

8.5 From the adjectives on the opposite page, choose two or three which could describe each of these people or things. (You can use the same adjective more than once.)

1 Wolfgang Amadeus Mozart   *famous, creative, musical*
2 the weather *cloudy area*
3 someone's driving *indratyabber*
4 an area of a city
5 a car *actor*
6 yourself *famoege*

9 Nouns and verbs with the same form

Many words in English function as noun and verb, or verb and adjective, or noun and adjective, with the same form.

What's the **answer**? (noun)   I must **clean** my room. (verb)   I don't like the **cold**. (noun)
Answer the question. (verb)   It's a **clean** room. (adj)   I don't like **cold** weather. (adj)

The same word form can have different meanings, but this unit looks at examples where the meaning is the same or similar, and concentrates on nouns and verbs with the same form.

A   Noun and verb

laugh   rain   smile   taste   kiss   smell   dream

brake (= stop a car using the **brake** on the floor)   **ring** (= telephone)
diet (= eat less to lose weight)   **queue** (= wait in a line of people)
guess (= give an answer without knowing the facts)   **murder** (= kill someone)

Many common words can function as noun and verb with the same form and meaning:
drink, *rest*, *look*, *cost*, *swim*, *wash*, *push*, *pull*, *reply*, *kiss*, **chat** (= a casual conversation *infml*) [also *practise* (v) and *practice* (n)].

B   Which verb?

It is often more natural in English to use the verb + noun structure (e.g. had a guess) and not the verb (e.g. guessed). You need to know which verbs to use with the nouns.

verb	*verb + noun*
I didn't know the answer, so I **guessed**.	I didn't know the answer, so I **had a guess**.
We **rested** for a while.	We **had** a short **rest**.
She **braked** suddenly.	She **put on** the **brakes** suddenly.
He needs to **diet**.	He needs to **go on** a **diet**.
I'm going to **ring** him.	I'm going to **give** him a **ring**.
I **looked** in the paper.	I **had a look** in the paper.
I **dreamt** about you last night.	I **had a dream** about you last night.
We had to **queue** for half an hour.	We had to **wait in a queue** for half an hour.

Exercises

9.1 What word is being defined? (The first letter has been given to you.)

1 Give an answer without knowing the facts   g...*predicter*
2 Eat less in order to lose weight   d...*disate*
3 Wait in a line of people   q...*ques*
4 Kill someone   m...*derer*
5 Telephone   r...*aide*
6 Press your lips against another person's lips   k...*iss*
7 Have a casual conversation   c...*onvertion*
8 Images in your mind when you are sleeping   d...*ream*

9.2 Rewrite these sentences using the <u>underlined</u> nouns as verbs. Change or add words if necessary.

Example   There was a lot of <u>rain</u> yesterday.
     It rained a lot yesterday.

1 We had a long <u>wait</u>.   We *had a long pg*
2 This apple has got a strange <u>taste</u>.   This *apple had a very strang*
3 We waited in the <u>queue</u> for half an hour.   We *are waiting*
4 The <u>cost</u> of the holiday was about £500.   The *cost to the century*
5 I wrote a <u>reply</u> to his letter yesterday.   I *wrote a later*
6 She gave me a <u>smile</u> this morning.   She *gave me a big hug*

9.3 Rewrite these sentences using the <u>underlined</u> verbs as nouns. The meaning must stay the same.

Example   They want to <u>rest</u> for a bit
     They want to have a rest for a bit.

1 I'll <u>ring</u> him this evening.   I'll *have ring him this*
2 I'll <u>diet</u> if necessary.   I'll *have diet*
3 If you don't know, just <u>guess</u>.   If you don't know, just *have guess*
4 I <u>braked</u> but I still couldn't stop in time.   I *have brake but I still*
5 I <u>dreamt</u> about my mother.   I *have about my mother*
6 Did you <u>look</u> in the paper?   Did you *have look in the paper*?

9.4 Sometimes the same word can be a verb and noun but the meaning changes. Read these pairs of sentences. Do the verb and noun have a similar meaning, or are they different in meaning?

1a We had a long <u>wait</u> for the bus.
 b If we <u>wait</u> any longer, we may miss the train.
2a I gave him the <u>book</u>.
 b Did you <u>book</u> the table in the restaurant?
3a They take a <u>break</u> after an hour's work.
 b Did he <u>break</u> his arm skiing?
4a I go for a <u>run</u> most mornings.
 b I was late so I had to <u>run</u> to get to school on time.

Compound nouns

A Formation

A compound noun is formed from two words, and occasionally three, to create a single new idea.

earrings   frying pan   tin opener   washing machine   sunglasses   credit card

toothbrush   traffic lights   hair dryer   cash machine   T-shirt

dining room (= room where you eat meals)
science fiction (= stories about the future)
writing paper (= paper for writing letters)
mother tongue (= your first language)
bus driver (= person who drives buses)
bus stop (= where buses stop for people to get on)
haircut (e.g. My hair's long; I need a haircut.)
traffic jam (= long line of cars moving very slowly)
babysitter (= person who looks after children when parents are out)
box office (= place where you buy cinema or theatre tickets)
travel agent (= job of a person who makes travel arrangements for us)

film star (e.g. Tom Cruise, Meg Ryan)
income tax (= tax you pay on your salary)
dishwasher (= machine for washing dishes)
brother-in-law (= your sister's husband *or* wife's brother)

B One word or two?

Some short common compound nouns are written as one word, e.g. **bedroom, postman**; a few are written with a hyphen, e.g. **T-shirt, make-up** (= stuff you put on the face, often on lips and around eyes, to be more attractive); but most are written as two words, e.g. **credit card, bus stop**. Use a dictionary to check if necessary.

C Pronunciation

The main stress is usually on the first part, e.g. <u>post</u> office, <u>income</u> tax, but sometimes it is on both parts, e.g. <u>science</u> <u>fiction</u>, <u>mother</u> <u>tongue</u>. Use a dictionary to check if necessary.

D Forming new compounds

One part of a compound often forms the basis for a number of compound nouns.

postman	film star	toothbrush	living room
postbox	pop star	toothpaste	waiting room
post office	rock star	toothache	chat room (= an area for communication on the internet)

Exercises

10.1 Find compound nouns on the opposite page connected with each of these topics.

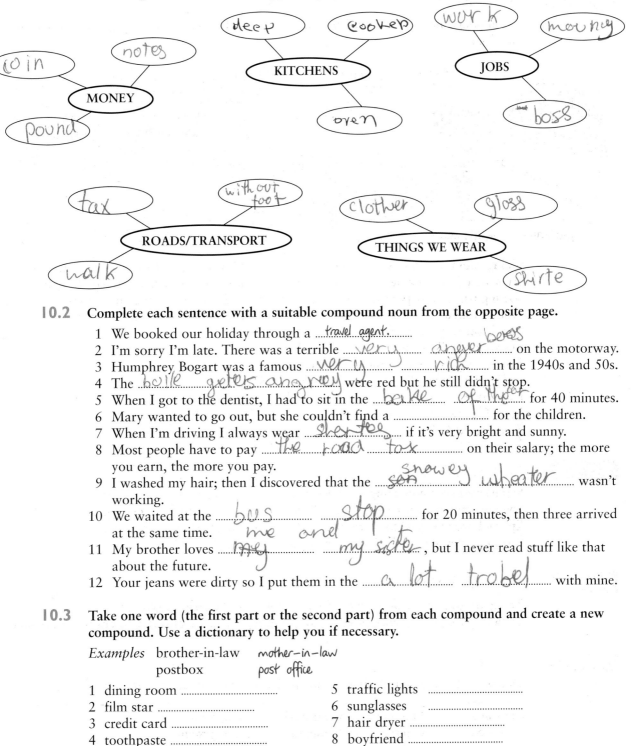

(handwritten answers on diagram)

MONEY: coin, notes, pound
KITCHENS: deep, cooker, oven
JOBS: work, money, boss
ROADS/TRANSPORT: tax, without foot, walk
THINGS WE WEAR: clother, gloss, shirte

10.2 Complete each sentence with a suitable compound noun from the opposite page.

1 We booked our holiday through a ...*travel agent*...
2 I'm sorry I'm late. There was a terrible ...*very*... *anever beres*... on the motorway.
3 Humphrey Bogart was a famous ...*very*... *rich*... in the 1940s and 50s.
4 The ...*balle getels anginey*... were red but he still didn't stop.
5 When I got to the dentist, I had to sit in the ...*barke of thget*... for 40 minutes.
6 Mary wanted to go out, but she couldn't find a .... for the children.
7 When I'm driving I always wear ...*shartee*... if it's very bright and sunny.
8 Most people have to pay ...*the road tax*... on their salary; the more you earn, the more you pay.
9 I washed my hair; then I discovered that the ...*snowey wheater*... wasn't working.
10 We waited at the ...*bus stop*... for 20 minutes, then three arrived at the same time.
11 My brother loves ...*may*... *my sicter*..., but I never read stuff like that about the future.
12 Your jeans were dirty so I put them in the ...*a lot trobel*... with mine.

10.3 Take one word (the first part or the second part) from each compound and create a new compound. Use a dictionary to help you if necessary.

Examples   brother-in-law   *mother-in-law*
         postbox   *post office*

1 dining room ....
2 film star ....
3 credit card ....
4 toothpaste ....
5 traffic lights ....
6 sunglasses ....
7 hair dryer ....
8 boyfriend ....

Now mark the main stress on each of the compound nouns you have created.

Compound adjectives

A Formation and pronunciation

A compound adjective is formed from two words, and occasionally three. The second part is often a present participle (e.g. good-_looking_) or a past participle (e.g. well-_known_). They usually have a hyphen before a noun, (e.g. **a well-known actress, a good-looking man**) and we usually pronounce both parts with equal stress.

B Describing people

Many compound adjectives describe a person's appearance, character and situation.

This is Bill. He isn't **well known** (= famous), he isn't **well off** (= rich), and nobody says he's **good looking** (= very nice/attractive to look at). But he's a nice man – kind, friendly and **easy going** (= relaxed and easy to be with). Here he's wearing a **short-sleeved** shirt and a **brand-new** (= completely new) hat.

C 'Well' and 'badly'

These adverbs combine with many past participles to form compound adjectives. We can use both of them with most of these participles, e.g. _well-paid_ or _badly-paid_ (NOT ~~badly-known~~).

a **well-organised** team
a **well-equipped** computer room
a **well-written** story
a **well-known** writer (= famous)

a **well-paid** job (= good salary)
a **badly-behaved** child (= acting in a bad way)
a **badly-dressed** young man (= wearing old or dirty clothes)

D A 'five-minute' walk

We often combine a number and a singular noun to form a compound adjective. The nouns in bold in these sentences, e.g. **walk, hotel** are often used with the particular adjectives.

It's a **ten-minute walk** to the shop. (= a walk of ten minutes)
He works in a **four-star hotel**. (= a hotel with a rating of four stars)
I gave her a **twenty-pound note**. (= a note with a value of twenty pounds)
Our flight finally left after a **two-hour delay**. (= the plane was two hours late)
The winner was a **ten-year-old girl**. (= a girl who is ten years old)
If you park your car there, you could get a **fifty-euro fine**. (= a penalty of €50 to pay for parking in the wrong place)

E Common compounds

She used to have a **part-time** job – just mornings – but now she works **full time**.
Most people are **right handed**, but about 10% are **left handed**.
I went **first class** to Paris, but it was more expensive.
Mary bought a **second-hand** BMW. (= the car was not **brand new**, but new for her)

Exercises

11.1 Match words from the left-hand box with words from the right to form ten compounds.

Example first-class

first	well		new	known
easy	good		class	time
five	short		looking	sleeved
brand	second		hand	handed
part	left		going	star

11.2 Complete the compound adjective in these sentences.

1 They were both wearing short-................................. shirts.
2 Goran Ivanisevic is probably the most famous left-................................. tennis player.
3 He's just bought a brand-................................. car.
4 One girl was very badly .... : she kept shouting and then threw food all over the floor
5 She's just got a ....-time job now. She works three hours a day, Monday to Thursday.
6 It was a very badly-................................. article: terrible punctuation and lots of spelling mistakes.
7 They're very well .... , so they can go to expensive restaurants.
8 She's got a little shop near the market, where she sells second-................................. things.
9 When I saw her, she was with a very good-................................. man in a white suit.
10 Have you ever met a well-................................. actor or politician?
11 I had a nice time with my cousin – he's good company and very easy ....
12 She has a seven-................................-old son.

11.3 Find two examples to complete these compound adjectives.

1 well- known ....

3 badly- ....

2 .... -time

4 .... -handed

11.4 Choose the most suitable noun to follow the adjectives in these sentences.

1 I stayed in a five-star .... in London.
2 We didn't get to Malaga until midnight because we had a two-hour .... at Heathrow.
3 She bought a paper and paid for it with a twenty-pound ....
4 It's just over a kilometre, so it's only about a fifteen-minute ....
5 I had to pay a forty-pound .... for not having a parking ticket.

11.5 Write about yourself using ten different compound adjectives from the opposite page. You can describe yourself, your personality, your family, your clothes, the place where you live, the journeys you make, etc. Compare your answers with someone else, if possible.

12 Collocation (word partners)

A What is collocation?

If you want to use a word naturally, you need to learn the other words that often go with it. This can be different from language to language. For example, in English we say:

I **missed the bus.** (= I didn't **catch the bus**) (NOT I ~~lost~~ the bus)
He had to go to hospital; it's a **serious injury.** (= a bad injury) (NOT a ~~grave~~ injury)
She was **bitterly disappointed** (= very disappointed/unhappy) with her exam result.

B Verb + noun

The meaning of many of these examples may be clear, but did you know these verbs and nouns go together? Are they the same or different in your language?

start { **a car** (= turn on the engine)
{ **a family** (= think about having a first child)

tell { **a story**
{ **a joke** (= a funny story)
{ **the truth** (*opp* tell a lie)

miss { **a person** (= be unhappy because a particular person is not there)
{ **a lesson** (= not go to a lesson)

get on a bus (*opp* **get off** a bus)   **waste time/money** (= use it badly)

C Adjective + noun

a **soft** { **drink** (= non-alcoholic drink)
{ **voice** (*opp* a **loud** voice)

dry { **wine** (*opp* **sweet** wine)
{ **weather** (*opp* **wet** weather)

a **strong accent** (*opp* a **slight accent**)
(a) **strong coffee** (*opp* (a) **weak coffee**)

heavy { **traffic** (= a lot of cars on the road)
{ **rain** (= raining a lot)
{ **smoker** (= a person who smokes a lot)

hard work (= difficult physically or mentally)
a **hard question** (= difficult to answer)

a **great** { **success** (= very successful)
{ **time** (= an enjoyable time)

I can't understand his English because he has such a **strong accent.**
The conference was **hard work** but everyone said it was a **great success.**
There was **heavy traffic** in the city centre because of the **wet weather.**
We had a **great time** in Brazil – the beaches are fantastic.

D Adverb + adjective

The underlined adverbs in 1–3 mean *very*, the adverbs in 4–5 mean *fully/completely*. In each case, we often use these adverbs with the adjectives that follow them. Notice also the phrases in bold.

1 I'm <u>terribly</u> **sorry to bother you** (= to disturb you), but is Steven there?
2 She is <u>well</u> **aware of the problem.** (= she knows all about the problem)
3 It is <u>vitally</u> **important** to make a note of common collocations in your notebook.
4 He's <u>fast</u> **asleep.** (= in a deep sleep)
5 She was <u>wide</u> **awake** (= fully awake) a minute ago.

Exercises

12.1 You can keep a record of common collocations using diagrams. They are very clear on the page and you can add to them. Complete these.

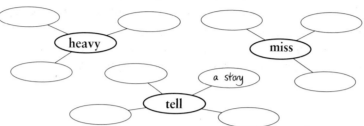

12.2 Write the opposite.

1 get on the bus *get off the bus*
2 a strong accent
3 strong coffee
4 a soft voice

5 an alcoholic drink
6 tell the truth
7 catch the bus
8 sweet wine

12.3 Complete these sentences with a suitable word.

1 I'm ......*terribly*...... sorry I'm late, but I .... the bus and had to wait ages for another one.
2 He .... everyone the same joke, and nobody laughed.
3 We had snow in the night and I couldn't .... the car this morning.
4 Everyone said the party was a .... success.
5 I think they want to get married and .... a family.
6 We carried the suitcases up to the fourth floor, and it was very .... work.
7 It's .... important that we finish this work by the end of the week.
8 If this .... rain continues, I don't think he'll come.
9 I don't drink .... coffee at night because it keeps me awake.
10 I really .... my family when I stayed in Australia on my own last year.
11 I'm sure she is .... aware of the problem.
12 I .... my time on that course; it was terrible.
13 When I went into the children's room, the boys were both .... asleep, but Angela was .... awake, reading a Harry Potter story.

12.4 The adjectives on the left can all mean 'very big', but we often use them with the nouns on the right. Use a dictionary to find the correct collocations, and then complete the sentences below. You will need to look at the example sentences in the dictionary, perhaps at the adjectives and the nouns.

wide	vast	size	range
large	broad	shoulders	majority

1 A: What .... do you take?   B: Medium or ....
2 Fortunately the shop I go to has a .... of shirts and jumpers to choose from.
3 I've got very .... , but my waist is quite small.
4 A few men can't find clothes to fit them, but the .... are small, medium or large.

13 Idioms and fixed expressions

A What is an idiom?

An idiom is a group of words with a meaning that is different from the individual words. Sometimes the meaning is easy to understand; sometimes it is difficult to understand from the individual words. These examples move from 'easy to understand' to 'more difficult to understand'.

I've **changed my mind** about those shoes. (= changed my decision or opinion)
I'm tired today because I had **a late night**. (= went to bed later than usual) (*opp* **an early night**)
I'm trying to write an essay but I'm **getting nowhere**. (= not making progress)
You find fast food restaurants **all over the place**. (= everywhere)
My wife and I **take it in turns** to cook. (= I cook one day, she cooks the next, etc.)
I'm sorry but I don't think I can **make it** (= come) on Friday. I'm really busy.
They asked us to **keep an eye on** (= watch/look after) the house while they're away.
I **feel like** (= want) a drink; I **feel like** going out this evening. (= want to go out)
We should **get rid of** some of this stuff. (= remove it/throw it away)
That boy really **gets on my nerves**. (= is very annoying; makes me angry)
The answer's **on the tip of my tongue**. (= I know it, but can't remember it at this moment)

B Pairs of idioms

These pairs are related in meaning and sometimes they are used together.

On the one hand/on the other hand (= used to contrast opposite points of view)
I'm not sure about these new apartments. **On the one hand** they provide homes for people, which is good. But **on the other hand**, we have lost the only piece of open land in the area.

In the short term/in the long term (= a short or long period of time in the future)
In the short term we can manage here, but **in the long term** we will need a bigger place.
If we do this, it will be cheaper **in the long term**. (= over a long period of time)

In theory/in practice (used to contrast a general idea with reality)
In theory your plan looks very interesting; but **in practice**, it may be too expensive for us.

C Common idioms

Some common idioms are used in everyday questions and replies.

A: Are you coming?
B: Yes, **hang on**. (= wait a minute)

A: **What's up?** (= What's the matter?)
B: Nothing.

A: I've forgotten to bring your book.
B: **Never mind**. (= it's OK, no problem)

A: Shall we go out?
B: Yeah, **if you like**. (= I am happy to do that)

A: Can I borrow your dictionary?
B: Sure, **go ahead**. (= help yourself; take it; do it)

A: I don't know which one to choose.
B: Well, **make up your mind**. (= make a decision)

A: What's the answer?
B: **I haven't a clue**. (= I don't know)

A: Would you prefer to stay in?
B: **It's up to you**. (= it's your decision)

Exercises

13.1 Replace the <u>underlined</u> word(s) with an idiomatic phrase from the opposite page.

1 A: Is Rebecca here?
  B: Yes, <u>wait a minute</u>. I'll get her.
2 A: How long does it take?
  B: <u>I've no idea</u>.
3 A: Could I borrow this for a minute?
  B: Yes, <u>take it</u>.
4 A: I'm sorry I broke that glass.
  B: <u>That's OK</u>. It's not important.
5 A: Would you like to go to the cinema?
  B: Yes, <u>I am happy to do that</u>.

6 A: What's <u>the matter</u>?
  B: Nothing. Why?
7 A: Could you <u>look after</u> my things for a minute?
  B: Yeah, sure.
8 A: Is John coming this evening?
  B: No, I'm afraid he can't <u>come</u>.
9 A: You'll have to <u>decide</u> soon.
  B: Yes, I know, but it's very difficult.
10 A: What time shall we leave?
  B: I don't mind. It's <u>your decision</u>.

13.2 Complete the idioms in these sentences.

1 **In the short** .... we don't need any help from the bank.
2 We **take it in** .... to look after the dog.
3 Tell the children to be quiet – they're **getting on my** ....
4 The new traffic system sounds like a good idea in .... ; but will it work?
5 Nowadays you can find internet cafés **all over the** ....
6 I planned to go to Greece for my holiday but I've **changed my** ....
7 I had to **get** .... of all my magazines because they were taking up too much space.
8 What's in the fridge? **I feel** .... something to eat.
9 I'm very tired this evening. I think I'll have **an** .... **night**.
10 The answer was **on the tip of my** .... but I just couldn't remember it.
11 It'll take us the whole day to drive to Scotland – the train is much faster. **On the other** .... , it'll be very convenient to have the car when we get there.
12 I'm .... **nowhere** with this crossword; I just can't do any more.
13 I was going to invite my cousins, but I've .... **my mind**.
14 I can't take all my furniture with me: I'll have to .... **rid of** some of it.

13.3 It can be difficult to guess the meaning of an idiom, especially if you do not have the full context. Look at these examples (they are not presented on the opposite page).

1 The exam was **a piece of cake**.
2 They've gone **for good**.
3 I can **make do with** a small flat.

Here is a fuller context for the above idioms. Can you guess the meaning now?

1 A: Was the exam difficult?
  B: No, it was **a piece of cake**.
2 A: Do you think they'll ever come back to England?
  B: No, they've gone **for good**.
3 A: Do you really need a large flat?
  B: Well, it would be nice to have a big place, but I can probably **make do with** a small flat.

14 Verb or adjective + preposition

A Verb + preposition

Some verbs are often followed by a particular preposition. Pay special attention to any that are different in your language.

I often **listen to** the radio.
Paul doesn't like it and I **agree with** him. (= have the same opinion)
I may go but it **depends on** the weather.
He **suffers from** (= has the illness of) a type of diabetes.
He **got married to** a girl he met in France. I don't know her name.
I think we should **apologise for** (= say sorry for) being late.
She has **applied for** (= made a written request for) a new job.
They were **waiting for** me at the airport.
Don't **worry** (= be nervous) **about** your exam; it'll be OK.
His teachers were **satisfied** (= pleased) **with** his progress.
She **complained** (= said she wasn't satisfied) **to** the manager **about** the food.
He **spends** a lot of money **on** clothes.
That dictionary **belongs to** Rolf. (= it is Rolf's dictionary)
They are going to **translate** the book **into** Spanish.
I'm **thinking of** going to France. (= it's a future possibility) [Used mostly in the continuous form.]

B Prepositions that change the meaning

He **shouted to** me. (= to communicate from a distance)

He **threw** the ball **to** me. (= for me to catch it)

He **shouted at** me. (= he was angry)

Someone in the crowd **threw** a bottle **at** the police. (= in order to hit them; he was angry)

C Adjective + preposition

I was never very **good at** mathematics. (*opp* **bad at**)
She is **afraid of** (= frightened of) flying.
I'm not very **keen on** fish. (= I don't like fish very much)
She is **similar to** (= in some ways the same as) her older sister, but very **different from** her brother.
He's very **interested in** photography.
I was **surprised at** (or **by**) the way he reacted – he's usually very calm.
I think she's **aware of** (= knows about) **the problems** in her class.
I'm **tired of** people telling me what to do. (= I've had enough and I want it to stop)
As it's the school holidays, the pool was **full of** children. (= lots of children in the pool)
There is something wrong with this TV. (= the TV is not working/functioning correctly)

Exercises

14.1 Finish these questions with the correct preposition, then write a short answer for each one.

1 A: What exactly is she worried ...*about*.. ?   B: *her exams* ....
2 A: What subjects is she good .... ?   B: ....
3 A: Who is she waiting ....?   B: ....
4 A: What job is she applying .... ?   B: ....
5 A: What programme is she listening .... ?   B: ....
6 A: What did she complain .... ?   B: ....
7 A: What did she apologise ....?   B: ....
8 A: Who does this car belong .... ?   B: ....
9 A: I know she's angry but who's she shouting .... ?   B: ....
10 A: What kind of films is she interested ....?   B: ....
11 A: What does the decision depend ....?   B: ....
12 A: What is she afraid .... ?   B: ....

14.2 Match the sentence beginnings on the left with the endings on the right.

1 He's tired
2 She wasn't aware
3 He threw the book
4 She complained
5 She said it was similar
6 She applied
7 She shouted
8 He said it depends
9 The suitcase was full
10 She spent over £200
11 She apologised
12 I was very surprised

a at me, but it missed.
b for a job in Australia.
c of working at weekends.
d to the man across the lake.
e for the mistake.
f at his choice.
g of clothes.
h to the one she has.
i on that coat.
j of her mistakes.
k on the time they get there.
l about the bad service.

14.3 Complete the sentences in a logical way. If possible, compare with someone else.

1 My steak was overcooked, so I complained ...*to the waiter about it.*......
2 When I was a child I sometimes wore clothes that belonged ....
3 Her teacher wasn't very satisfied ....
4 In the summer a lot of people suffer ....
5 I'm afraid there's something wrong ....
6 The book is very successful and has been translated ....
7 A lot of people are afraid ....
8 I've always been interested ....
9 I'm not very keen ....
10 People in my country are very different ....
11 For my next holiday, I'm thinking ....
12 In the summer, places like Spain and Greece are full ....

14.4 A good dictionary will tell you if a verb or adjective is usually followed by a special preposition. Use a dictionary to find the preposition that often follows these words.

fond (adj)   concentrate (v)   rely (v)

15 Preposition + noun

A Common patterns

Sometimes a preposition is used with a particular meaning in a number of expressions.

A **book by** Stephen King; a **film by** Steven Spielberg; a **song by** Elton John

I heard it **on the radio**; I saw it **on TV**; we spoke **on the phone** (but I read it **in the newspaper**)

You can go **for a walk, for a swim, for a drive, for a run**

You can visit **in the morning, in the afternoon, in the evening** (but **at night**)

You can travel **by car, by train, by plane, by bus** (but **on foot**)

The man **in the blue jumper, in the dark glasses** (= wearing the blue jumper/dark glasses)

B Fixed expressions

I took his pen **by mistake**. (= I thought it was my pen)

I did all the work **by myself/on my own**. (= without help from others)

The shoes are **made by hand**. (= not by machine)

The workers are **on strike**. (= they won't work because of a problem over pay, hours, etc.)

I met them **by chance**. (= it wasn't a planned meeting; it was luck)

The children are **on holiday**. (= they are having a holiday)

There are two million **out of work**. (= without a job)

I think Marianne's **in love** with him. (= she loves him)

The building's **on fire**. (= it is burning)

Why are they always **in a hurry**? (= need to do things or go somewhere very quickly)

He broke the plate **by accident**. (= he did not want to do it; it was a mistake)

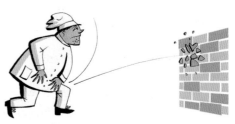

He broke the plate **on purpose**. (= he wanted to do it and intended to do it)

C 'In time' or 'on time'?

Sometimes two prepositions can be used with the same noun, but the meaning is different.

Lessons begin at 8.30 and the students are usually here **on time**. (= at 8.30)

If we hurry, we'll be there **in time**. (= before the time we need to be there; we won't be late)

We were tired of waiting, so **in the end** we went home. (= finally, after a long period)

At the end of the book they get married. (= in the last part)

The two men have been **in business** (= worked as businessmen) for many years.

They're both in Germany **on business**. (= they are there for work, not a holiday)

I'll see you **in a moment**. (= very soon)

I can't speak to you **at the moment**. (= **right now**/at this moment)

Exercises

15.1 Complete these sentences with the correct preposition. Cover the opposite page first.

1 I saw it .... TV.
2 They came .... car.
3 They are all .... strike.
4 He is here .... business.
5 I did it .... my own.
6 It was written .... Goethe.
7 We went .... a walk.
8 I read it .... a magazine.
9 He's .... holiday this week.
10 She took it .... mistake.
11 I went .... the afternoon.
12 He came .... foot.
13 The clothes are made .... hand.
14 She broke it .... accident.
15 He did it .... purpose.
16 I'll see you .... a moment.
17 She's always .... a hurry.
18 It's very quiet .... night.
19 We met .... chance.
20 I think they're .... love.

15.2 Replace the <u>underlined</u> words with a suitable phrase from the opposite page.

Example The meeting was planned for 11 and we got there <u>at 11</u>.
The meeting was planned for 11 and we got there *on time*.

1 I wrote the reports <u>without help from anyone else</u>.
2 Did you get to the cinema <u>before the film started</u>?
3 Most of the factory is <u>burning</u>.
4 She's <u>making a phone call</u>.
5 I saw the advertisement <u>when I was watching TV</u> last night.
6 He opened her letter <u>because he thought it was addressed to him</u>.
7 It was a very long journey but <u>finally</u> we got there.
8 He gets killed <u>in the last scene</u> of the film.
9 I'm afraid I'm very busy <u>right now</u>.
10 I saw her yesterday <u>but we didn't plan to meet</u>.

15.3 Respond to these questions using a suitable prepositional phrase. Look at the example first.

Example A: Was it the man wearing the blue shirt?
B: No, the one *in the white shirt*.

1 A: Did she hit him on purpose?
  B: No, she did it ....
2 A: Did the others help him?
  B: No, he did it ....
3 A: Did they go by car?
  B: No, they went ....
4 A: Are they here on holiday?
  B: No, they're here ....
5 A: Did you read about the accident in the newspaper?
  B: No, I heard about it ....
6 A: Has he got a job at the moment?
  B: No, I'm afraid he's ....
7 A: Did they fly?
  B: No, they went ....
8 A: Do they really like each other that much?
  B: Yes, they're .... Isn't that sweet?

16 Apologies, excuses and thanks

A Apologies (= saying sorry)

We can **apologise** (= say sorry) in different ways in different situations.

	situation
(**I'm**) **sorry.** **I'm (very/terribly) sorry.** **I beg your pardon.** (*fml*)	When you close the door in someone's face, or sit in someone's seat
I'm sorry to disturb you. **I'm sorry I'm late.** (**I'm**) **sorry to keep you waiting.**	When you interrupt/speak to someone who is working When you are late for an appointment Someone is waiting to see you and you are busy. You can also say: **I won't be long.** (= I will be free soon)

In formal situations we often use **apologise** and **apology**.

I must **apologise for** being late.   I would like to **apologise for** the delay. Unfortunately, ...

Please accept our apologies for the delay in sending out your order. [a common phrase in business letters]

B Excuses and promises

NOTE
Be/get delayed means to be late because of a problem that you cannot control.

If the situation is important we can give an explanation or **excuse** after the apology. An excuse is the <u>reason</u> for the apology – it may or may not be true.

I'm sorry I'm late, but I **was delayed/got held up** at the airport.
I'm sorry I'm late, but my train **was cancelled.** (= the train was on the timetable but did not run)

If you are responsible for a problem, you can offer or promise to do something about it.
I'm sorry about the mess in here – **I'll clear it up.** (= I will make everything tidy/in order)
I'm sorry about the confusion over the plans – **I'll sort it out.** (= I will solve the problems)

C Reassuring people

When people apologise to us, it is common to **reassure** them (= tell them that 'everything is OK'). Sometimes we use two expressions to emphasise that 'it's OK'.

A: I'm sorry I'm late.
B: **That's OK. Don't worry.**

A: I'm afraid I forgot to bring the books.
B: **Never mind. It doesn't matter.**

D Thanks and replies

These are the most common ways of thanking people in everyday situations, with typical replies.

A: Here are the books you wanted.
B: Oh, **thank you (very much).**
A: **That's OK.**

A: I'll answer that.
B: Oh, **thanks (a lot).**
A: **No problem.**

A: I'll post those letters for you.
B: Oh, thank you. **That's very kind of you.** [This is polite and a bit more formal.]

Exercises

16.1 Complete these dialogues with a suitable word. Contractions (e.g. I'm) count as one word.

1 A: I'm ...*very*.................... sorry.
   B: That's OK.

2 A: I'm sorry .... late. The 7.30 train was .... and I had to catch the 7.50.
   B: That's OK. No ....

3 A: Sorry to .... you waiting.
   B: That's OK. Never ....

4 A: I think the boss has got a real problem with this contract.
   B: Yes, but I'm sure he'll .... it out.

5 A: I've got your CDs.
   B: Oh, thanks a ....

6 A: I must .... for missing the meeting.
   B: That's OK. It doesn't ....

7 A: I'm busy right now but I won't be ....
   B: That's OK. Don't ....

8 A: I'll carry your bags for you.
   B: Thanks. That's very .... of you.

9 A: I .... your pardon.
   B: That's OK. No ....

10 A: I'm sorry .... the room; it's very untidy.
   B: That's OK. I'll clear it .... later.

16.2 What could you say in these situations? (If it is an apology, give an explanation.)

1 You get on a bus at the same time as another person and he/she almost falls over.
   I'm terribly sorry. / I beg your pardon. I didn't see you there.

2 You arrange to meet friends in the centre of town but you are 20 minutes late.

3 Your car has broken down. You're pushing it to the side of the road and a stranger offers to help.

4 A friend borrows a pen, then loses it. When they apologise, you want to reassure them.

5 You need to see your boss, but she's busy. What do you say as you go into her office?

6 A colleague at work tells you that a number of files are in the wrong order and he doesn't know what to do. When he apologises, how can you reassure him, and what can you offer to do?

7 You were unable to go to a meeting with a client. Now you phone to explain.

8 Your company promised to send some information about new products to a customer last week. You still haven't sent the information and must now write to explain.

17 Requests, invitations and suggestions

A Requests and replies

Notice that the phrases get longer when the requests get bigger.

1 A: **Could you** pass me the salt?
   B: Yeah, **sure**.

   A: **Could I possibly** borrow your dictionary?
   B: Yes, **help yourself**. (= yes, take it)

2 A: **Do you think you could (possibly)** lend me two or three pounds?
   B: Yeah, sure.   *or*   No, **I'm afraid I can't.**
                           No, **I'm afraid not.** } I haven't got any money **on me**. (= with me)

3 A: **I was wondering if I could (possibly)** leave work half an hour early today?
   B: Yeah, **no problem.**   *or*   Well, **it's a bit difficult (actually)**, because …

B Invitations and replies

A: **Would you like to** go out this evening?

B: Yeah, **great/I'd love to.**

or **I'm sorry, I can't.**

A: We're going to a restaurant and **we were wondering if you'd like to** come with us?

B: **I'd love to, but I'm afraid I can't.** I've got to write an essay.

C Suggestions and replies

Suggestions are ideas for things to do/say/make, etc.

Asking for suggestions
What **shall we** do tonight?
Where **shall we** go this evening?
What do you **fancy doing** (= want to do) this evening? (*infml*; notice the *-ing* form after **fancy**)

Making suggestions
How about (or **What about**) go**ing** to the cinema? (notice the *-ing* form)
Perhaps **we could** just get a pizza or something like that.
Why don't we try that new club in the main square?
Do you **fancy going** to that Italian restaurant? [This can be a suggestion or an invitation.]

Replies
Positive: Yeah, **great/fine/that's a good idea/that sounds great.**
Neutral: Yeah, **if you like.** (= if you want to go, then I am happy to go)
            Yes, **I don't mind.** (= it's OK for me) (NOT ~~for me it's the same~~)
Negative: I think **I'd rather** (= I would prefer to) stay in and watch TV.

Exercises

17.1 Correct the mistakes in this dialogue. There are six, including the example.

      Would
A: ~~Do~~ you like to go out this evening?
B: I'm afraid but I haven't got any money.
A: That's OK, I'll pay. How about go to see a film?
B: No, I think I'd rather to stay in and do my homework.
A: Why you don't do your homework this afternoon?
B: I'm busy this afternoon.
A: OK. We could go tomorrow.
B: Yeah, great.
A: Right. What film shall we see?
B: For me it's the same.

17.2 Complete the dialogues with a suitable word. Contractions (e.g. *isn't*) count as one word.

1 A: Could you ...*possibly*............... open that window? It's very hot in here.
  B: Yeah, ...*sure*.............
2 A: Clive and Sally are here at the moment and we were .... if you'd like to come over for a meal this evening?
  B: Yes, I'd .... to.
3 A: What do you .... doing this evening?
  B: I don't know really. Any ideas?
  A: Why .... we go to the cinema? We haven't been for ages.
  B: Yeah, that's a great ....
4 A: OK. Where .... we go on Saturday?
  B: How .... going to the beach if the weather's nice?
  A: Yeah. Or we .... try that new sports centre just outside town.
  B: Mmm. I think I'd .... go to the beach.
  A: Yeah, OK, if you ....
5 A: What .... you like to do this weekend?
  B: I don't .... You decide.

17.3 Respond to each of these requests, invitations and suggestions. If possible, do this activity with someone else: one of you asks the questions, the other answers.

1 Could I borrow a pen for a minute?
2 Do you think you could post a letter for me?
3 I was wondering if you've got a suitcase you could lend me?
4 Would you like to go out this evening?
5 I've got some tickets for a concert. Do you fancy coming with me?
6 How about going to a football match at the weekend?
7 Why don't we meet this afternoon and practise our English for an hour?
8 We could invite some other people from our English class to meet us as well.
9 I know you're busy but could you help me with this essay?
10 Do you fancy going to the cinema?

18 Opinions, agreeing and disagreeing

A Asking someone for their opinion

What do you think of his new book/girlfriend? (= asking about a specific person/thing)
What do you think about cosmetic surgery? (= asking about a general topic)
How do you feel about working with the others?

B Introducing your own opinion

(Personally) I think Paula was probably right.
(Personally) I don't think it's a good idea. (NOT I ~~think it's not~~ a good idea)
In my opinion we need to change the direction of the company. [This is more formal.]

C Having strong opinions

These adjectives are common when we give opinions.

I thought it was a **brilliant idea**. (= a fantastic idea)
She thought the pictures were **disgusting**. (= terrible, very unpleasant, not acceptable)
His plan is just **ridiculous**. (= absurd and stupid)
I think it's a really **original** book. (= new and different from anything else)

D Giving the opinion of others

According to the newspaper (= in the opinion of the paper), she knew nothing about it.
The newspaper **says** the President knew weeks ago. (NOT It ~~is written~~ in the newspaper.)

E Agreeing with someone

If we want to show we agree with someone, we can do it like this:

A: I think we should put the money in the bank.
B: Yes, **I agree (with you)**.   *or*   Yes, **I think you're (absolutely) right**.

F Disagreeing with someone

It is common to begin by agreeing before you give a different opinion.

	possibly,	but don't you think …
Yes,	**perhaps/maybe,**	but I'm not sure that …
	you could be right,	but don't forget …

If we disagree but not completely, we often use these expressions:
Yes, **I see what you mean,** but …
Yes, **I take your point,** but …

G Strong disagreement

I **totally disagree** (with you).
I'm afraid I **don't agree** (with you) **at all**.

Exercises

18.1 Complete these questions in three different ways to ask people their opinion.

1 .... these shoes? Do they look OK?
2 .... the plan to change the examination system?
3 .... having more responsibility?

18.2 Fill the gaps with a suitable word from the opposite page.

1 A: What did you think .... the film?
   B: Well, ... I didn't like it.
2 .... to the radio this morning, we won't know the result until tomorrow.
3 Yes, I take your .... , but I still think the book was too long.
4 I .... disagreed with her, which is unusual.
5 I know she has very strong .... on this subject – she talks about it all the time.

18.3 Rewrite these sentences using the words on the right. The meaning must stay the same.

1 I think you're right.   AGREE
   I agree with you.
....

2 I think the club needs new players.   OPINION
....

3 I totally disagree with you.   AT ALL
....

4 The newspaper says terrorists started the fire.   ACCORDING
....

5 Yes, I take your point, but I'm not sure I agree.   MEAN
   Yes, I ....

6 How do you feel about giving children more freedom?   THINK
....

18.4 Match the words on the left with the correct definition on the right.

1 disgusting   a absurd and stupid
2 ridiculous   b fantastic
3 original   c terrible and very unpleasant
4 brilliant   d new and different

18.5 Continue these conversations. You can agree and add another reason, or disagree and add a different point of view. Remember, if you disagree, start with a short expression of agreement first. If possible, compare your answers with someone else.

1 A: A lot of women are very happy to stay at home and be housewives.
   B: ....
....

2 A: The state shouldn't give money to people who don't want to work.
   B: ....
....

3 A: People from developing countries need all the help we can give them.
   B: ....
....

19 Likes, preferences and interests

A What do you like?

NOTE
Most verbs and expressions on the left can also be followed by an -ing form:
I love driving;
I don't mind working at the weekend.

	agree	disagree
I love rock music.	**So do I/me too.**	**Really? I don't.**
I'm really into dance music. (*infml*)	**So am I/me too.**	Really? **I'm not.**
I **like** a lot of pop music.	So do I/me too.	Do you? I hate it.
I **quite like** salsa and samba.	So do I/me too.	Oh, I'm not very keen on it.
I **don't mind** jazz.	Yeah, it's OK.	Oh, I can't stand it.
I'm **not very keen on** folk music.	**Neither am I/me neither.**	Really? I love it.
I don't like reggae.	**Neither do I/me neither.**	Oh, I quite like it.
I **can't stand** opera.	**Neither can I/me neither.**	Really? I quite like it.
I **hate** classical music.	So do I/me too.	Oh, I really like it.
(= I dislike it very much)		

B And things like that

We can describe a list of things, e.g. likes or dislikes, with one or two examples, then finish with general phrases like these. We can also use them to ask about likes or dislikes.

She's very keen on poetry and drama and **that sort of thing**.
I try to eat healthy food – simple pasta and salads, and **stuff like that**.
My husband likes boxing and wrestling, but I hate **things like that**.
What **kind of things/sort of stuff** do you like?

C Look forward to

I'm **looking forward to** going home. (= pleased and excited about going home soon)
I always **look forward to** my birthday. (= pleased and excited when it is going to happen)
I'm **not looking forward to** the exams because I haven't done much work.
I **look forward to hearing from you.** [This is a common way to end a formal letter.]

D Which do you prefer?

In general
A: Which **do you prefer,** tea or coffee?
B: **I prefer** coffee **to** tea in the morning. But in the afternoon I usually drink tea.

Specific occasion
A: We can go to the cinema or the theatre – it doesn't matter. Which **would you prefer?**
B: **I'd prefer to** go to the cinema.   *or*   **I'd rather go** to the cinema.

'I'd rather' is the same as 'I'd prefer to', but is more common in spoken English.

E What are you interested in?

A: Are you **interested in** Latin American music?
B: Yes, **very (much).**   *or*   **No, not really.**   *or*   No, **it doesn't interest me (at all).**

Exercises

19.1 Correct the mistakes in these dialogues (one mistake in each).

1 A: I love modern art.
   B: Yes, so I do.
2 A: Do you like this?
   B: Yes, I like very much.
3 A: Would you like to go out?
   B: No, I'd prefer stay here.
4 I'm looking forward to see you next week.

5 A: Do you like tea?
   B: Yes, but I prefer coffee than tea.
6 A: Does he like football?
   B: No, he's not interesting in sport.
7 A: I don't like his new CD.
   B: No, so do I.
8 I don't mind to help them.

19.2 Complete the phrases in bold in these sentences.

1 My sister loves Robbie Williams, but I **can't** .... him.
2 He likes windsurfing and waterskiing and **that sort of** ....
3 They're not very **keen** .... sightseeing.
4 Do you really enjoy **things** .... **that?**
5 **Are you looking** .... **to your holiday?**
6 I love the cinema, but this particular film **doesn't** .... **me at all.**
7 Carole **is really** .... modern art at the moment. Personally, I hate it.
8 (*formal letter*) **We look forward to** .... **from you.**

19.3 Rewrite the sentences using the word on the right. The meaning must stay the same.

1 I hate these new shoes.   STAND
   I can't stand these new shoes.
2 I think they'd prefer to go home.   RATHER
....
3 I don't find his books interesting.   INTEREST
....
4 I don't really like that sort of thing. THINGS
....
5 I find archaeology very interesting. INTERESTED
....
6 I think the new building is OK.   MIND
....

19.4 Agree with each of these sentences using 'so' or 'neither' and the correct verb.

1 I love this ice cream. *So do I.*
2 I like strawberries.
3 I don't like cold tea.

4 I can't work with music on.
5 I'm single.
6 I'm not married.

Now write 'me too' or 'me neither' next to each of your answers.

19.5 Complete these sentences about yourself. Compare with someone else if possible.

I really like .... and ....
and things like that.
I don't mind ....
I can't stand ....
I prefer .... to ....

I'm looking forward to ....
I'm not looking forward to ....
I'm interested in ....
.... doesn't interest me.

20 Frequently asked questions

It will help you to learn these common questions as fixed expressions.

A Personal questions

questions	possible answers
Where are you from? Where do you come from?	Italy.
What do you do? (= What's your job?)	I'm a film director.
What are you doing at the moment?	I'm making a film.
Are you married?	No, **I'm single.**
How old are you? (= What's your age?)	I'm 27.
What's your address/phone number?	It's …

B Everyday questions

NOTE
The last two constructions are very similar in meaning. Often you can use either, but remember not to confuse the forms. (*How's …?* and *What's … like?* NOT ~~How's it like?~~)

questions	typical answers
How are you? *or* How's it going? (*infml*)	**Fine, thanks.** *or* **Not bad. How about you?**
What are you doing this evening?	**Nothing special/much.** (= I have no plans)
What's the matter? (= What's the problem?)	Nothing. Why?
Have you got the time? (= Do you know the time?)	Yeah, it's five past three.
How much is that (necklace)? (= what's the price?)	It's £35.99.
What sort/kind of (cheese do you like)?	I like most cheese – especially hard cheese.

How was (the party)? (= tell me your opinion of it)
What's (the flat) **like?** (= describe it to me and tell me what you think of it)

C Place and distance

A: I live in Italy.
A: **How far** is it? (= what distance is it?)
A: **How do I get to** the (railway station)?

B: **Whereabouts?** (= where exactly in Italy)
B: About ten miles.
B: **Sorry, I don't know.**

D 'Time' questions

SITUATION: You are on holiday in Ireland for two weeks. On the evening of the fourth day you meet someone in a bar. These are typical questions they may ask you.

questions	answers
How long have you been here?	Four days.
How long are you staying? How long are you here for?	Two weeks. *or* Another ten days.
How much <u>longer</u> are you staying?	Ten days.
Is this the first time you've been to (Dublin)?	Yes, it is. *or* No, I've been before. I came …

Exercises

20.1 Complete each dialogue with a suitable word.

1 A: What do you ...*do*........... ?
  B: I make TV programmes.
2 A: Are you .... ?
  B: No, I'm married, actually.
3 A: What are you doing this evening?
  B: Nothing .... Why?
4 A: How do I .... to the Tourist Information Office from here?
  B: I'm sorry, I don't know.
5 A: .... was the film like?
  B: Brilliant.
6 A: They've been in the flat for a year now.
  B: Yeah. And how much .... are they planning to stay?
7 A: .... was the lecture?
  B: Very interesting.
8 A: What .... of car does he drive?
  B: I don't know.

20.2 Here are some answers. What could the questions be?

1 I'm a doctor.   *What do you do?*
2 Yes, it's almost four o'clock.
3 I'm 23 next month.
4 It's about five kilometres.
5 Usually French or Italian, but occasionally Chinese food.
6 Sorry, I don't know. I'm a stranger here myself.
7 It's very large – there are six bedrooms and the kitchen is fabulous.
8 I have no plans at all. I'll probably watch TV.
9 We arrived last Sunday.

20.3 Replace the underlined word or phrase with a word or phrase of similar meaning.

1 A: How long are you <u>staying</u>? *here for*
  B: Two weeks.
2 A: How <u>are you</u>?
  B: Fine. And you?
3 A: <u>Where exactly</u> do you live in Italy?
  B: In Rome.
4 A: <u>How's your steak</u>?
  B: Oh, it's delicious.
5 A: Is this <u>your first visit</u> to Spain?
  B: Yes, it is.
6 A: What's the <u>problem</u>?
  B: Nothing.

20.4 You are on holiday in Prague. Complete this conversation with a person you meet on the third day.

A: How .... here?
B: Just a couple of days.
A: Really? And .... ?
B: Until next Friday.
A: Is this the .... ?
B: No, I came last year.

21 Common responses

A Short responses

questions	short response
Are you going to the party tonight?	**I think so.** *or* **I don't think so./I doubt it.**
Is Tom going to meet us?	Yes, **I hope so.** (= I don't know but I want it to happen)
Is it going to rain?	**I hope not.** (NOT I ~~don't hope so~~)
Are you working this weekend?	**I'm afraid so.** (= Unfortunately, I am)
Can you come to the match?	**I'm afraid not.** (= I'm sorry, but no I can't)

B Responding with interest and enthusiasm (= strong feeling of interest and enjoyment)

statements	enthusiastic responses
She finally got her visa to travel.	**Really? That's great.**
He's passed his driving test.	**Oh, that's brilliant.**
We're going camping in Greece.	**Oh, that sounds wonderful.**
I'm going to meet some actors.	**Really? That sounds interesting.**
They're having a baby.	**Oh, how fantastic.**
I've got a new job.	**Wow! How exciting.**

We can respond to bad news using the same constructions but different adjectives.
Really? That's dreadful.   **Oh, that sounds terrible.**   **Oh, no. How awful.**

C Responding with disappointment

I can't go to the party this evening.	**Oh, what a pity/that's a pity.**
Sam isn't feeling well, so he's staying here.	**Oh, what a shame/that's a shame.** (= what a pity)
I think it's going to rain for our picnic.	**Oh, what a nuisance/pain.** [We use this when we are angry about a situation.]

D Responses of agreement

These responses all agree to do something, or they permit the speaker to choose and make the decision. The way we say these phrases makes it clear if we are happy or unhappy.

What time shall we go?	**Whenever you like.** (= We can go when you want)
What do you want to do?	**Whatever you like.**
Where shall we put these chairs?	**Wherever you like.**
Do you want to go out?	**I don't mind.** (= I am happy to go out, or stay in)
Shall we take a taxi?	Yeah, **if you like.** (= that's OK with me)

E Remember to respond!

It is important to show you are listening. These are common ways we do it.

mmm	**uh huh**	**yeah**	**OK**	**I know**	**sure**	**right/I see** (= I understand)

Exercises

21.1 Check the pronunciation of the <u>underlined</u> words in the Index at the back of the book. Practise saying the phrases.

> I <u>doubt</u> it. I'm <u>afraid</u> so. Oh, what a <u>nuisance</u>. That sounds <u>dreadful</u>.

21.2 Complete the last word of these dialogues. Practise them with a partner if possible.

1 A: Can we still get tickets?
  B: I hope ....
2 A: Are you working tomorrow?
  B: Yes, I'm afraid ....
3 A: Is the price going up?
  B: Well, it's already expensive, so I hope ....
4 A: Are you going?
  B: I doubt ....
5 A: Are there any left?
  B: I don't think ....
6 A: Have you got any change for the coffee machine?
  B: I'm afraid ....

21.3 Choose the best response on the right for each of the questions or statements on the left.

1 Tom can't come because he's working.   a Whenever you like.
2 We're staying in a very expensive hotel.   b I'm afraid so.
3 Do you want to watch the end of the film? c Oh, what a pity.
4 Does he often get angry like this?   d Oh, that's a nuisance.
5 We can't get in – Joe's got the key.   e Yeah, if you like.
6 What time do you want to start?   f Oh, that sounds great.

21.4 Replace the <u>underlined</u> word or phrase with another word or phrase that has the same meaning.

1 A: She's ill.   4 A: Is it still busy at this time of year?
  B: Oh, what a <u>pity</u>.   B: No, I <u>don't think so</u>.
2 A: Do you want to go?   5 A: What do you want to do?
  B: <u>I don't mind</u>.   B: <u>I don't mind</u>.
3 A: We're going on Concorde.   6 A: He fell off his bike and broke his arm.
  B: Oh <u>that's</u> exciting.   B: Oh, <u>how awful</u>.

21.5 Respond to these statements in a suitable way. Practise with someone else if possible.

1 I'm going to spend three weeks in Australia.
2 Alex has lost your watch.
3 Do you want to finish this later?
4 Where shall we go?
5 I've just won £1,000.
6 I can't go tomorrow. I have to work.
7 Peter has lost his wallet with all his credit cards.
8 I wanted to speak to Karen, but she's out all day.

22 Greetings, farewells and special expressions

A Greetings: 'hello'

How do you do? *or* **Hello. Nice to meet you.**	Used in formal situations when you meet someone for the first time. The reply can also be **How do you do?** or **Pleased/nice to meet you.**
Hi/Hello. How are you?	A common greeting when you meet someone you already know. (Also **How's it going?** *infml*) The usual reply is: **Fine, thanks. And you?** Or possibly: **Not bad. How about you?**
Good morning, good afternoon, good evening	These expressions are used at different times of the day (most people say **Good morning** until lunchtime). British people do not usually say **Good day**, but Australians do.

B Farewells: 'goodbye'

Nice to meet you. *or* **Nice to have met you.**	In formal situations, when you say goodbye to someone you have just met for the first time.
See you later/tomorrow.	If you plan to see someone you know later the same day/ the next day.
Bye. See you soon.	You know you will see someone again, but have no plans to meet them.
Goodnight.	When you say goodbye to someone late at night, or if you (or they) are going to bed.
A: **Have a nice weekend.** B: **Yes. Same to you.**	When you say goodbye to a colleague/friend on Friday afternoon. You can also reply: **You too.**

C Happy occasions and celebrations

Happy Birthday	To someone on his/her birthday. You can also say **Many happy returns.**
Happy/Merry Christmas	To someone just before or on Christmas Day (25 December).
Happy New Year	To someone at the beginning of the year.
Congratulations	To someone who has just achieved something, e.g. passed an exam, got a job, etc. We can also say **Well done.**

D Expressions for special situations

NOTE
There is no special phrase when people start eating. In restaurants, waiters may say: **Enjoy your meal.**

Excuse me	a	To get someone's attention, e.g. **Excuse me.** Is this your hat?
	b	When you want to get past other people (on a bus or in a crowded room).
	c	To tell others you are going to leave the room.
Sorry	a	To say **sorry**, e.g. you stand on someone's foot.
	b	When you want someone to repeat what they said. (With this meaning, the voice must rise at the end of the word.)
Cheers		Used to express good wishes when you have a drink with other people. Informally it can also mean 'goodbye' and 'thank you'.
Good luck		To wish someone well before a difficult situation, e.g. exam or job interview.
Bless you		To someone when they sneeze. They can reply: **Thank you.**

Exercises

22.1 **What message could you write in a card to these people?**

1 A friend. Next week is 25 December.   *Happy Christmas*
2 A friend who is 21 tomorrow.
3 A friend. It will be 1 January in three days' time.
4 A very good friend who has just passed some important exams.
5 A friend who is going to take his driving test in three days' time.
6 A friend you will visit when you return from your holiday, but you're not sure when.

22.2 **Complete the conversations in a suitable way.**

22.3 **What could you say in these situations?**

1 You are in a meeting. Someone enters the room and says you have an important
   telephone call. What do you say as you leave?   *Excuse me. I won't be long.*
2 Someone says something to you but you didn't hear all of it. What do you say?
3 You met a new business client for the first time 15 minutes ago, and now you are
   leaving. What do you say?
4 You are in a crowded bus. It is your stop and you want to get off. What do you say to
   other passengers as you move past them?
5 You are staying with some English friends. What do you say to them when you leave
   the room in the evening to go to bed?
6 You are in the street. A woman walks past you and at the same time something falls out
   of her bag. She has her back to you. What do you say?
7 A friend tells you they have just won some money.
8 Another friend is going for a job interview this afternoon.

22.4 **When do we use these expressions? Do you have similar ones in your language?**

| Hard luck. | Say 'cheese'. | Watch out! | Keep your fingers crossed. |

23 Phrasal verbs (1): form and meaning

A Formation

A phrasal verb is a verb + adverb <u>or</u> preposition, and occasionally a verb + adverb <u>and</u> preposition.

The price of petrol is **going up** (= increasing) again.
He **fell over** (= fell to the ground) and hurt his knee.
She's trying to **find out** (= learn/discover) the name of that new hotel.
Who's going to **look after** (= take care of) the children when their mother is in hospital?
If you don't understand the meaning, **look it up**. (= find the meaning in a dictionary)
He doesn't **get on with** (= have a good relationship with) his parents. (verb + adv + prep)

B Meaning

Sometimes the adverb or preposition doesn't change the meaning, but makes it sound more natural.

I didn't **wake up** until 7 o'clock.
Hurry up or we'll be late.
Sit down and be quiet.

I'm **saving up** for a new computer.
She **stood up** and went over to the door.
He told me to **lie down** on the bed.

Sometimes an adverb adds a particular meaning. For example, **back** can mean 'return'.
I'm going to **take** that jacket **back** to the shop; it's too small.
You can look at the books but remember to **put** them **back** on the shelf.

More often, the adverb or preposition changes the meaning of the verb: 'take off' doesn't mean the same as 'take', and 'get on' doesn't mean the same as 'get'. Here are some examples:

It took her a long time to **get over** (= get better/recover from) her illness.
We'll take a short break and then **carry on** (= continue) with the meeting.
My wife has decided to **give up** (= stop) smoking.
I can't make any sandwiches – we've **run out of** bread. (= no bread is left; it is finished)
I've told them we can't **put** the meeting **off**. (= change the time of the meeting to a later date)

C Multiple meanings

Be careful: many phrasal verbs have more than one meaning.

It was so hot I had to **take off** (= remove) my jacket.
I'm always nervous when the plane **takes off**. (= leaves the ground)

I've got a lot of work to **get through** (= finish) before Friday.
I tried phoning him, but I couldn't **get through**. (= make contact and talk to him)

My alarm clock didn't **go off** (= ring) this morning.
The bomb could **go off** (= explode) at any minute. [See picture.]
The fish will **go off** (= go bad) if you don't put it in the fridge.

I **picked up** most of the rubbish. (= took it from a place, using my hands)
I have to **pick** Jane **up** (= collect her in my car) from the station.

Exercises

23.1 Complete the phrasal verbs. Remember to put the verb into the correct form.

1 I don't think they ever ....found.......... out how the man escaped.
2 The children went round the school and .... up all the rubbish.
3 This milk smells horrible; I think it has .... off.
4 I rang the tourist information office but I couldn't .... through. It's engaged all the time.
5 The relationship was difficult at first, but I think she .... on with him quite well now.
6 If she's still ill tomorrow, we'll have to .... off the trip to France until later in the month.
7 I agreed to .... after my sister's cat when she goes to France.
8 We can .... on with this exercise while the others are in the library.
9 Our English teacher said we should .... through the textbook by the end of the course.
10 I'm afraid this photocopier has .... out of paper, but you can use the one in my office.

23.2 Complete these sentences in a logical way.

1 It will take her a long time to get over ...her illness...........................
2 The plane took off ....
3 He had to look it up ....
4 I don't really get on with ....
5 She came in and took off ....
6 I've decided to give up ....
7 Who is going to look after .... ?
8 I went to the garage to pick up ....
9 I'm afraid we've run out of ....
10 My rent is going up ....

23.3 Look at the dictionary entry for 'go off', and match the meanings with the sentences below.

> **go off 1** [LEAVE] to leave a place and go somewhere else *She's gone off to the pub with Tony.*
> **2** [FOOD] *UK informal* If food goes off, it is not good to eat any more because it is too old.
> **3** [STOP] If a light or machine goes off, it stops working. *The heating goes off at 10 o'clock.*
> **4** [EXPLODE] If a bomb or gun goes off, it explodes or fires. **5** [MAKE NOISE] If something that makes a noise goes off, it suddenly starts making a noise. *His car alarm goes off every time it rains.*

1 When the light goes off, the machine has finished.
2 My alarm clock went off early this morning.
3 I think this meat has gone off.
4 The bomb went off without any warning.

23.4 Write two sentences for each of these phrasal verbs to show their different meanings.

pick up   take off   go off   get through

24 Phrasal verbs (2): grammar and style

Grammar: intransitive verbs

Some phrasal verbs are intransitive. They don't need an object after the verb, and we cannot put another word between different parts of the verb.

He **grew up** in a city. (= spent his childhood/developed into an adult) (NOT He grew ~~in a city up.~~)
Don't wait out there. Please **come in**. (= enter)
I'm going to **stay in** (= stay at home) this evening.
We **set off** (= started the journey; usually a long journey) at about 7.30.

Grammar: transitive verbs

Many phrasal verbs are transitive: they need a direct object after the verb. You can usually put the object between the different parts of the verb, or after the phrasal verb.

Put on your shoes. ✓   **Turn on** the TV. ✓   **Take off** your coat. ✓
Put your shoes **on**. ✓   **Turn** the TV **on**. ✓   **Take** your coat **off**. ✓

If the object is a pronoun, it <u>must</u> go in the middle.

Put them **on**. ✓ (~~Put on them.~~)   **Turn** it **on**. ✓ (~~Turn on it.~~)   **Take** it **off**. ✓ (~~Take off it.~~)

In dictionaries

You can use a dictionary to check the grammar. Most dictionaries show it like this:

carry on, get by (= intransitive phrasal verb)
I can **get by** in French. (= I can manage in French, but I don't speak it well.)

put sth←→on, throw sth←→away (= transitive phrasal verb)
Did you **throw** <u>those books</u> **away**? (= get rid of them/put them in a rubbish bin)
Did you **throw away** <u>those books</u>?

get over sth, look after sb/sth (= verb + preposition + object)
Maria will **look after** (= take care of) the children. (Maria will **look after them**.)

Style: formal or informal?

Most phrasal verbs are more common in spoken English. In written English there is often a more formal word with the same meaning. (The other words in bold are often used with these verbs.)

make sth up = invent/create sth (from your imagination), e.g. We had to **make up a story**.
leave sth out = omit sth (= decide not to do sth), e.g. You can **leave out** question 7.
sort sth out = solve sth (such as a problem), e.g. We asked the computer guy to **sort it out**.
turn sb/sth down = reject sth (= say *no* to sth), e.g. I offered him £50, but he **turned** it **down**.

Some phrasal verbs are used in written English if there is no other easy way to express the meaning.

wake up, e.g. I always **wake up** early, even at weekends.
break down (= go wrong/stop working), e.g. The **car broke down** on the motorway.
take off (= leave the ground), e.g. The **plane** couldn't **take off** because of bad weather.
break into sth (= enter by force, often illegally), e.g. **Thieves broke into** the house and stole £500.

Exercises

24.1 Correct any mistakes with word order in these sentences. Be careful: some are correct.

1 He's putting his boots on.
2 I told the children I'd pick up them after school.
3 She grew on a farm up.
4 We set off very early this morning.
5 It's a big problem but the man will sort out it.
6 I think she made that story up.
7 We know there were two thieves, but do you know how they broke the house into?
8 I said I'd look after them if necessary.

24.2 Make these texts more informal by changing the <u>underlined</u> verbs to phrasal verbs.

1 The cost of living is <u>increasing</u> all the time and I am now finding it quite difficult to <u>manage</u> on my salary. I can probably <u>continue</u> for a few months, but after that I may have to look for another job.
2 She told us to <u>enter</u>, but then we had to <u>remove</u> our shoes.
3 The teacher told half the class to <u>invent</u> a story to go with the picture in our books, while the other half did Exercise 5. She said we could all <u>omit</u> Exercise 4 if we wanted to.
4 I don't know why he <u>rejected</u> my offer of help because the company is in a lot of trouble and they've got no one to <u>solve</u> the problems.

24.3 Fill the gaps to complete the phrasal verbs in these sentences.

1 I'm afraid the photocopier has just **broken** ....
2 I couldn't do the second question, so I **left** it ....
3 **Put** your coat .... if you're cold.
4 If there are problems with the computer, I usually have to **sort** it ....
5 He told me he was 25, but I don't believe him. I think he's **making** that ....
6 You're not going to **throw** .... that food, are you?
7 Why couldn't the plane **take** .... ?
8 I think she **grew** .... in a small village.
9 We'll get there by seven if we **set** .... now.
10 They offered him the job but he **turned** it ....

24.4 Complete these sentences in a logical way.

1 Could you lie down ...*on the floor*............... ?
2 I'm not very good at making up ....
3 She asked me to turn on ....
4 Two men tried to break into ....
5 We have asked an engineer to come and sort out ....
6 Are you going to stay in .... ?
7 Why did you leave out .... ?
8 I'm afraid we broke down ....
9 Can you get by .... ?
10 I grew up ....

24.5 There are many phrasal verbs in other units. Find three phrasal verbs in each of these units: 52, 53, 61, 79, 80.

25 Have and have got

A Have vs have got

We can use *have* or *have got* to talk about possessions, relationships, illnesses and some other states. *Have got* is more common in spoken English.

I've **got** an old CD player.	I **haven't got** a car at the moment.
She's **got** two brothers.	**Have** you **got** the time? (= What time is it?)
He's **got** a headache.	It **hasn't got** a swimming pool.

1 In negative sentences, we can use *haven't got* or *don't have*.
   I **haven't got** a car/I **don't have** a car. (NOT I haven't a car.)
2 We don't use *got* in short answers, and it isn't common in the past tense.
   A: **Have** you **got** any brothers or sisters?   B: No, I **haven't**. (NOT No, I haven't got)
   I **had** a car when I was at college. (NOT I had got)
3 The verb form used in the question is usually the same in the answer.
   A: **Do** you **have** a car?   A: **Have** you **got** a car?
   B: Yes, (I **do**).   B: Yes, (I **have**).

B Have + noun

When the same word can be a noun or a verb, e.g. *wash*, it is common to use *have* + the noun, and not the verb on its own, e.g. *I'm going to have a wash.* (NOT I'm going to wash.) *Have got* is not used here.

I always **have a** quick **shower** when I get up. (= shower)
Let's **have a rest** before we go on. (= rest/stop doing an activity and relax)
I often **have a sleep** after lunch. (= sleep) [We use this expression for a short period of sleep.]
This computer game is really hard. Would you like to **have a try**? (= try it)
I **had a dream** about you last night. (= dreamt)
Let me **have a think** before I decide. (= think about sth for a period of time)

We use *be* + adjective and not *have* + noun in these expressions:

She **was lucky**.   I'm **hungry**. (= I want something to eat.)   I'm **thirsty**. (= I want a drink.)

C Have + object

have breakfast/lunch/a meal, etc. (= eat)	I **had** steak but Paul just **had a sandwich**.
	What time do you have breakfast?
have a drink (= drink sth)	Let's **have a drink** before dinner.
have a party	I'm **having a party** for my birthday.
have a baby (= be pregnant or give birth)	Mary is **having a baby** next month.
have a look (= read or examine)	Could I **have a look** at your paper? (= read it)
	The doctor **had a look** at my knee. (= examined it)
have a nice/great/terrible/etc. time	We **had a very nice time** in Switzerland.
have an argument (= angry discussion)	They **had an argument** about the holidays.
have a word with sb (= speak to sb)	I **had a word with** the teacher about my homework.
have the bill (= receive it in a restaurant)	Could I **have the bill**, please?
have a problem + (with) or (-*ing*)	I'm **having a problem with** this exercise.
	I **had a problem** opening the door.

Exercises

25.1 Transform these sentences from *have* to *have got*, or *have got* to *have*.

1 I have a new CD player. *I've got a ...*
2 I don't have a job at the moment.
3 Has he got any change for the machine?
4 She hasn't got much money.
5 We don't have a video at school.
6 A: Do you have an English dictionary?
   B: Yes, I do.

25.2 Now change the form of *have* to *have got* <u>where possible</u>. Make any other changes that are necessary.

1 Do you have a car? *Have you got a car?*
2 Have you seen her today? *You can't change the form here.*
3 We have a small garden.
4 I think I have a cold.
5 A: Do you have a spare pen?   B: No, sorry.
6 Someone told me she has a new boyfriend.
7 Let's have lunch.
8 They had an exam yesterday.
9 I have a new computer.
10 Excuse me. Do you have the time?

25.3 Fill the gaps with a suitable word.

1 I'm tired. I think I'll have a *sleep.*
2 I had a funny .... about you last night. I woke up laughing.
3 I'm exhausted. Can we have a .... ?
4 She's having her 21st birthday .... next week. Are you going?
5 I need to have a .... before I decide what to do.
6 Did you have a .... finding the place without a map?
7 The weather was terrible on our holiday. We didn't have a very good ....
8 We had .... in a little restaurant, then went for a walk in the afternoon.
9 There's a problem with the car, so I asked the garage to have a .... at it.
10 I had a terrible .... with my sister; I haven't spoken to her for days.

25.4 What can you ask in these situations? Use *have* + a noun and start each question *Could I ...?*

1 You want to pay in a restaurant. *Could I have the bill, please?*
2 You would like to look at someone's newspaper.
3 You want to speak to your teacher.
4 You are in a friend's house and you are thirsty.
5 Someone asks you if you want to buy their CD player, but you're not 100% sure if you want it.

25.5 Express these sentences in a different way using *have* + a noun. Keep the meaning the same and start each one with *Mary ...*

1 Mary is speaking to one of the boys. *Mary is having a word with one of the boys.*
2 Mary is pregnant.
3 Mary found it very difficult to work the video.
4 Mary examined my bad shoulder.
5 Mary really enjoyed herself in Ireland.

26 Make, do and take

A Things we make

a mistake (= an error)	He **made** a few **mistakes** in the test.
a meal (= prepare)	I don't usually **make a meal** in the evening if I'm busy. I'll **make** lunch today.
money (= become rich)	He **made** a lot of **money** when he was in America.
friends	I **made** a lot of **friends** in Australia last year.
a decision	Think about it before you **make a decision**.
a noise	I can't work when the children **make** a lot of **noise**.
progress (= become better)	Her English is good now; she's **made** a lot of **progress**.
a difference (= have an effect on a situation)	Sarah tried to help but it didn't **make any difference**. The extra money **makes a big difference** to us.

B Things we do

homework	I forgot to **do** my **homework** last night.
the housework (= cleaning)	My mother **does** all **the housework** in our house.
a subject (= study a subject)	What **subjects** do you **do** at school? Did you **do English** at school?
a course	I **did** a one-week **course** in word processing.
the shopping (= buy food)	I always **do the shopping** at the weekend.
research (= detailed study)	He's **doing research** in physics at Rome University.
sb a favour (= do sth to help sb)	Could you **do me a favour**? I haven't got any coffee. Could you lend me some?
well (= succeed; *opp* badly)	I **did well** at Spanish, but my sister **did** very **badly**.
something/nothing/anything	Those kids **do nothing** all day. I didn't **do anything** last night.

C Things we take

an exam (also 'do')	I'm going to **take** four **exams** next month.
a photo	She **took** lots of **photos** on holiday.
a break (= short period of rest)	OK, let's **take a break** for ten minutes, then we'll continue.
a decision (also 'make')	I'm not very good at **taking decisions**.
a shower (also 'have')	I'm just going to **take a shower** before lunch.
a bus/train/plane/taxi (also 'get')	We were late, so we **took a taxi** to the airport.
periods of time (= time we need to do sth)	It **takes** me **half an hour** to walk to school. **How long** does **it take** you to do an exercise?
a seat (= sit down)	Please come in. **Take a seat**.
time off (= time away from work for holidays or to do sth)	I **took** a few days **off** work and we went away. Could I **take** this afternoon **off**?

Exercises

26.1 Underline the correct verb(s) in italics. Be careful: in some sentences both verbs are correct.

1 I couldn't *do/make* my homework last night.
2 When do you *take/do* your next exam?
3 Did he *do/make* many mistakes?
4 I don't often *make/do* the housework.
5 Did you *make/take* many photos?
6 I think I've *done/made* a lot of progress.
7 I want to *do/make* a course in English.
8 We must *take/make* a decision soon.
9 He is *doing/making* research in chemistry.
10 They *did/made* a lot of noise during the party.

26.2 Replace the underlined phrase with a phrase from the opposite page. Use the verb in brackets.

Example I'll <u>clean the house</u> at the weekend. (do)   *do the housework*

1 I <u>buy my food</u> on Saturday morning. (do)
2 He is definitely <u>improving</u>. (make)
3 OK, let's <u>stop work and relax</u> for 15 minutes. (take)
4 Could you <u>help me</u> and post this letter for me? (do)
5 Now I have a car it <u>changes things a lot</u>. (make)
6 They both want to <u>become rich</u>. (make)
7 When are they going to <u>decide</u>? (make)
8 I'm afraid she <u>failed</u> in both exams. (do)
9 Please <u>sit down</u>. (take)
10 I want to <u>have a week's holiday</u>. (take)

26.3 Complete the sentences in the past tense about each of the pictures. Use verbs from the opposite page.

1 Sally / this morning   2 Maria / after dinner   3 Simon / of me this morning   4 Michael / in his exams

26.4 Choose three of these things. How long does it usually take you to do them? Write sentences, and compare with someone else if possible.

Example It usually takes me about 25 minutes to get to work.

get to college/work	eat lunch	do your English homework
check your e-mail	wash your hair	put on your make-up

Give, keep, break, see

A Give

I'll **give** you **a ring** this evening. (= phone you this evening)
Could you **give** me **a hand**? (= help me)
I'll **give** you **a lift** home. (= take you home in my car)

In spoken English *give* + noun is often used instead of a verb
on its own, e.g. He **gave** me a **kiss**, instead of He **kissed** me.
Other examples are:
He **gave** me a **push**. (= pushed me)
He **gave** me a (big) **smile**. (= smiled at me)
He **gave** me some **advice**. (advised me)
He **gave** me a **hug**. [See picture.]

B Keep

Keep (+ noun/pronoun) + adjective (= to make sth/sb stay in a particular state)

These gloves will **keep** your hands **warm**.   That raincoat will **keep** you **dry**.
Running helps me to **keep fit**. (= stay healthy)   Please **keep quiet**. (= remain quiet)

Keep + *-ing* (= to do sth <u>again and again</u>; often sth that you don't want to happen)
I **keep** losing my glasses.   She **keeps** interrupting me.   I **keep** getting backache.

I try to **keep in touch** with old school friends. (= stay in contact, e.g. phone/write to them)
I'm sorry to **keep you waiting**.

C Break

If you **break a record**, you do something faster or better than anyone else before, e.g.
He **broke the** world 100 metres **record** with a time of 9.79 seconds.
I didn't know I was **breaking the law**. (= doing something wrong/against the law)
Who's going to **break the news** to her family? (= give her family the news)
It'll **break her heart** (= make her very unhappy) to see her son like this.

D See

A: She didn't have your number, so she couldn't phone.
B: Oh, **I see**. (= I understand)

A: It's easier to carry two smaller suitcases.
B: Yes, **I see what you mean**. (= I understand
what you are saying.)

They're doing experiments to **see** (= find out)
how people react when they are under stress.

A: Do you think we need the car?   A: Is that John at the door?
B: **I'll see** (= find out) **what** the others think.   B: Yes, **I'll see** (= find out) **what** he wants.

I don't see the point of practising six hours a day. (= I don't understand the reason/I think
it's crazy.)

Exercises

27.1 Match each verb with two nouns on the right to form common phrases.

1 break	in touch	the law
2 give	somebody a hand	somebody's heart
3 keep	somebody waiting	somebody a lift

27.2 Fill the gaps with verbs from the opposite page.

1 She ..*gave*.............. me a big smile when I got to work this morning.
2 He said he was sorry to .... us waiting.
3 That's the second time she's .... the record.
4 Before we make a decision, let's .... what Patricia says.
5 He just came up to me and .... me a big hug.
6 I don't know what the problem is, but I .... getting headaches.
7 I don't know when the next bus is due – I'll go and .... what the timetable says.
8 A: There's something wrong with this door. B: Yes, I .... what you mean.
9 I'll have to .... the news when they get here.
10 I don't .... the point of spending a lot of money on children's clothes – they only last for a few months and then they're too small.

27.3 Complete these dialogues using a verb + noun construction with the same meaning as the underlined words and phrases.

1 A: Did you take them in your car?
   B: Yes, I ..*gave them a lift.*......
2 A: Did you phone her?
   B: Yes, I .... last night.
3 A: Have you ever committed a crime?
   B: No, I've never .... in my life.
4 A: Have you stayed in contact all this time?
   B: Yes, I've tried to .... as much as possible.
5 A: This is going to make her terribly unhappy.
   B: Yes I know. It'll ....
6 A: Could anyone help me with this?
   B: Yeah, I'll ....

27.4 Complete the sentences with a suitable adjective or *-ing* form.

1 This umbrella should keep you ....
2 I don't know why she keeps .... – it wasn't a very funny story.
3 I never drink coffee at night; it keeps me ....
4 If you do lots of exercise, it'll keep you ....
5 It's really stupid, but I keep .... to lock the door when I go out.
6 They're making a lot of noise in there. Could you tell them to keep .... ?

27.5 Can you translate the phrases in bold on the opposite page into your own language? If so, do you use the same verb in your own language?

28 Leave, catch and let

A Leave

leave home/work (= depart/go out from)	I always **leave home** before 8 am.
leave school/work/a husband/a wife (= permanently)	She **left her job** last year to have a baby.
	No one really knows why she **left her husband**.
leave sth/sb somewhere (= allow sb/sth to stay/remain in a place)	You can **leave** your coats in my bedroom.
	I **left** my things at home; I'll pick them up later.
leave sth somewhere (= forget sth)	I **left** my books on the bus. It was so stupid.
have got sth left (= the amount that remains)	I had £100 yesterday, and now **I've** only **got** £20 **left**.
	Have we got any coffee **left**, or did we drink it all?
leave a message	He wasn't in, so I **left a message** on his answerphone.
leave sb alone (= go away/don't disturb sb)	**Leave** Boris **alone** – he's working.

B Catch

catch a bus (= take/travel by)	We can walk or **catch a bus**; I don't mind.
catch a criminal (= find and take)	The police **caught the man** outside the bank.
catch a cold/flu (= get)	My girlfriend has **a cold** and I think I **caught** it from her.
not catch (= not hear what sb said)	I **didn't catch what he said**. Is it platform 3 or 4?
	I'm sorry, I **didn't catch your name**.
catch a ball	I had to run to **catch the ball**.
catch sb doing sth (= see sb when they are doing sth wrong)	My mother **caught** me taking food out of the fridge.

C Let

let sb do sth (= permit sb to do sth)	I **let** my sister borrow my car.
	My parents won't **let** me stay in the flat.
let sb know (= tell sb 'yes' or 'no')	I'll **let you know** tomorrow about the holiday.
	If you want to come, could you **let me know**?
let's ... (= introducing a suggestion)	Oh, come on, **let's** go out this evening.
	Let's try that new bar in the main square.
let me see (= a phrase we use to give ourselves time to think)	A: What time shall we leave?
	B: Er ... **let me see** ... er ... how about six o'clock?
let me do sth (= offering to do sth)	**Let me** help you (with the washing up).
	Let me give you a lift (to the station).

Exercises

28.1 Fill the gaps in these sentences and dialogues with a suitable verb.

1 We can walk to the High Street and then .... a bus to the cinema.
2 (*on the phone*) I'm afraid Paul's out. Do you want to .... a message?
3 I asked Dad, but he won't .... me borrow the car.
4 The teacher .... them talking to each other in the exam, so they could be in trouble.
5 I put everything in my bag for school, then .... it on the kitchen table.
6 A: Is it OK if I .... my bike in front of the apartment?
   B: Yes, sure.
7 A: I'm sorry, I didn't .... your name.   B: Michael.
8 A: What shall we do?
   B: Er, ... go to the swimming pool.

28.2 Complete the phrases in bold in these sentences.

1 **Please leave me** .... ; I'm trying to finish this essay.
2 I'm sorry, **I didn't quite** .... **what you said.**
3 If you want any more tickets, just **let me** ....
4 A: How many people can we take in the bus?
   B: Ooh … er, **let me** .... … er … about 30, I think.
5 We can't make an omelette – **we haven't got** any eggs .... You had the last one yesterday.
6 Do you want me to **leave a** .... **on his answerphone?**
7 You have to .... **the ball,** then throw it to someone else.
8 I **caught a** .... on holiday and I've still got it. I feel terrible.

28.3 Each sentence beginning below has two possible endings. Choose the correct combinations.

1 She left   a me use her mobile.
                 b her bags at the station.
2 She let   c the bus outside the supermarket.
                 d the man trying to steal her handbag.
3 She caught   e her job because it was boring.
                 f us go home early today because it's my birthday.

28.4 Complete these dialogues in a suitable way.

1 A: I don't know how to do this.   3 A: I have to go to the station.
   B: OK, let *me have a look* ....   B: Well, let ....
   A: Oh, thanks.   A: Oh, that's very kind of you.
2 A: I'm just going to do the washing-up.   4 A: Do you want to come next week?
   B: Oh, let ....   B: I don't know. I'll let ....
   A: No, you don't have to do that. Sit down.   tomorrow.

28.5 Would you let your best friend do these things? Ask somebody else the same questions if possible.

| borrow your bike or car for the weekend | choose clothes for you in a shop |
| live in your home while you're away | decide where you are both going for a holiday |

Get: uses and expressions

A Meanings

Get is an informal word and is very common in spoken English. It has many meanings.

RECEIVE	I **got** a couple of letters this morning. You **get** a certificate at the end of the course.
FIND/BUY	I **got** my ticket for the match yesterday. Where did you **get** those shoes? She's trying to **get a new job**.
BECOME	It **gets** dark very early in December. My hands are **getting** cold.
ARRIVE/REACH	When did you **get** here? I can't **get** there before 7 pm. I'll phone when I **get home**.
FETCH	Could you **get** the books from the cupboard? Wait here while I **get** the car.

B Get + past participle

We use this structure in particular expressions. It is more natural than just using the verb.

get married (= marry) **get divorced** (= divorce)	Rob and Sarah have just **got married**. They **got divorced** last year. (= the marriage ended officially)
get dressed (= dress) **get undressed** (= undress) **get changed** (= change clothes) **get lost** (= lose your way)	I **got dressed** quickly and went out. He **got undressed** and got into bed. I need to go home and **get changed** first. I **got lost** on my way to the station.

C Get + adjective

Get (= become) combines with many adjectives that often describe a change in state.

It's getting	hot/cold dark (*opp* light) late better/worse busy	I'm getting	hot/cold tired better/worse hungry ready (= preparing)

D Phrases and phrasal verbs

I **get on** very well **with** my sister. (= have a very good relationship with my sister)

How are you getting on? (= What progress are you making? e.g. with an exercise or in general)

Is it difficult to **get to know** people? (= meet people and make friends)

We should **get rid of** these books. (= sell them/throw them away; remove them)

My alarm wakes me up at 7, but I don't usually **get up** (= get out of bed) until 7.15.

Those boys **get on my nerves** (= annoy me and make me angry). They don't do any work.

Exercises

29.1 Write a synonym for 'get' in each of these sentences.

1 Where can I get something to eat round here?
2 I'm just going to get some paper from the office. I'll be back in a minute.
3 What time did they get here last night?
4 He got very angry when I told him what you did with his CDs.
5 I couldn't get a room; all the hotels were full.
6 I normally get about four or five letters a week.
7 This book is getting quite interesting.
8 I must get some stamps before I go home.
9 He sent the letter last week but I didn't get it until yesterday.
10 Do they often get here early?

29.2 Complete the dialogues using *getting* + a suitable adjective. Add other words if necessary.

1 A: It's *getting cold in here.*
   B: Yes, it is. I'll turn on the heating.
2 A: I'm ....
   B: OK, let's have something to eat then.
3 A: I'm ....
   B: Yes, me too. I'll open the window.
4 A: It's ....
   B: Yes, it is. I think I'll go to bed.
5 A: It's ....
   B: Yes, it is. I'll put the lights on.
6 A: I'm ....
   B: No, you're not. You're getting much better. You understand a lot now.

29.3 Rewrite each of these sentences using an expression with 'get'. The meaning must stay the same.

1 I had to put on my clothes very quickly.
   I had to *get dressed very quickly.*
2 How do you meet people and make friends in this country?
   How do you .... ?
3 I have a good relationship with my boss.
   I ....
4 We would like to throw away most of the furniture in this room.
   We would like to ....
5 Someone told me you're doing a new course. How's it going?
   Someone told me you're doing a new course. .... ?
6 The people in my class really annoy me.
   The people in my class ....
7 They're preparing to go out.
   They're ....
8 My sister told me to get out of bed.
   My sister told me to ....

29.4 Write down examples of 'get' that you see or hear, then try to group your sentences according to the different meanings. This will help you to get an idea of the ways in which this important word is used in English.

30 Go: uses and expressions

A Come vs go

NOTE
There is a similar difference between **bring** and **take**: **Take** the mobile phone with you, then Peter can use it. He can **bring** it back here tomorrow.

With **go** the movement is usually away from the speaker; with **come** the movement is towards the speaker. For example, you are at school and the time is 9.30 am.

> I had to **go** to Jimmy's to pick up some books. Then I **went** to the post office before I **came** to school.

Sometimes the speaker imagines they are in another place. When Thomas meets Marta in Spain, he invites her to stay at his home in Switzerland. He says:
'Would you like to **come** and visit me in Bern?' (He lives there, so her movement is towards him.)

We can also imagine that the listener is in a different place. Talking to Marta, Thomas says:
'I'll **come** to your flat at 7.30 pm.' (She will be at home, so his movement is towards her.)

B Different meanings of 'go'

- When you leave a place <u>in order to do an activity</u>, you often express it in these ways.

  go + -ing form
  We could **go shopping.**
  They all **went sightseeing.**
  I'd like to **go swimming.**

  go (out) + for a + noun
  Why don't we **go (out) for a** walk/drive?
  They decided to **go (out) for a** drink.
  She wants to **go (out) for a** meal.

- **Go** can describe a changing state (usually a bad one) with certain adjectives.
  My dad's **going grey** (= his hair is going grey) and I'm **going bald.** (= losing my hair)
  The company **went bankrupt** last year. (= lost all its money and had to stop operating)
  My grandmother is **going deaf.** (deaf = cannot hear)
  Our 12-year-old dog is **going blind.** (blind = cannot see)
  He'll **go mad** (= get very angry *infml*) if you wear his jacket.

- When you want to say/ask if a road or form of transport takes you somewhere.
  Does this bus **go** to the National Gallery?
  This road **goes** through the mountains.

- **Go and get** means fetch.
  Could you **go and get** the glasses from the kitchen?

- When you talk about the usual position for something.
  The dictionaries **go** on the bottom shelf.
  Does this table **go** next to the wall?

C Expressions with 'go' as noun and verb

I've never tried bungee jumping but I'd love to **have a go.** (= try it)
How's it going? (*infml*) (= How are you? or What progress are you making? e.g. with an exercise)
I'd like to see the film. Why don't we **go together**? (= go somewhere with another person/people)
It's **time to go.** (= time for us to leave)

Exercises

30.1 Complete the dialogue using the correct form of *come, go, bring* or *take*. (Two verbs are possible in one of the answers.)

A: What time are you (1) ...*going*........................ to Jim's party this evening?

B: I'm not sure because Chris is (2) .... here first, and then we'll
(3) .... together.

A: Right. Do you know what's happening about the music?

B: Yeah, I'm going to (4) .... some CDs, and Sue is (5) .... her
guitar. But I'll probably leave quite early, so could you (6) .... my CDs
back here tomorrow?

A: Yeah, sure. What time?

B: Well, I want to (7) .... to the shops in the morning. Could you
(8) .... before ten?

A: Yeah, no problem.

30.2 Replace the <u>underlined</u> words with a different word or phrase. The meaning must stay the same.

1 Excuse me. Does this road <u>go</u> to the bus station?   *take me*
2 Some people aren't interested in scuba diving but I've always wanted to have a <u>go</u>.
3 Hi, Sue. Nice to see you again. How<u>'s it going</u>?
4 Could you <u>go and get</u> my handbag from the other room?
5 If you want, we could go <u>with each other</u>.

30.3 Complete these sentences with an *-ing noun* (e.g. riding), or *for a + noun* (e.g. for a walk).

1 I went .... this morning and bought some books and clothes.
2 We didn't have much food in the house, so we decided to go out ....
3 Why don't we go .... in that nice new bar near the square?
4 I wanted to go .... because it was my first time in Rome.
5 My brother has just got a new sports car. We could go .... at the weekend.
6 The pool is at the end of the road, so we often go ....

30.4 Complete these sentences with a suitable word.

1 Don't put the desk in the corner. It doesn't go ...*there*........................
2 You can always wear a hearing aid if you go ....
3 If business doesn't improve they could go ....
4 You can always dye your hair (= change the colour) if you start going ....
5 And you can wear a wig (= false hair) if you go ....
6 If the dog comes into the house with wet feet, my aunt will go ....
7 He's going .... , but he's hoping to get a guide dog next year.
8 You don't need to go on your own. We could go ....

30.5 Look up 'go' in a good English dictionary. Find two or three new meanings (including
phrasal verbs and idioms) that you think may be useful to you. Try to learn them. Write
down the meanings with example sentences in your notebook. Write a translation as well
if you want.

The senses

 A ## The five basic senses

These are: **sight, hearing, taste, touch** and **smell**. For each one we use a basic verb, which can be followed by an adjective or noun in these constructions.

It **looks** terrible. (= from what I could see)   It **looks like** a wedding cake.
He **sounds** German. (= from what I heard)   It **sounds like** a good idea.
It **tastes** strange. (= from tasting it)   This **tastes** a bit **like** chicken.
It **feels** soft. (= from touching it)   It **feels like** wool.
It **smells** wonderful. (= from smelling it)   This **smells like** garlic.

We can also use the verbs as nouns.

I didn't like **the look of** the fish.   We could hear **the sound of** church bells.
Do you really like **the taste of** olives?   She hates **the smell of** petrol.

 B ## See, look (at) and watch

Compare these examples of **see** (= able to see) with **look (for)** sth (= search for, try to find), **look (at)** sth (= pay attention to sth, usually not moving and for a short time) and **watch** (= pay attention to sth not moving, usually for a long time).

I can't **see** a thing without my glasses. (= I'm not able to see anything)
I can't find my keys and I've **looked** (= searched/looked carefully) everywhere.
The police have been **watching** that man for weeks.
If you **look at** (= look carefully) the map, you can **see** (= are able to see) the mountains on the left.
He ran into me because he wasn't **looking**. (= paying attention) [the speaker seems angry]
He ran into me because he didn't **see** me. (= wasn't able to see me) [the speaker is not angry]

Sometimes two verbs are possible in one context; sometimes only one.

I **saw/watched** a great programme on TV last night. [For TV, we can use either verb.]
I **saw** a great film last night at the cinema. [For the cinema, we only use **see**.]

C ## Hear and listen (to)

Hear means <u>to be able</u> to hear; **listen (to)** means <u>to pay attention</u> to things you hear. Compare:

I couldn't **hear** what she said. (= I was physically unable to hear)
I can sometimes **hear** the trains from my bedroom. (= I am able to hear without trying)
I don't know what she said because I wasn't **listening**. (= I wasn't paying attention)
I was **listening to** the radio (= paying attention to it), when I **heard** a strange noise outside.

Sometimes we can use **hear** (but not in the progressive form) to mean 'listen to'.

I know he's dead – I **heard** it on the radio last night. (= I heard it when I was listening)

 D ## Touch

Don't **touch** those wires – they're dangerous.
You have to **press** that button to start the machine.
I don't feel safe up here. Could you **hold** my hand?

Exercises

31.1 Complete the sentences using words from the box. Use a dictionary to help you if necessary.

> banana sore brother salmon photograph silk
> ~~new~~ ripe doorbell horrible fresh old socks

1 Those shoes look ....*new*........... When did you buy them?
2 I don't think I'll try these peaches yet; they don't feel ....
3 This milk smells .... I'll open another bottle.
4 We had some fruit which tasted a bit like ....
5 My feet are feeling very .... after that run.
6 I love the smell of .... bread.
7 That painting actually looks like a ....
8 I met Malcolm the other day and he really looks like his ....
9 It's a pink fish but it doesn't taste like ....
10 This cheese is terrible – it smells like ....
11 Your telephone sounds just like a ....
12 This dress was quite cheap but it feels like ....

31.2 Complete the sentences below the pictures using *looks/tastes/feels* + adjective.

1 This man .... 2 This pillow .... 3 This apple ....

31.3 <u>Underline</u> the correct verb in brackets. (Both verbs are correct in one case.)

1 I was (listening to/hearing) the radio when I (listened to/heard) a terrible noise outside.
2 The government is going to introduce new laws about noisy neighbours – I (listened to/heard) it on the radio this morning.
3 She turned up the volume but I still couldn't (listen to/hear) it.
4 I don't know if this is an antique; we'll get an expert to come and (look at/see) it.
5 They wanted to stay and (watch/look at) the programme, but it was a bit late.
6 I was very angry with Tom – he just wasn't (hearing/listening to) what I was saying.
7 Can you bend over and (touch/press) your toes?
8 You have to (touch/press) the eject button if you want to get the video out.
9 Could you (touch/hold) this video for a moment while I move the TV?
10 If you (watch/look) carefully, you can (look/see) how the man does the trick with those cards.

31.4 Complete these sentences about your own likes and dislikes.

> I love the smell of .... I hate the smell of ....
> I love the sound of .... I hate the sound of ....
> I love the taste of .... I hate the taste of ....

32 Partitives: a bag of ..., a bit of ...

There are many different words used to describe a particular quantity of something.

A Containers (e.g. a bag) and contents (e.g. of shopping)

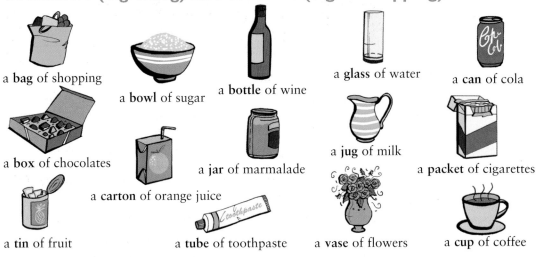

a **bag** of shopping

a **bowl** of sugar

a **bottle** of wine

a **glass** of water

a **can** of cola

a **box** of chocolates

a **jar** of marmalade

a **jug** of milk

a **packet** of cigarettes

a **carton** of orange juice

a **tin** of fruit

a **tube** of toothpaste

a **vase** of flowers

a **cup** of coffee

B With uncountable nouns

Certain words make uncountable nouns countable in order to describe a specific quantity, e.g. Has anyone got **a sheet of paper** I can have? Other examples are:

a **piece** of toast	a **piece** of cake	a **piece** of wood
a **slice** of ham	a **slice** of bread (= a thin piece)	a **drop** of milk (= a little)

We use **piece** with the nouns above and some abstract nouns, e.g. **a piece of advice**, but the most common phrase in spoken English is **a bit**: we use it with a wide range of nouns.

a **bit** of advice   a **bit** of bread   a **bit** of luck   a **bit** of time   a **bit** of news

C A pair of ...

Some nouns have two parts, e.g. trousers (two legs) and shoes (left and right). You can use **pair of** to specify the number, e.g. a **pair of** skis, two **pairs of** shoes, three **pairs of** shorts.

D Groups of things

a **herd** of cows

a **group** of people

a **bunch** of flowers

a **gang** of youths/ kids/teenagers

a **bunch** of grapes

Exercises

32.1 Complete the phrases below the pictures.

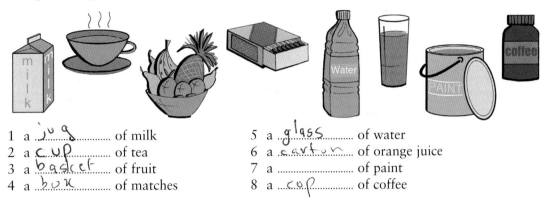

1 a _jug_ of milk
2 a _cup_ of tea
3 a _basket_ of fruit
4 a _box_ of matches

5 a _glass_ of water
6 a _carton_ of orange juice
7 a .... of paint
8 a _cup_ of coffee

32.2 Contents come in different containers. Are these normal or unusual? If they are unusual, change them and make them normal.

Example a glass of soup   Unusual: It's usually a bowl or cup of soup.

1 a vase of coffee _of flower_
2 a jug of wine
3 a jar of mustard
4 a carton of toothpaste

5 a bowl of milk
6 a tube of cigarettes
7 a bag of salt
8 a tin of tomatoes

32.3 Complete these sentences with a suitable noun.

1 I gave her a big _bunch_ of flowers from my garden.
2 The police are looking for a .... of youths who may be responsible for the damage.
3 I cut about six .... of ham and put them on a plate.
4 They own a large .... of land on the coast.
5 I did a .... of homework last night, then went out.
6 The teacher told us to take a blank .... of paper, then write our names at the top.
7 A small .... of people gathered outside the embassy.
8 I need at least two .... of socks inside these shoes.
9 I asked him for a .... of advice.
10 I like to put a .... of cream in my coffee.
11 Have you seen that old .... of boots I use for gardening?
12 I've got a .... of time, so I can help you now if you like.

32.4 <u>Underline</u> any words in (brackets) which are wrong in these sentences.

1 I asked her for a (bit/piece) of advice.
2 I asked for a (piece/sheet) of cake.
3 There was a (group/gang) of journalists outside her house.
4 My lunch consisted of two (slices/pieces) of bread and a small (bunch/group) of grapes.
5 She hit me over the head with a small (piece/bit) of wood.
6 I'm in a hurry, but I've still got a (bit/piece) of time.
7 We had a (piece/bit) of luck this morning: we won some money!
8 Could I have a (piece/bit/drop) of milk in my coffee?

33 Uncountable nouns and plural nouns

A Uncountable nouns

NOTE
You can make many uncountable nouns singular using different nouns, e.g. **a piece of toast, a news item**, etc. In spoken English we use **a bit** with many nouns, e.g. **a bit of information, a bit of advice**.

Uncountable nouns, e.g. information, homework, advice:
- don't have a plural form, e.g. **information** (NOT ~~informations~~)
- are not used with the indefinite article, e.g. (**some**) **homework** (NOT ~~a~~ homework)
- are used with a singular verb, e.g. my **advice is** … (NOT my advice ~~are~~ …)

The uncountable nouns below are often countable in other languages. Look at them carefully, and also notice the other words in **bold** that are often used with them.

Perhaps we could **get** some more **information about** the concert off the internet.
She **gave me** lots of **advice** about the best dictionary to buy.
Are we going to sell all the **furniture**? (= tables, chairs, armchairs, desks, etc.)
My **knowledge** (= what I know) **of** German is **very limited**. (= very little)
You need a lot of **camping equipment**. (e.g. tent, sleeping bag, things for cooking, etc.)
She's worked hard and she's **making good progress**. (= she is improving/getting better)
Is there any more **news** about the rail strike?
The teacher **gave us** a lot of **homework** last night.
I always put my camera in my **hand luggage**. (= bags you carry with you on the plane)
Would you like some more **toast**? (= bread that is heated and brown on both sides)

B In dictionaries

Learners' dictionaries show countable nouns with a (C) and uncountable nouns with a (U). Some nouns can be countable with one meaning and uncountable in another.

book (C)	The books are on the table.
housework (U)	I did a lot of housework (= cleaned the house) this morning.
hair (U)	My hair is getting very long. I must get it cut.
hair (C)	I'm starting to get a few grey hairs now.

C Plural nouns

Plural nouns, e.g. trousers, stairs, sunglasses:
- have a plural form and aren't used with 'a/an', e.g. **trousers** (NOT ~~a trouser~~)
- usually take a plural verb, e.g. These stairs **are** dangerous (NOT These stairs ~~is~~ …)
- can sometimes be made singular using **a pair of**, e.g. **a pair of sunglasses**

Here are some other nouns that are usually plural:
I've just bought **a pair of trainers**.
These **shorts** are too long.
I bought new **pyjamas** when I went into hospital.
The **scissors** are on the table.
I often wear **sunglasses** for driving.
You can **weigh yourself** on the **scales** in the bathroom.
He couldn't hear me because he was **wearing headphones**.

Exercises

33.1 Check the pronunciation of the <u>underlined</u> words in the Index. Practise saying the phrases.

my <u>knowledge</u> of German   camping <u>equipment</u>   buy some <u>furniture</u>
hand <u>luggage</u>   a pair of <u>pyjamas</u>   I want to <u>weigh</u> myself

33.2 Correct the mistakes in these sentences.
1 I need some informations.
2 The teacher has a news about the school trip.
3 The furnitures are very old.
4 I'm looking for a new jeans.
5 Your hairs are getting very long.
6 Do you have a scissors?
7 We had a lot of homeworks yesterday.
8 Do you think she's making a progress with her English?
9 These trousers is too small.
10 She gave me some good advices.

33.3 Mark these nouns countable, uncountable, or countable and uncountable. If they can be both, write sentence examples to show the difference.

cup   housework   coffee   spaghetti   money   coin   work   travel

33.4 Complete these dialogues using a suitable plural noun or uncountable noun from the opposite page. Make sure the form of each word is correct. Look at the example first.

Example A: It's too hot for jeans.   B: You need *a pair of shorts*.

1 A: I have to cut this paper into three pieces.
  B: You need ....
2 A: I can't see because the sun is in my eyes.
  B: You need ....
3 A: I don't know what to do when I leave school.
  B: You need ....
4 A: My room looks so empty.
  B: You need ....
5 A: I want to find out how much I weigh.
  B: You need ....
6 A: I can't play my music loud because my mother always complains.
  B: You need ....

33.5 Read this short text from a radio broadcast. Find two uncountable nouns and one noun always used in a plural form. (These words are not included on the opposite page.)

Traffic on the M3 motorway has been terrible this morning because of the bad weather and the roadworks near Basingstoke, and there have been long delays for motorists heading into London. Drivers are advised to choose an alternative route if at all possible.

34 Verbs + -*ing* form or infinitive

A Verb + -*ing* form

Some verbs are followed by an -*ing* form if the next word is a verb. Here are some of them.

enjoy	finish	imagine	admit	avoid
feel like (*infml*)	(don't) mind	can't stand	give up	deny

I've lived in New Zealand all my life; I can't **imagine** liv**ing** anywhere else.
Some people **can't stand** (= hate) work**ing** at the weekend but **I don't mind.**
(= for me it's OK)
His doctor told him to **give up** smok**ing**. (= stop smoking)
I always try to **avoid** go**ing** through the city centre. (= stay away from it)
At the police station, he **admitted** steal**ing** her money, but **denied** tak**ing** the computer.
(= he said 'yes' he took the money, but 'no' he didn't take the computer)
Do you **feel like** go**ing** out (= want to go out) this evening?

B Verb + infinitive

Some verbs are followed by an infinitive if the next word is a verb.

decide	want	seem	appear
hope	forget	expect	mean
manage	refuse	promise	offer

It's a long walk so **I offered** to take them in the car.
I **expect** (= think or believe something will happen) to get the results before next week.
I **meant** (= planned/intended) to get the information, but I **forgot** (= didn't remember) to
phone.
It was hard work but we **managed** to finish it. (= we were able to finish it but it was
difficult)
I asked her to carry the suitcases but she **refused** to help. (= she said 'no')
They **promised** to phone me as soon as they arrived. (= they said they would)

C Verb + -*ing* form or infinitive

Some verbs can be followed by an -*ing* form or infinitive and the meaning is very similar,
e.g. **love**, **like** and **prefer**. But with some verbs there is a difference in meaning:

I **remembered** to buy my grandmother a birthday card. (= I <u>didn't forget</u> to buy one)
I **remember** making cards for her when I was small. (= it's one of my memories from the
past)

D Verb + infinitive without 'to'

Two common verbs are followed by an object + infinitive without 'to': **make** someone do
something, and **let** someone do something.

My parents **make** me **do** my homework every night. (= They **force** me **to do** my homework.)
My parents **let** me **go out** at the weekend. (= They **allow**/permit me **to go** out.)

Exercises

34.1 <u>Underline</u> the correct word(s). Be careful: in two sentences, both possibilities are correct.

1 We decided (to work/working) during our holiday.
2 She promised (to help/helping) us.
3 I don't feel like (to go/going) for a walk at the moment.
4 She hopes (to spend/spending) some time in the mountains this summer.
5 Do you actually like (to go out/going out) when it's raining?
6 I can't imagine (to eat/eating) pasta every day of the week.
7 Most of the time she prefers (to work/working) on her own.
8 I don't remember (to go/going) to the zoo when we stayed in Madrid.
9 He hopes (to finish/finishing) his thesis by the end of the month.
10 I don't mind (to help/helping) you if I'm not busy.

34.2 Complete part (c) of each sentence in a suitable way, starting with a verb.

1 Most people want:
  a to be rich   b to get married   c ....
2 A lot of people can't stand:
  a getting wet   b getting up early   c ....
3 Most people enjoy:
  a going to parties   b lying on a beach   c ....
4 On hot days most people don't feel like:
  a working   b eating big meals   c ....
5 Most people expect:
  a to be happy   b to find a job they will like   c ....
6 A lot of people don't mind:
  a washing up   b ironing   c ....
7 Some parents make their teenage children:
  a wear certain clothes   b do housework   c ....
8 Other parents let their teenage children:
  a wear what they like   b stay out all night   c ....

Now think about each of the above statements. Are they true, and are they (or were they) true for you?

34.3 Read the story and answer the questions below.

> When Julie was 17, her father said she could go on holiday with two school friends. He also said that he would lend her the money for the hotel, but she must pay for the flight and her entertainment. Julie was delighted and said she would bring him back a wonderful present, and pay him back in six months. First they had to decide where to go. They looked at lots of brochures and finally agreed on a two-week holiday in the south of France. They had a great time, but unfortunately Julie spent all her money and forgot to buy a present for her father.

1 What did Julie's father let her do?   He let *her go on holiday with friends.*
2 And what did he offer to do?   He offered ....
3 But what did he refuse to do?   He refused ....
4 In return what did Julie promise?   She promised ....
5 What did the three girls decide?   They decided ....
6 What did Julie forget?   She forgot ....

35 Verb patterns

A Verb + object

subject	verb	object
They	discussed (= talked about)	the film for hours.
Did she	answer	the question?

B Verb + object + question word

NOTE
There is no direct object after **explain**: He explained ~~me~~ what to do.

subject	verb	object	question word	
I	told	them	where	to find it.
She	asked	(us)	why	we were late.
He	showed	everyone	what	to do.

C Verb + object + infinitive

subject	verb	object	infinitive
She	asked	everyone	to leave.
They	told	us	to wait outside.
The doctor	advised	him	to stay in bed.
I	wanted	the others	to help us.
He	persuaded	me	to go to the party.
She	warned	them	to **be careful**. (= think/pay attention)

Warn (= tell someone of a possible danger, and often tell them what they should(n't) do)
She **warned** the children not to swim near the boats.
Persuade (= make somebody change their mind/opinion)
John wanted to get the new car now, but I **persuaded** him to wait.

D Verb + 'that' clause

subject	verb	(that) clause
He	said	(that) it was good.
She	suggested	(that) we go together.
He	mentioned	(that) the film was tonight.

She warned me not to try rollerblading.

Mention (= say or write a fact or piece of information)
When I spoke to the secretary, she didn't **mention** (that) our teacher was ill.

E Verb + (object) + preposition

I **asked** the taxi driver **for** directions to the hotel.
They **blamed** me **for** the accident. (= they said I was responsible for it/it was my **fault**)
She **complained** (to the manager) **about** the service. (= said she was not satisfied with it)
The manager **apologised for** the noise outside the restaurant. (= the manager said sorry)

Exercises

35.1 Correct the mistakes in these sentences.

1 She said me the film was terrible.   *She said the film was terrible.*
2 He told it's impossible.
3 The teacher is going to explain you what to do.
4 She suggested us to go to an Italian restaurant.
5 Can we discuss about my report?
6 I want that he leaves.
7 You must answer to the question.
8 I apologised my mistake.
9 She advised me buy a dictionary.
10 I asked to the waiter for a knife.

35.2 Complete the sentences with a suitable verb. (There may be more than one answer.)

1 They watched the film together and then they ...*discussed*... it in small groups.
2 I didn't understand the exercise but she .... me what to do.
3 She wasn't satisfied with her room, so she .... to the manager.
4 My suitcase was very heavy, so I .... the hotel porter to carry it.
5 Martin knew the area was dangerous but he didn't .... me when I went there.
6 I didn't want to go at first but she .... me.
7 I didn't feel well and my mother .... me to stay at home and rest.
8 She lost all her money but she didn't .... it when I phoned her.
9 I don't think it was my fault but they still .... me for it.
10 She didn't know the way, so I .... how to get there.

35.3 Complete these sentences in a logical way.

1 Some of them were getting hungry so I suggested ....
2 They were making a lot of noise next door and I told ....
3 Paula went to that new Greek restaurant and said ....
4 We read the book for homework and discussed ....
5 She didn't have any money, so she wanted ....
6 It was only a few minutes to the beach, but I still couldn't persuade ....
7 She said there were strange noises outside her flat, so I advised ....
8 The team played badly but most of the newspapers blamed ....
9 The water can make you ill and I warned ....
10 If you don't understand the instructions, someone will explain ....

35.4 When you learn new verbs, you may need to know the constructions that are used with them. So look at the grammar information about a word in a good dictionary, and always look carefully at the example sentences, then write one or two of your own. Do it for these three examples. What patterns from the opposite page are used after these verbs?

> order   recommend   prevent

Example   ask   1 + object + question word, e.g. I asked her what to do.
2 + object + infinitive, e.g. I asked them to help me.
3 + (object) + preposition, e.g. I asked (her) for some advice.

36 Adjectives

A 'Scale' and 'limit' adjectives

NOTE

We usually don't use 'very' with limit adjectives (NOT ~~very marvellous~~) or 'absolutely' with scale adjectives (NOT ~~absolutely good~~), but we can use 'really' with both (**really marvellous** and **really good**).

LIMIT	SCALE		SCALE	LIMIT
terrible	(very) bad	OK	(very) good	marvellous
awful				**terrific**
dreadful				**great**

Adjectives such as 'good' and 'bad' can be anything from weak to strong, e.g. **quite good** or **very good**. Adjectives at the end of the scale only have one extreme meaning and are often used on their own. We can make them stronger with 'absolutely' or 'really', e.g. **absolutely great, really awful**.

scale	*limit*	*scale*	*limit*
(very) small	(absolutely) **tiny**	(very) pleased	(absolutely) **delighted**
big	**huge/enormous**	cold	**freezing**
tired	**exhausted**	nice	**delicious** (food only)
interesting	**fascinating**	frightened (= afraid of)	**terrified**
surprised	**astonished**	hungry	**starving** (*infml*)

B Adjectives ending in *-ing* and *-ed*

A large group of adjectives can have an *-ing* or *-ed* ending. The *-ing* ending describes a person, thing or situation; the *-ed* ending describes the effect on someone of this person, thing or situation.

It was such a **boring** party. Most people left before 11 pm – they were so **bored**.
I think the students are **depressed** because the weather is very **depressing** at the moment.

Other examples of adjectives ending *-ing* and *-ed* are:

surprising/ed	astonishing/ed
tiring/ed	exhausting/ed
interesting/ed	fascinating/ed
frightening/ed	terrifying/ed
confusing/ed	exciting/ed
embarrassing/ed	disappointing/ed

I'm exhausted.

John isn't very good at French, so I was quite **surprised** when he passed the exam – and I was absolutely **astonished** at his result. He got 98%.
I thought it was very **exciting** when I first got on a plane. Then we took off and flew into bad weather. I was **terrified**.
London has lots of streets with the same name; it's very **confusing** for tourists.
Greg was very **disappointed** when they lost the match. Then, the next day, his girlfriend left him, so now he's really **depressed**.
One of our teachers often forgets my name. It was funny at first, but now it's a bit **embarrassing**.

Exercises

36.1 Write one limit adjective with a similar meaning to these scale adjectives. Cover the opposite page before you begin.

1 bad ....*awful*........   6 good ....
2 small ....   7 cold ....
3 tired ....   8 big ....
4 surprised ....   9 hungry ....
5 interesting ....   10 frightened ....

36.2 Rewrite this postcard using limit adjectives where possible to give a more positive and/or more extreme effect. Make any other changes that are necessary and include *absolutely* once or twice.

Dear Sandy
Arrived on Sunday evening after ~~a very tiring~~ *an exhausting* journey. We're very pleased with the hotel – our room is big and the food is nice. We've been lucky with the weather as well – it's been hot every day so far, so we've spent most of the time on the beach. Tomorrow we're planning to walk to a village a couple of kilometres along the coast. In this weather, I'm sure we'll be really tired by the time we get back, but it does sound an interesting place, so I'm looking forward to it.
I'll write again in a couple of days and tell you about it.

Love,
Benita

36.3 Complete the dialogues using a suitable 'limit' adjective in the correct form (*-ing* or *-ed*).

1 A: I was very <u>interested</u> in her talk.
   B: Yes, it was absolutely ....*fascinating*...........
2 A: You weren't <u>frightened</u>, were you?
   B: Yes, it was absolutely ....
3 A: It was a <u>surprising</u> decision, wasn't it?
   B: Yes, everyone was ....

4 A: Was the journey very <u>tiring</u>?
   B: Yes, I was ....
5 A: Are you <u>hungry</u>?
   B: Yes, I'm absolutely ....
6 A: I expect you were very <u>pleased</u> with your score.
   B: Yes, I was absolutely ....

36.4 Think of an adjective from the opposite page to describe how the people felt in these situations.

1 They walked ten miles, then spent the afternoon cutting down trees.   *exhausted*
2 From the description in the travel brochure, they expected a beautiful big villa by the sea. In actual fact it was quite small, not very nice, and miles from the beach.
3 They wore jeans to the party but when they arrived everyone was wearing very formal clothes.
4 One person told them the street was on the left, another told them to turn right, and a third person said they had to go back to the station.
5 My brother has a flat and it's usually in a terrible mess – he's very untidy. But yesterday when I visited him, the place was incredibly tidy. In fact everything looked new.

37 Prepositions: place

A At, on, in

NOTE

She lives **in Danver Road.** BUT She lives **at 43 Danver Road.**

at a point/place	I met her at the bus stop.	She lives at 43 Danver Road.
	He's at work (i.e. not at home).	They're at a party tonight.
on a surface	The book's on the desk.	We put the picture on the wall.
	They sat on the floor.	Don't put it on the sofa.
in an area or space	A country in Africa.	She lives in Poland.
	He's in the kitchen.	The key's in the top drawer.

B Opposites

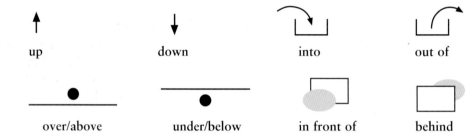

up   down   into   out of

over/above   under/below   in front of   behind

Over/above and **under/below** are very similar in meaning, but **over** and **under** sometimes suggest movement. For example:

When we flew **over** Paris we couldn't see much because we were **above** the clouds.
Below us was the river which ran **under** the bridge.

C Other common prepositions of place

We drove **along** one side of the lake, then **round** the top shore, **past** the old castle, and finally **through** the village.

We came **over** the bridge and parked **next to** the house, which was **opposite** the hotel.

Our house is **between** two shops and it's **near** a bus stop. You just go **across** the road and walk **along** the other side **towards** the church.

Exercises

37.1 **Fill the gaps with *at*, *on* or *in*.**

1 I put the books .... the table.
2 The butter is .... the fridge.
3 We saw them .... the bus stop.
4 I met her .... a party.
5 She works .... Moscow.
6 The dictionary is .... my desk.
7 I sat .... the bed and wrote the letter.
8 I left my books .... school.
9 There was still a lot of snow .... the ground when I arrived.
10 He lives .... a very nice area.

37.2 **Complete these dialogues using the opposite preposition.**

1 Was he standing in front of you?
   No, _behind me._
2 Is it up the hill to his house?
   No, it's ....
3 Did you climb over the fence?
   No, we got ....
4 Did you see her get into the car?
   No, but I saw her get ....
5 Does she live in the flat above you?
   No, she's ....

37.3 **Look at this picture and complete the description of the route you took on the first day.**

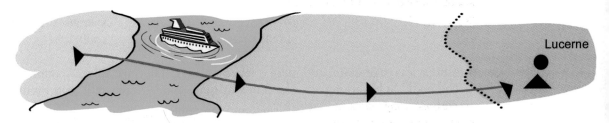

Lucerne

We took the boat (1) .... the channel, then we drove (2) .... France and
(3) .... Switzerland, where we spent the first night (4) .... a small town quite
(5) .... Lucerne.

Now look at this picture and complete the description of the second day.

The next morning we walked (6) .... a river which ran (7) .... two
mountains. We had lunch (8) .... a small restaurant and then walked (9) ....
the small town of Stans before heading back.

38 Adverbs: frequency and degree

A Frequency (= how often)

← ─── →

always	often	quite often	sometimes	occasionally	seldom *(fml)*	never
	frequently				hardly ever	
					rarely	

- Adverbs of frequency usually go before the <u>main</u> verb, but not if the main verb is 'to be':
  I **occasionally** <u>see</u> them.   They **hardly ever** <u>go</u> to the cinema now.
  She <u>is</u> **often** late these days.   I've **never** <u>tried</u> Korean food.

- **Sometimes, occasionally** and **often** can go at the beginning or end of the sentence:
  They go to the zoo **quite often**.   I play tennis **occasionally**.
  Sometimes my parents give me money.   **Occasionally** I work at the weekend.

B Degree (= how much)

These adverbs are used with adjectives. They are more common in spoken English. Each group has a similar meaning, but read the notes below carefully.

I was **a bit** bored	It's **quite** large	They were **very** interesting
slightly	fairly	extremely
	rather	incredibly
	pretty	really

- **A bit** = less than **quite**, and **quite** = less than **very**. They are all very common.
  The book's **a bit** boring.   The film was **quite** good.   She tells **very** funny stories.

- **A bit, pretty** and **really** are *informal* and much more common in spoken English. **A bit** is mostly used before negative adjectives or adjectives with a negative prefix.
  The food was **pretty** good.   This watch must be **really** expensive.
  The hotel was **a bit** disappointing.   The explanation was **a bit** unnecessary.

- **Rather** is like 'quite' and 'fairly', but we often use it when something is a surprise.
  Her cooking is **rather** good actually. (= better than I thought and a very nice surprise)
  People don't usually like factories, but I think they're **rather** interesting places.

- **Incredibly** and **extremely** are stronger than 'very'.
  We're **extremely** busy at the moment.   I was **incredibly** tired at the end.

C Almost/nearly

It's **almost/nearly** five o'clock. (= it is probably about 4.57)
I **almost/nearly** lost the match. (= I won but only just; only by a small amount)

D Hardly

I **hardly** had **anything** to eat for lunch. (= I had almost nothing)
She could **hardly** walk after her operation. (= it was difficult for her to walk)

Exercises

38.1 Organise these mixed-up words into correct sentences.

1 brother often us Sundays visits on my
2 me ever phones she hardly
3 have leg my broken never I
4 summer ever saw I hardly him the during
5 get occasionally I early up
6 lose often I glasses quite my

38.2 Replace the <u>underlined</u> adverb with a different adverb that has the same meaning.

1 She <u>seldom</u> goes to conferences now.
2 The cinema was <u>fairly</u> full.
3 There were <u>almost</u> 50 people there, you know.
4 I thought it was <u>a bit</u> disappointing, didn't you?
5 I'm afraid I'm <u>extremely</u> busy next week.
6 We <u>frequently</u> ask them to turn their music down.

38.3 Respond to these sentences using 'rather' to show a positive surprise. (You can also add 'actually' at the end of the sentence; this is very common in spoken English.)

1 A: Was it a boring evening?
  B: No, it ....*was rather interesting, actually.*......
2 A: Were the children very noisy?
  B: No, they ....
3 A: I've heard it's a very dirty town. Is that true?
  B: No, it ....
4 A: Was the weather bad?
  B: No, it ....

38.4 Change the <u>underlined</u> adverbs to make these sentences more positive.

1 I thought they were <u>very</u> good. *I thought they were incredibly good.*
2 He's been getting <u>quite</u> good marks in his exams.
3 It's a <u>pretty</u> nice house.

Change these adverbs to make them <u>less negative</u>.

4 John said the flat was <u>very</u> small.
5 They said it was <u>fairly</u> boring.
6 The clothes were <u>very</u> expensive.

38.5 Put a frequency adverb into each of these sentences to make a true sentence about yourself. Make sure you put the adverb in the correct place.

1 I buy clothes I don't like.
2 I remember my dreams.
3 I give money to people in the street.
4 I clean my shoes.
5 I speak to strangers on buses and trains.
6 I lose things.

Now think about each of your answers to the above sentences. Do you think they are:
a fairly typical? b slightly unusual? c extremely unusual?

If possible, compare your answers with someone else.

39 Time and sequence

A When/as soon as

I'll phone my uncle **when** I get home.
As soon as I get home I'll phone my uncle.
When you've finished this exercise you can go home.
You can go home **as soon as** you've finished this exercise.

> The meaning is the same, but **as soon as** suggests it is more immediate. **When** and **as soon as** can be followed by the present tense or the present perfect [but not *will*].

B Two things happening at the same time

Pat got ready **while** I cooked the dinner. [Two actions that need similar periods of time.]
The accident happened **while** I was on my way to work. [A longer action 'on my way to work' and a shorter action 'the accident'. We can also use **when** or **as** here.]
I saw him (**just**) **as** I came out of the office. [For two <u>short</u> actions happening at the same time we use **as**, and we can add **just** for emphasis, e.g. He opened the door **just as** I rang the bell.]

C One thing after another

We met the others in the café, and **then/afterwards** we went to the match.
I finished my homework, and **after that/afterwards** I played some computer games.
After my visit to New York, I decided to have a rest.
We had something to eat **before** we went out.

We can also follow **before** and **after** with an *-ing* form:

After visit**ing** New York, I ...   We had something to eat **before** go**ing** out.

D A sequence of actions

We had a great holiday. **First of all** we stayed in St Moritz. **Then/After that** we drove down the coast for a few days. **Finally**, we went back to Switzerland to visit friends.

- We can use **afterwards** instead of 'after that', and especially if one thing happens soon after another, e.g. We had a couple of drinks, then **afterwards** we went back to the flat.

- If something happens after a lot of time or problems, you can use **eventually** or **in the end**, in place of **finally**, e.g. The weather was bad and the traffic was awful, but **eventually** we got there.

E A sequence of reasons

There are different combinations of words and phrases we can use here:

WORKER: Why can't we buy the new photocopiers now?
MANAGER: **First(ly)** we haven't got enough money. **Second(ly)** the new models are not available yet. And **third(ly)** the ones we have will be OK for at least six months.

- In spoken English we can start with **for one thing**, followed by **and for another (thing)**.
  A: What's wrong with that washing machine?
  B: Well, **for one thing** it's too big to go in the space. **And for another**, it's very noisy.

- For a second or final reason, we also use **anyway** in spoken English.
  We can't go to that club because it's too far. **Anyway**, I'm not a member.

Exercises

39.1 <u>Underline</u> the correct word(s) in brackets. Sometimes both answers are correct.

1 We can have lunch (when/as soon as) we've finished this.
2 I'll give them your message as soon as I (get/will get) there.
3 Maria cleaned the kitchen (as/while) I did the bathroom.
4 We must go to that gallery before (leave/leaving).
5 I had problems at the shop but (eventually/finally) they gave me back my money.
6 The phone rang (while/just as) I was shutting the front door.
7 The letter arrived (while/just as) we were having lunch.
8 We spent the morning in the park and (after that/afterwards) we went home for lunch.

39.2 Complete these sentences in a suitable way.

1 I'll give you the answers when ...you've finished...
2 We had a game of squash and afterwards ....
3 I'll meet you as soon as ....
4 I must remember to lock the back door before ....
5 He thinks he dropped the letter as ....
6 I worked with a partner. I looked up half of the words while ....
7 We had to wait for hours but eventually ....
8 If we phone his home, he probably won't be there. Anyway, ...
9 I saw him break the window just as ....
10 I knew she was angry as soon as ....

39.3 Add a final sentence (starting with a suitable link word or phrase) to each of these dialogues.

1 A: Why do you want to stay in this evening when we could go to Karl's party?
   B: Well, for one thing because my ex-boyfriend will be there and I really don't want to see him. And ....

2 A: What did you do?
   B: First of all we spent a few days in Paris. After that we took the train down to Marseilles and stayed with friends. ....
   ....

3 A: Why can't we send one of our staff to the conference?
   B: Firstly, I don't think that the company should send anyone to the conference.
   ....

39.4 You spent a weekend at a hotel and had these problems:

- There was very little variety in the food.
- The service was very slow.
- When you mentioned this to the staff, they were very rude.

The manager was on holiday during your stay, so you have decided to send a letter of complaint. Write the next part of this letter and then look at the model answer for the whole letter on page 219.

> Dear Sir,
> I have just returned from a weekend break at The Royal Hotel, and I'm
> afraid it was not a very enjoyable stay. Firstly, ...

40 Addition and contrast

A Also, as well, in addition

NOTE

In addition and **what's more** are more common in written English.

You can link two ideas in one sentence using **and**, e.g. The food is excellent **and** very good value. When we put this information in two sentences, we can use these link words.

The restaurant has excellent food. It's **also** very good value.
The food is excellent in that restaurant. It's very good value **as well** (or **too**).
You get very good food in that restaurant. **What's more**, it's open every day of the week.
The set menu is £15, which is excellent value. **In addition**, they give you a free glass of wine.

B Although, despite, in spite of

NOTE

It is common to include **still** for emphasis in these sentence contrasts.

When you contrast two ideas in <u>one sentence</u>, and the second idea is surprising or unexpected after the first, you can use these link words at the beginning or in the middle of the sentence.

She <u>still</u> won the game, **although/though** she had a bad knee.
Although/though some people were getting tired, we decided to carry on for a bit longer.

They went for a walk **despite the fact that** it was raining.
Despite having no money, he <u>still</u> seemed very happy.
They got there on time **in spite of** the delay.
In spite of all the problems, we <u>still</u> enjoyed the trip.

Despite/in spite of can be followed by a noun, an *-ing* form, or a clause beginning **the fact that** ...; **although** is only followed by a clause, e.g. Although she had ...

C However

But contrasts two ideas in one sentence; **however** contrasts two ideas in <u>two sentences</u>. **Though** can be used in a similar way in spoken English, but it comes at the end of the clause.

I don't agree with a lot of his methods. **However**, he is a good teacher.
We didn't like the town that much. **However**, the hotel was wonderful.
I didn't like the film at all. It was better than sitting at home, **though**.
They told us the shop was next to the station. We never found it, **though**.

D Whereas, however

Whereas and **however** can contrast a fact or opinion about one person, place or thing, with something different about other people, places or things. The second fact is a contrast but not always a surprise. Notice that **whereas** contrasts two ideas in a single sentence.

Sarah is careful **whereas** Christopher makes lots of mistakes.
The south is hot and dry **whereas** the north gets a lot of rain.
Most big cats such as tigers like to live alone. Lions, **however**, spend a lot of time in groups.
Marcel said it was very interesting. **However**, most of them thought it was a fairly stupid film.

Exercises

40.1 Organise these words into two groups: words that link ideas with a similar meaning, and words that show a contrast between ideas.

although	in addition	whereas	as well
however	also	what's more	despite

40.2 <u>Underline</u> the correct word(s) in brackets. Both answers may be correct.
1 (Although/In spite of) we left late, we still got there in time.
2 It was a fantastic evening (although/in spite of) the terrible food.
3 We have decided to go (in spite of/despite) the cost of the tickets.
4 They enjoyed the course, (although/whereas) it was very difficult.
5 I love the sea (what's more/whereas) most of my friends prefer the mountains.
6 We've found a lovely villa near the lake. (In addition/What's more) it has its own swimming pool, and we have free use of the owner's car.
7 We told John the car was too expensive. (However/Although), he still bought it.
8 Most people tried to help us. They were very friendly (too/as well).
9 It's busy during the week. At the weekend, (however/whereas), it's very quiet.
10 My uncle owns the factory opposite. He (also/however) runs the restaurant next door.

40.3 Combine parts from each column to form five short texts.

A	B	C
He went to school today	although	it's not really what he wants.
He always worked hard at school	in spite of	he's the most experienced.
He's got the right qualifications.	However,	the help I gave him.
He didn't pass the exam	whereas	he didn't feel very well.
He decided to take the job.	What's more,	most of his classmates were lazy.

40.4 Fill the gaps with a suitable link word or phrase.
1 .... the fact that they were busy, they still helped us.
2 It took me two hours to do it .... the others finished in half an hour.
3 People say the hotel is very good. ...., it's quite cheap.
4 People say the hotel is terrible. ...., it's quite cheap.
5 She managed to get there, ... she didn't have a map like the others.
6 It's not the best dictionary you can buy. .... , it's better than nothing.
7 She's the youngest in the group, and she's better than most of them ....
8 I think you can do it. It won't be easy, ...
9 Mike is always here on time .... his brother is late at least twice a week.
10 The food's not as good as it was. .... , they've put their prices up.

40.5 Complete these sentences in a logical way.
1 I understood what she was saying although ....
2 I was able to follow what she was saying whereas ....
3 We enjoyed the holiday in spite of ....
4 If you buy a season ticket, you can go when you like. What's more, ...
5 The exam was very difficult. However, ...
6 Although it's a long film, ...

41 Similarities, differences, comparisons, exceptions

A Similarities

These are ways of saying that two or more things are similar, or have something the same.

Peter is **like** his brother/**similar to** his brother in many ways. (= they are the same in many ways)
Tom and Mark are **very similar**.
We **have similar taste** in music/art/etc. (= we like the same music/art/etc.)
There is **a similarity between** them.
Maria and Rebecca **both** passed their exams. (= Maria passed and Rebecca passed)
But **neither** wants to go to university. (= Maria doesn't want to go and Rebecca doesn't want to go)
I really like my cousin, and we **have a lot in common**. (= we have many of the same interests)

B Differences

His early films are **very different from** his later ones.
The two brothers are **completely different**. (= different in every way)
Paula is **quite unlike** (= completely different from) her sister.
They **have nothing in common**. (= they have no hobbies, interests or beliefs that are the same)

C Comparisons

When we **compare** two or more things, we study them to see how they are similar or different.

We want to **compare** the prices before we decide which one to buy.
If you **compare** this one **with** the others, I'm sure you'll see a difference.
House prices in the north are very low **in comparison with** London and the south.
Our new flat is very big **compared with/to** our old one. (= if you compare it with/to our old one)

D Exceptions

An 'exception' is when we make a general statement about things or people and then say that <u>one</u> thing or person is not included, or is different from the others.

It snowed everywhere **except** (= but not) the west coast.

The museum is open every day **except/apart from** Sunday(s).
Everyone heard the fire alarm **except/apart from** the two boys in room 7.
We all agreed it was a good idea **with the exception of** George – but he always disagrees.

'Except' and 'apart from' have a similar meaning, but 'except' is more common. 'Except' can also be followed by 'for'.

Except for a few tourists, the streets were empty.

Exercises

41.1 Fill the gaps with the correct preposition(s).

1 He's similar .... my brother.
2 She's different .... the others.
3 It's cheap compared .... the others.
4 They have a lot .... common.
5 There is a similarity .... them.

6 Everyone came apart .... Sean.
7 We all agreed .... the exception
.... Pat.
8 It's nice .... comparison
.... the other one.

41.2 Read the information, then complete the sentences below with a word or phrase.

MICHEL	PHILIPPE	PAUL
is 21 and lives with his parents. He works in a shoe shop. He is shy, works hard, and is good at sport. He would like to become manager of a sports shop.	is 22 and lives alone. He is at university. He is clever but lazy, and spends most of his time at parties. He has no plans for the future.	is 20 and lives with his parents. He works in a bank and one day he wants to be manager. He's good at football.

1 Michel and Paul are very ...similar...................
2 Philippe is quite .... the other two.
3 Paul and Michel have a lot ....
4 Paul and Philippe have almost nothing ....
5 Paul and Michel both ....
6 Neither of them ....

41.3 Rewrite the sentences using the words on the right.

1 She's like the others.
She's ...similar to the others...........................   SIMILAR
2 Manuela is quite unlike her brother.
Manuela is completely ....   DIFFERENT
3 When you see their houses, you realise that our house is very small.
Our house is very small ....   COMPARED
4 In her class, Carla was the only one who didn't pass the exam.
Everyone ....   EXCEPT
5 The two girls have completely different interests.
The two girls have ....   COMMON
6 It's free every day except Saturday.
It's free ....   APART
7 Everyone liked it except William.
Everyone liked it ....   EXCEPTION
8 We like the same sorts of clothes.
We ....   SIMILAR

41.4 Complete these sentences about yourself and your country.

1 In my family, I think I am quite similar to ....
2 I am .... compared with the rest of my family.
3 In comparison with Britain, my country is ....
4 I think Britain is very different from my country because ....

42 Reason, purpose, result, condition

A Reason

I went home early **because/as** I was feeling a bit tired.
As I was feeling tired, I went home early. [We don't usually start a sentence with 'because'.]
I was feeling a bit tired, **so** I went home early. [This is very common in spoken English.]
The reason I went home early **was that** I was feeling tired.

We can also use **because of**, but with a different construction. Compare:
They go there **because** the weather is wonderful. [because + noun + verb]
They go there **because of** the wonderful weather. [because of + (adjective) + noun]

Due to means the same as **because of**, and is often used to explain the reason for a problem:

The plane was late **due to** bad weather. [**Due to** is often used after the verb 'to be'.]

B Purpose

A 'purpose' is an intention or reason for doing something:

The purpose of the meeting is to plan the timetable. (= the reason for the meeting is ...)

We often introduce a purpose using **so (that)** or **in order to**:
I bought this book **so (that)** I can improve my English.
They went home early **(in order) to** watch the match on television.
We moved house **so (that)** we could send our children to this school.
She went into town **(in order) to** do some shopping.

> In spoken English, we often say **so** (without **that**) and **to** (without **in order**).
> It is also common to use a modal verb, e.g. *can* or *could*, after **so that**.

C Result

I left my ticket at home, **so** I had to buy another one.
They are a very big team **and therefore** they can get the best players.
I forgot to send the letters. **As a result,** no one knew about the meeting.

So is very common in spoken English, and usually links ideas in a single sentence.
Therefore is more formal, and can be used in a single sentence or to connect two sentences.
As a result is more common in written English, and usually connects ideas in two sentences.

D Condition

You probably know **if**, but we also use other words to express conditions. Notice the tenses used.

We'll be late **unless** we leave now. (= <u>if we don't</u> leave now)
Unless the weather improves (= <u>if the weather doesn't</u> improve), we won't be able to go.

I have to go now, **otherwise** (= because if I don't) I'll miss the last bus.
You'll have to turn up the music, **otherwise** (= because if you don't) they won't be able to hear it.

You can borrow it **as long as** you bring it back by Thursday. (= but you must bring it back)
You can wear what you like **as long as** you look smart. (= but you must look smart)

Exercises

42.1 Combine the two sentences into one sentence using 'so', 'so that' or 'because'. More than one answer is possible in some sentences.

1 I didn't phone you. It was very late. *I didn't phone you because it was very late.*
2 I turned up the radio in the lounge. I could hear it in the kitchen.
3 The restaurant was full. We went to the bar next door.
4 I stayed at home. I was expecting a phone call.
5 It's a very large city. You have to use public transport a lot.
6 I learned to drive. My mother didn't have to take me everywhere.

42.2 Rewrite these sentences using 'because of'. Make any changes that are necessary.

1 He couldn't play because his arm was broken. *He couldn't play because of his broken arm.*
2 She got the job because her qualifications are excellent.
3 The weather was terrible, so we couldn't eat outside.
4 She didn't go to school because she had a bad cold.
5 The light was very bad, so the referee had to stop the game.
6 The traffic was very heavy; I was half an hour late.

42.3 Fill the gaps with 'unless', 'otherwise' or 'as long as'.

1 I must write that letter now, ... I'll forget to do it.
2 I can meet you for dinner on Friday .... I have to work late at the office.
3 We agreed to buy my daughter a dog .... she takes it for a walk every day.
4 .... there's a problem, I won't disturb you.
5 You can borrow my dictionary .... you bring it back on Monday.
6 You'd better tidy your room, ... your mother will get very angry.

42.4 Read this memo from a manager to the staff. Fill each gap with a suitable link word/phrase.

To: All staff
From: The Manager
Date: 9th August
Subject: Temporary roadworks

From next Monday, there will be roadworks on all major approach roads to the factory.
(1) .... this will create long delays, could I please ask staff to leave home
a few minutes early in the morning (2) .... everyone arrives on time. The
roadworks also mean that you won't be able to park on the street. (3) ....
it may be a good idea to leave your cars at home (4) .... it is absolutely
impossible for you to use public transport.

Thank you for your cooperation in this matter.

42.5 These sentences are all about learning English. Complete them in a logical way.

1 I want to improve my English because ....
2 I bought myself a personal stereo so that I ....
3 I usually study English at the weekend as I ....
4 I always write words down in my notebook, otherwise I ....
5 I don't get many opportunities to practise my English, and therefore ....
6 My brother has got a number of American friends. As a result, ...

43 The physical world

A The world and parts of the solar system

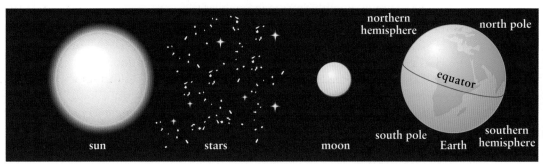

sun   stars   moon   northern hemisphere   north pole   equator   south pole   Earth   southern hemisphere

Why do people want to go **into space**? (= the area outside the earth where the stars and planets are)

I'd love to travel **round the world.**   You find oil **in many parts of the world.**

It's the coldest place **on earth.**   The hottest place **in the world.** (NOT ~~of~~ the world)

There's a five-hour **time difference between** Britain and New York.

Rio de Janeiro is only three hours **behind** London.

They're nine hours **ahead of us** in Sydney.

B Physical features

NOTE
Sometimes we need the definite article *the*, e.g. **the** Red Sea; sometimes no article is used, e.g. Mount Everest.

I travelled through the **continent** of Asia.

China is an enormous **country.**

We **flew** over the **Atlantic Ocean.**

We've got a small house near **Lake Como.**

The Nile is the longest **river** in Africa.

We went **diving** in the **Red Sea.**

We travelled into **the Sahara Desert.**

Parts of **the Amazon rainforest** are disappearing.

Few people have **climbed Mount Everest.**

Elba is an **island** just off the coast of Italy.

Elba — ITALY — Rome

C Natural disasters

A **disaster** is when something terrible happens. There is physical damage and people often die.

earthquake

hurricane

flood

volcano/volcanic eruption

The **earthquake destroyed** many homes. (= many homes are so badly damaged, they don't exist)

They say the **hurricane** could **hit** Florida today. (= reach Florida today with great force)

The **floods** have been terrible – hundreds of people have **drowned.** (= died from being under water)

There are many **active volcanoes** in the world, such as Mount Etna.

Exercises

43.1 Fill the gaps with the correct word.

1 Would you like to go round the ....._world_.............. if you had the chance?
2 Neil Armstrong was the first man to walk on the ....
3 On a clear night you can see lots of ....
4 Australia is in the .... hemisphere.
5 If you think of time, is your country .... Britain or .... of Britain?
6 Is China the largest country .... the world?

43.2 Complete the sentences.

1 The Nile is a ...._river_........................
2 The Atlantic is ....
3 Greece is ....
4 The Sahara is ....
5 The Amazon is ....
6 The Mediterranean is ....
7 Africa is ....
8 Crete and Corsica are ....
9 Everest is the highest ....
10 Michigan and Eyrie are two of the Great ....

43.3 Fill the gaps in the text with the definite article (*the*) if necessary.

My journey took me across (1) .... Atlantic Ocean from (2) .... Europe to
(3) .... South America. I travelled through (4) .... Amazon rainforest and
down through the interior of (5) .... Brazil. From there I headed north again, through
Bolivia, round (6) .... Lake Titicaca and up to Cuzco. Then I crossed (7) ....
Andes and finally arrived in Lima. For the last part of the journey I flew to (8) ....
Jamaica in (9) .... West Indies.

43.4 What type of disaster is being described in each of these sentences?

1 It lifted a car off the ground, and then we saw it disappear down the street.
2 It was about two metres deep and we watched as our furniture just floated away.
3 The walls began to move visibly, and large cracks opened up in the ground.
4 The heat was incredible and we watched as the red hot lava came down the mountain.

43.5 Complete the sentences below using the correct form of the verbs in the box.

destroy	hit	dive	drown	climb	fly

1 Two children .... in the floods when their boat capsized.
2 The earthquake .... the village – there is nothing left.
3 It's a fantastic place to go .... because the water is so clear.
4 The plane .... over the Alps on the way back from Geneva.
5 They say the hurricane may .... the islands later today.
6 They're going to .... the south face of the mountain.

44 Weather

A Weather conditions

Notice that it is very common to form adjectives by adding '-y'.

noun	adjective	noun	adjective
sun	sunny	wind	windy
cloud	cloudy	ice	icy
fog	foggy	shower	showery
heat	hot	humidity	humid

It was very **cloudy** in the morning, but then the **sun came out** (= appeared) in the afternoon. The accident happened in **thick fog** (= bad fog) on the motorway.

B Rain

For **light rain** (= raining a bit) we can use **drizzle**, e.g. It was cloudy with a bit of **drizzle**. For **heavy rain** (= raining a lot) we often use **pour**, e.g. It's **pouring** (**with rain**) outside. Rain for a short period of time is a **shower**, e.g. We had several **showers** today – some quite **heavy**.

C Temperature

thermometer

boiling   hot   warm   not very warm   cold   freezing
(= very hot)   (also **chilly**)   (= very cold)

A: **How hot does it get** in the summer?
B: It can **reach** about 35°. (= 35 degrees)
A: **How cold does it get** in the winter?
B: It often goes below 0. (= zero)

D Wind

a **breeze**   a **wind**   a **strong wind**   a **gale**   a **hurricane**

A **breeze** is gentle and pleasant; a **hurricane** is over 100 km per hour and can be dangerous.

It was a hot day but there was a **gentle breeze**.   Her hair was **blowing** in the **wind**.
The trees were **damaged** in the **gale** last night.   The **hurricane destroyed** many buildings.

E Thunderstorms

A period of very hot weather is sometimes called a **heatwave**, and it often ends with a **thunderstorm**. First it becomes very **humid** (= when the air feels wet), then you get **thunder and lightning**, and finally very **heavy rain**. Afterwards, it is often cooler and feels fresher.

Exercises

44.1 Identify the weather conditions in these pictures.

1 ....   2 ....   3 ....

4 ....   5 ....   6 ....

44.2 Fill the gaps with a suitable word.
1 We had really thick .... this morning.
2 When it's hot, you still get a lovely .... off the sea.
3 I hope we don't get any more thunder and ....
4 We had a heavy .... of rain this morning, but it only lasted a few minutes.
5 The hurricane completely .... the village. There's nothing left.
6 It's quite hot when the sun .... out.
7 What's the .... today? It feels much colder than yesterday.
8 They said it was ten degrees below .... in New York yesterday. That's too cold for me.

44.3 True or False? (If a sentence is false, change it to make it true.)
1 When it's foggy you need sunglasses.   *False (When it's foggy you can't see very well.)*
2 It gets quite chilly in the desert in the evening.
3 Thunder makes a noise.
4 Lightning can kill people.
5 A shower is a type of wind.
6 If it is humid, the air will be very dry.
7 Heavy rain means that it is pouring with rain.
8 It often pours with rain in the desert.

44.4 Complete this text with suitable words.

> An important influence on Japanese weather is the wind. During the summer it
> (1) .... from the Pacific, causing (2) .... and humid weather,
> but in winter, the north-westerly (3) .... from Siberia are very cold and it
> (4) .... heavily on the mountains in the north-west. The south-eastern parts
> receive cold dry air. Between June and mid-July, there is a period of very wet weather when
> the rice fields get the water they need. After that, there is less heavy rain, but the air is still
> (5) .... Autumn, however, is drier and usually very pleasant.

Write a paragraph about the weather in your own country, or a specific part of your country, e.g. your own region. Try to use as many words as possible from the opposite page.

45 Animals and insects

A Pets and farm animals

NOTE
The word 'sheep' is the singular and plural form. A young sheep is called a **lamb**.

Many people **keep pets** (= own and look after domestic animals that live with people) in Britain.

The most common are dogs and cats, but people also keep **mice** (singular = a **mouse**), **rabbits** and **goldfish**.

Farm animals include: sheep, pigs, cows, horses, chickens and goats.

sheep

goat

rabbit

mouse

pig

B Wild animals

You will find these animals **in a zoo** or **in the wild**. (= living free, e.g. in parts of Africa)

camel

bear

tiger

leopard

giraffe

gorilla

elephant

lion

monkey

zebra

Some animals that live in the wild are **in danger of extinction** (= they may not exist much longer), so it is important that we **protect** them. (= make sure they stay safe)

C Insects

bee

ant

mosquito

butterfly

fly

spider

D In the water, in the air and on the ground

Here are some **creatures** (= living things, e.g. animals and birds) that swim, fly or **move along the ground** (e.g. a snake).

whale

shark

eagle

snail

snake

Exercises

45.1 Look at the <u>underlined</u> letters in each pair of words. Is the pronunciation the same or different? Use the pronunciation guide in the Index to help you.

Examples   wh<u>a</u>le   w<u>a</u>ter (different)
            c<u>a</u>t   c<u>a</u>mel (same)

1	l<u>i</u>on	t<u>i</u>ger	6	m<u>o</u>nkey	m<u>o</u>squito
2	le<u>o</u>pard	mosquit<u>o</u>	7	c<u>a</u>mel	sn<u>a</u>ke
3	b<u>ea</u>r	<u>ea</u>gle	8	leop<u>ar</u>d	sh<u>ar</u>k
4	<u>g</u>orilla	<u>g</u>iraffe	9	m<u>o</u>nkey	b<u>u</u>tterfly
5	sp<u>i</u>der	w<u>i</u>ld	10	m<u>ou</u>se	c<u>ow</u>

45.2 Fill the gaps with a suitable word.

1 I've only ever seen .... animals on television, or in a zoo.
2 Some animals are in .... of extinction.
3 I don't just hate spiders and mosquitoes – I hate all ....
4 We used to .... animals on our farm.
5 Snakes can move along the .... really fast if they want.
6 Some animals are disappearing – it's very important that we .... them, so they continue to exist.

45.3 Arrange these words into three groups: farm animals, wild animals, and insects.

monkey	horse	goat	fly
lion	zebra	elephant	pig
mosquito	tiger	bee	sheep
camel	ant	leopard	bear

45.4 Complete the sentences with a suitable word.

1 They've got lots of pets: two dogs, four cats, and a ....
2 Their farm animals include cows, sheep and ....
3 The children love to see the 'big cats' at the zoo such as lions, tigers and

....
4 I hate most insects, but particularly mosquitoes and ....
5 We saw some really large animals at the safari park: elephants, giraffes and

....

45.5 Start each sentence with a suitable creature from the opposite page.

1 ....*Eagles*............ can fly at a great height.
2 ....*shark*............ can swim very long distances.
3 ....*whale*............ can understand lots of human commands.
4 ....*Tiger*............ can run very fast.
5 ....*Camel*............ can travel through the desert for long distances without water.
6 ....*giraffe*............ can be 30 metres in length.
7 ....*giraffe*............ can eat leaves from tall trees.
8 ....*snake*............ change their skin several times a year.
9 .... can pick things up with their trunk.
10 ....*Bear*............ provide us with wool.

46 Countries, nationality and language

A Who speaks what where?

country	nationality	language
Argentina	Argentinian	Spanish
Brazil	Brazilian	Portuguese
Britain	British	English
China	Chinese	Mandarin (also Cantonese)
Egypt	Egyptian	Arabic
France	French	French
Germany	German	German
Greece	Greek	Greek
Israel	Israeli	Hebrew
Italy	Italian	Italian
Japan	Japanese	Japanese
Korea	Korean	Korean
Mexico	Mexican	Spanish
Poland	Polish	Polish
Russia	Russian	Russian
Saudi Arabia	Saudi Arabian	Arabic
Spain	Spanish	Spanish
Switzerland	Swiss	Swiss-German, French, Italian
The United States (USA)	American	English
Turkey	Turkish	Turkish

I **come from** Argentina, so I am **Argentinian** and my **first language** is Spanish. The **capital** is Buenos Aires, which has a **population** of more than 10 million people.

B Regions

There are some names for regions of the world that we often use.

Europe (e.g. Britain, Spain, etc.)   **the Mediterranean** (e.g. Italy, Spain, etc.)
the Far East (e.g. China, Japan, etc.)   **the Middle East** (e.g. Egypt, Iran, etc.)
the Caribbean (e.g. Jamaica, Trinidad, etc.)   **South/Latin America** (e.g. Brazil, Chile, etc.)

C The people

When we are talking about people from a particular country, nationalities ending in '-i' or '-(i)an' can be made plural with an 's', but most others are formed with the definite article (and no 's').

(The) Thais/Israelis
     Brazilians/Russians } are ...   The British
          The French } are ...

D Talking about people in general

These are common ways of talking about people 'in general'.

The British are **generally** ...   **I think most** French people are ...
Russians **tend to be** very ...   **In general**, Polish people are quite ...

Exercises

46.1 Answer these questions without looking at the opposite page.

1 Write down three countries whose first language is English.
2 What language is spoken in Brazil?
3 Write down three languages spoken in Switzerland.
4 What language is spoken in Saudi Arabia?
5 What nationality are people from Poland?
6 What language is spoken in Mexico?
7 Where do people speak Hebrew?
8 Where do people speak Mandarin?

46.2 What regions of the world are these countries in?

1 Germany *Europe*
2 Saudi Arabia
3 Jamaica
4 Corsica and Sardinia
5 Japan
6 Argentina

46.3 <u>Underline</u> the main stress on the words in the box, and practise saying them.

Bra<u>zi</u>lian	Japan	Japanese	Egyptian
Arabic	Italian	Austria	Korea
Chinese	Germany	Saudi Arabia	Egypt

46.4 Complete these sentences with the name of the people from the country on the right.

Examples I've worked a lot with *Germans/German people.* GERMANY
I've spent lots of time with *the French/French people.* FRANCE

1 We do a lot of business with .... JAPAN
2 I used to know a lot of .... ISRAEL
3 I have always found .... very friendly. BRAZIL
4 People often say that .... are reserved. BRITAIN
5 .... are very organised. SWITZERLAND
6 I met a lot of .... on my trip to Moscow. RUSSIA

46.5 Complete these sentences.

1 Athens is the capital of ....
2 Ankara is the capital of ....
3 Seoul is the capital of ....
4 Moscow is the capital of ....
5 Warsaw is the capital of ....
6 Madrid is the capital of ....

46.6 Answer these questions about yourself. If possible, ask somebody from a different country.

1 Where do you come from?
2 What's the total population?
3 What's your first language?
4 What's the capital city?

46.7 Write this sentence in three more different ways to make it more of a generalisation.

'British people are polite.' *I think most British people are polite.*

47 The body and what it can do

A Parts of the body

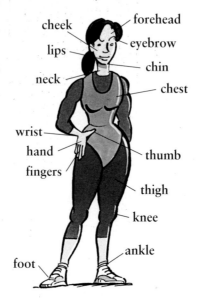

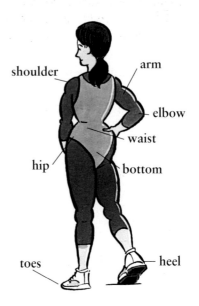

The outer part of the body is covered in **skin**, e.g. Too much sun is bad for your **skin**.

B Physical actions

People **breathe** through the nose or mouth, and **breathe in and out** 12–15 times a minute.
People **smile** when they're happy, and sometimes **smile at** people to be polite.
Funny things **make people laugh** – for example, when someone **tells a joke**.
People sometimes **cry** if they're unhappy or receive bad news.
They **yawn** when they're tired or bored.
People in some countries **nod their head** to mean 'yes', and **shake their head** for 'no'.

C Common expressions

shake hands with somebody   bite your nails   fold your arms   blow your nose   comb your hair

Exercises

47.1 Find 13 more words describing parts of the body, either across or down, in this word square.

47.2 How much of the picture can you label without looking at the opposite page?

1 forehead

2 ....

3 ....

4 ....

5 ....

6 ....

7 ....

8 ....

9 ....

10 ....

11 ....

12 ....

13 ....

14 ....

15 ....

16 ....

17 ....

18 ....

19 ....

20 ....

47.3 Match the verbs on the left with a part of the body on the right to form common expressions.

1 shake   your arms
2 bite   your nose
3 comb   your nails
4 fold   your head
5 blow   hands
6 nod   your hair

47.4 What do these actions often mean? (There may be several possible answers.)

1 People often smile when ...they're happy.........................

2 They often breathe quickly after ....

3 They laugh when ....

4 They may bite their nails ....

5 They blow their nose ....

6 They shake their head ....

7 And nod their head ....

8 They cry ....

9 They yawn when ....

48 Describing people's appearance

A General descriptions

Positive: **beautiful** is generally used to describe women; **handsome** is used to describe men; **good-looking** and **attractive** are used for both. **Pretty** is another positive word to describe a woman (often a girl), meaning 'attractive and nice to look at'.
Negative: **ugly** is a very negative word; **plain** is negative but more polite.

B Height and build

tall and slim

medium height
and build

medium height and
very muscular

short and fat

Another word for **slim** is **thin**, but with a more negative meaning, e.g. John is lovely and **slim**, but his brother is very **thin**. It is not very polite to say someone is **fat**; **overweight** is a bit less rude.

C Hair

blond(e)   fair   brown   dark   black

straight   wavy   curly hair

D Special features

The man on the left has very **pale skin** (= light skin). He also has **broad shoulders**, with a **scar** on his forehead. The other man has **dark skin**. He also has a **beard** and **moustache**.

E Asking questions about a person's appearance

Q: What does she **look like**?   A: She's **tallish**, with short fair hair.
Q: **How tall** is she?   A: **About** 1 metre 65.
Q: **How much** does she **weigh**?   A: I don't know – **roughly** 50 kilos, I guess.

We can use **about** and **roughly** to mean 'more or less' when talking about **height** (= how tall someone is), **weight** (= how heavy is someone) or **age**. The suffix '-ish' can be used at the end of some adjectives to mean 'quite' and at the end of some numbers to mean 'more or less'.

She's got **longish** hair.   He's **twentyish**.   She's **roughly** 40.

Exercises

48.1 Complete these sentences in a suitable way. (More than one answer may be possible.)

1 He's got very muscular ....*arms*............
2 She's got blonde ....
3 He's got very pale ....
4 They've both got curly ....
5 I would say he was medium ....
6 Her brother has got very broad ....
7 Last time I saw him he had grown a beard and ....
8 Both men were very good- ....

48.2 Replace the <u>underlined</u> word with a word which is more suitable or more polite.

1 He told me he met a <u>handsome</u> girl in the disco last night.   *beautiful*
2 She's beautiful but her younger sister is really quite <u>ugly</u>.
3 I think Peter is getting a bit <u>fat</u>, don't you?
4 I think she's hoping to meet a few <u>beautiful</u> men at the tennis club.
5 Paul is very <u>thin</u>.

48.3 You want to know about the following: someone's general appearance; their height; their weight. What do you need to ask? Complete these questions.

1 What .... ?
2 How .... ?
3 How much .... ?

48.4 Make these sentences less exact. Do it in a different way each time.

1 She's 20.   *She's 20, more or less.*
2 I'm 75 kilos.
3 She's 1 metre 70.
4 They're both 30.

48.5 Now answer these questions.

1 How tall are you?
2 How would you describe your build?
3 How much do you weigh?
4 What kind of hair have you got?
5 What colour is it?
6 Would you like it to be different? If so, what else would you like to change about your appearance?
7 Do you think you have any special features?
8 Are there any special features you would like to have?
9 Do you like beards?
10 Can you think of a famous woman you would describe as beautiful, and a famous man you would describe as good-looking?

If possible, ask another person these questions.

49 Describing character

A Opposites

NOTE

Sympathetic doesn't mean 'nice' in English. We use it to describe a person who understands other people's feelings/ problems, e.g. She was very **sympathetic** when I explained the problem.

positive	negative
warm and **friendly**	cold and **unfriendly**
kind (= cares about others)	**unkind**
nice, **pleasant**	horrible, **unpleasant**
generous (= happy to give/share)	**mean** (= never gives to others)
optimistic (= thinks positively)	**pessimistic** (= thinks negatively)
easy-going (= relaxed, calm)	**tense** (= nervous; worries a lot; not calm)
sensitive (= thinks about people's feelings)	**insensitive**
honest (= always tells the truth)	**dishonest**
good fun (= enjoyable to be with)	boring
broad-minded	**narrow-minded** (= unable to accept new ideas)

My parents are great and don't mind what I wear – they're very **broad-minded**.
When I tried on the dress, the shop assistant said it would look better on a younger person. I know she was trying to be **honest**, but it was a bit **insensitive** of her.

B What's he/she like?

He's very **self-confident**. (= feels he can do things, and is relaxed in social situations)
When you first meet her she seems **shy**. (= finds it difficult to talk to people and make conversation)
She doesn't **show her feelings**. (= you don't know what she is thinking or feeling)
He's got a great **sense of humour**. (= laughs a lot and sees the funny side of life)

C Describing character in work situations

positive	negative
hard-working	**lazy** (= never does any work)
punctual (= always on time)	not very punctual; always late
reliable	**unreliable** (= you cannot trust/depend on someone like this)
clever	stupid
flexible	**inflexible** (= a fixed way of thinking and unable to change)
ambitious	not ambitious (= no desire to be successful/get a better job)
has lots of **common sense** (= thinks in a practical way; doesn't do stupid things)	has no common sense; **an idiot** (= a stupid person)

D First impressions

We use **impression** to talk about the effect that a person has on another person.

She **made** a very **good impression** at her interview. (= had a positive effect on the interviewer)
My **first impression** of him was a bit negative.
She **comes across as** (= appears to be) quite serious.

Exercises

49.1 Organise these words into pairs of opposites and put them in the columns below.

| mean | clever | nice | lazy | relaxed |
| hard-working | tense | generous | unpleasant | stupid |

positive	*negative*
clever	....
....	....
....	....
....	....
....	....

49.2 Which prefix forms the opposite of these words? (You need three different prefixes.)

| unhappy | flexible | friendly | honest |
| reliable | sensitive | kind | pleasant |

49.3 How would you describe the person in each of these descriptions?
1 She's always here on time.   punctual
2 He never bought me a drink in ten years.
3 She often promises to do things but half the time she forgets.
4 I don't think he's done any work since he's been here.
5 She finds it difficult to meet people and talk to strangers.
6 He can work in any of the departments – on his own or part of a team.
7 One of her qualities is that she is so aware of what other people think or feel.
8 I know Mike wants to be head of the department and then go on to a bigger company.

49.4 Fill the gaps with a suitable word.
1 At work, James .... across as serious and a bit boring, but outside of work he's completely different; he's really good ....
2 It's important to .... a good impression on your first day in a new job.
3 I'm sure he can find the place; he just needs to use his common ....
4 Meeting new people doesn't worry her; she's a very self-................................. young woman.
5 It's hard to know what Sam thinks – he doesn't really .... his feelings.
6 Do you think .... impressions are very important? I do.
7 I always have a laugh with my cousin – he's got a great sense of ....
8 She is so ....-minded: she cannot accept any ideas different from her own.

49.5 What nouns can be formed from these adjectives? Use a dictionary to help you.

| kind | kindness | optimistic | punctual | lazy | confident | ambitious |

49.6 Choose three words from the opposite page which describe you. Is there one quality you do not have but would like to have? What, in your opinion, is the worst quality described on the opposite page? If possible, compare your answers with a friend.

50 Human feelings and actions

A Feelings/emotions

noun	adjective(s)
love (*opp* **hate**)	–
happiness *(opp* **sadness)**	happy (*opp* sad)
anger	**angry**
fear	afraid (of)/frightened (of)
pride	**proud (of)**
jealousy	**jealous (of)**
embarrassment	embarrassed/embarrassing (see Unit 36)

Pride can be a positive feeling when you (or people you know) have done something well.
  I'm not a great photographer, but I'm **proud of** my pictures because I taught myself.
  He was very **proud** when his wife became the first president of the organisation.
Jealousy is a negative feeling of anger/unhappiness, often if someone you love shows a lot of interest in others, or if someone has something you want and don't have.
  My boyfriend gets very **jealous** when I talk to other boys.
  He's **jealous of** his sister because she's more intelligent.
Upset is a common adjective, and means unhappy, sad, and sometimes angry.
  He was **upset** when they didn't invite him.   She **gets upset** if you shout at her.

B How do you feel?

I **felt** very sad when I left university and all my friends.
It was a **great feeling** when I finished all my exams.
She had **mixed feelings** (= not sure what to think or feel) about leaving her job.

C Ways of speaking, looking and walking

whisper (= speak very quietly)   **shout** (= speak in a very loud voice)
glance (at) (= look at sb/sth very quickly)   **stare (at)** (= look at sb/sth for a long time)
stroll (= walk in a slow casual way)   **march** (= walk quickly and with a clear reason)

These words can also function as nouns with no change in form.

I heard **a shout** from inside.   We had **a stroll** on the beach.

D Things we do with our hands

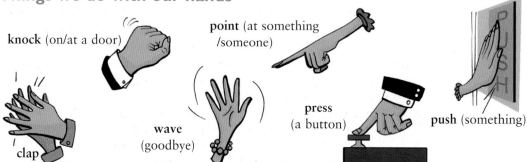

knock (on/at a door)

point (at something /someone)

clap

wave (goodbye)

press (a button)

push (something)

Exercises

50.1 **What nouns can be formed from these adjectives?**

1 sad *sadness*	3 angry	5 happy
2 proud	4 jealous	6 embarrassed

50.2 **Find the logical ending on the right for each of the sentence beginnings on the left.**

1 He was very proud when   a someone stole his money.
2 He was very jealous when   b his father appeared on TV.
3 He was very embarrassed when   c he heard his aunt had died.
4 He was very angry when   d he saw the man had a knife.
5 He was very sad when   e he sent her a birthday card on the wrong day.
6 He was very frightened when   f his best friend went out with a girl he liked.

50.3 **What are these people doing? Describe their actions using words from the opposite page.**

1   2   3   4   5

50.4 **Replace the underlined words with a single verb that has the same meaning.**

1 She stopped working and <u>looked quickly</u> at the clock.
2 As we were in the library, he <u>spoke very quietly</u> in my ear.
3 We <u>walked casually</u> along the beach and then stopped for a drink.
4 He made us all <u>walk quickly</u> up the hill.
5 The man <u>kept looking</u> at Susan, but she didn't seem to notice.
6 He kept <u>talking in a very loud voice</u>.

50.5 **Fill the gaps with the missing preposition.**

1 I knocked .... the door.	4 Why is he pointing .... the clock?
2 She glanced .... her watch.	5 He's very proud .... them.
3 She's jealous .... her sister.	6 What are they afraid .... ?

50.6 **Answer the questions. If possible, ask someone else the same questions.**

1 How would you feel if you forgot your mother's birthday or your father's birthday?
2 How do you feel when you are in a car that is going very fast?
3 How do you feel when other people ask you to do things that you don't want to do?
4 If you made a stupid mistake in English, how would you feel?
5 Is there any one thing that you are very proud of?
6 Are there any common situations where you sometimes feel embarrassed?
7 How do you feel about going home after a wonderful holiday?
8 Have you left school? If so, did you have mixed feelings when you left? If you haven't left school, do you think you'll have mixed feelings when you leave?

51 Family and friends

A Relatives (= members of your family)

NOTE
In English we usually say 'my uncle's daughter' (NOT ~~the daughter of my uncle~~) or 'Anna's sister' (NOT ~~the sister of Anna~~).

	male	*female*
Your parents' parents	grandfather(s)	grandmother(s)
Your parents' brother and sister	uncle(s)	aunt(s)
Your aunt's/uncle's children	cousin(s)	cousin(s)
The father and mother of the person you marry	father-in-law	mother-in-law
The brother and sister of the person you marry	brother-in-law	sister-in-law
Your brother's/sister's children	nephew(s)	niece(s)
If the person you marry dies, you are a ...	widower	widow
If your mother or father remarries, you have a ...	stepfather	stepmother

B Talking about family and friends

I've got two brothers and a sister. My brothers are **twins** (= two children born to one mother at the same time), and they are three years younger than me. I'm the oldest and I **take after** my father (= I am similar to him in appearance and/or character). My sister takes after my father in some ways, but she **looks like** my mother (= her appearance is similar to my mother's). We're **a close family** (= we have a good relationship/see each other a lot). My **best friend** Pete is **an only child** (= without brothers or sisters); he spends a lot of time with us and he's almost one of the family.

C Family names

Your parents give you a **first name**, e.g. James and Sarah are common first names in Britain. Your **family name**, usually called your **surname**, is the one that all the family have, e.g. Smith and Jones. Your **full name** is all the names you have, e.g. Sarah Jane Smith.

D Changing times

In some parts of the world, couples may live together but do not get married. In this relationship they often call each other their **partner**. Where the child or children live(s) with just one parent, especially after the parents have **separated** (= they don't live together any more), these are sometimes called **single-parent families**.

E Friends

an **old** friend (= someone you have known for a long time)
a **close** friend (= a good friend/someone you like and trust)
your **best** friend (= the one friend you feel closest to)
classmates (= other people in your class)
flatmates (= people you share a house/flat with, who are not your family)
colleagues (= people you work with; they may or may not be friends)

F Ex-

We use this for a relationship that we had in the past but do not have now:
The children stay with my **ex-husband** at the weekend.
I saw an **ex-girlfriend** of mine at the disco last night.

Exercises

51.1 Look at the family tree and complete the sentences below.

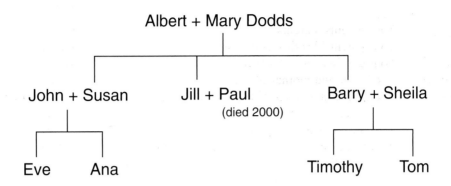

Albert + Mary Dodds

John + Susan   Jill + Paul
                (died 2000)   Barry + Sheila

Eve   Ana   Timothy   Tom

1 John is Jill's ...... *brother* ......
2 Timothy is Jill's ...... *niece(s)* ......
3 Eve and Ana are Timothy's ...... *cousins* ......
4 Eve is Sheila's ...... *aunt* ......
5 Albert Dodds is Tom's ....
6 Barry is Eve's ....
7 Susan is Timothy's ....
8 As Paul died in 2000, Jill is a ....
9 Tom is Mary's ....
10 The only two people who are not related are .... and ....

51.2 Fill the gaps with the correct word.

1 Did you say his .... name was Boris?
2 He looks like his mother but definitely takes .... his father in character.
3 There is an increasing number of single-........................ families in Britain.
4 Most of my .... at work are married, and I don't see them socially.
5 I've known him for years; he's an .... friend.
6 They're not married any longer, but she still sees her ....-husband.

51.3 Answer these questions about yourself.

1 What's your first name?
2 What's your surname?
3 Are you an only child?
4 Are you part of a very close family?
5 Do you look like your father or mother?
6 In character, who do you take after?
7 Do you know any twins?
8 Who is your best friend?
9 Do you work? If so, how many of your work colleagues are also your friends?
10 Do you have any ex-boyfriends or girlfriends who are still close friends?

51.4 Draw your own family tree. Are there any relationships you cannot describe in English?

52 Ages and stages

A Growing up and growing old

NOTE
The period between 13 and 17 approximately is called **adolescence**, and the boy/girl is an **adolescent**.

age	stage
0–1 approximately	a baby
1–2	a **toddler**
2–12 approximately	a child – this period is your **childhood**
13–17 approximately	a **teenager** (14 = early teens)
18 +	an **adult**
20–29	**in your twenties** (24–26 = **mid-twenties**)
30–39	**in your thirties** (38 = **late thirties**)
40 +	people are **middle-aged**
60 or 65	**retirement** (= when people stop work; they are **retired**)
75 +	**old age** (you can describe people as **elderly**)

B Childhood and adolescence

Sam (on the right) **was born** in Scotland but when he was two, his father got a new job in Los Angeles, and he **grew up** in California. He **went to university** at 19 where …

C Romance

… he **met** Anthea. He **went out with** her (= she was his **girlfriend**; he was her **boyfriend**) for three years, but towards the end they had lots of **rows** (= arguments) and finally they **split up** (= separated/ended their relationship). In his **mid-twenties** he met Marie. They **fell in love** and …

D Marriage

… **got married** within six months. One year later she got **pregnant** and they had their first child, a boy. But the marriage was not a success. Sam **left** two years afterwards and they **got divorced** (= the marriage ended officially). Four years later, Marie **remarried** (= got married again), and as you can see in the picture, she is now **expecting** a second baby (= she's pregnant).

Exercises

52.1 **What stage of life are these people at?**

1 Paul isn't two yet, so he's still a ...*toddler.*...............

2 Albert was a bus driver for 40 years but stopped work two years ago, so he's now
....

3 Susan is 25, so she is in her ....

4 Caroline is 48 this year so she is now in her ....

5 Ron is 33 and his wife is 32, so they are both in their ....

6 Joan is 75 this year, so she is quite ....

7 Jason was born six weeks ago, so he's a ....

8 Leyla is 13 this year, so she'll soon be a ....

9 Ravi is 18 this year, so legally he becomes an ....

10 15 is often a difficult age for boys going through ....

52.2 **Are these sentences true or false about the people on the opposite page? If false, write the correct answer below. Try to answer the questions first without looking at the opposite page.**

1 Sam was born in Ireland.   True/*False*
  Sam was born in Scotland.........................

2 He grew up in the south of Ireland.   True/False
  ....

3 He went out with Anthea for two years.   True/False
  ....

4 They split up because Sam went to live in Japan.   True/False
  ....

5 Sam fell in love with Marie.   True/False
  ....

6 They had a baby a year after they got married.   True/False
  ....

7 Marie is now expecting her third child.   True/False
  ....

8 Marie left Sam.   True/False
  ....

52.3 **Find the logical ending for each of the sentence beginnings on the left and construct Rebecca's life.**

1 Rebecca was born	a was a boy at her secondary school.
2 She grew up	b in her early thirties.
3 Her first boyfriend	c on a farm with lots of animals.
4 She went out with him	d when she was in her late twenties.
5 She went to university	e in a small local hospital in 1972.
6 She fell in love	f for six months.
7 They got married	g just after the baby was born.
8 She had a baby	h with another student doing medicine.
9 Her father retired	i when she left school.

How many of the sentence beginnings on the left can you complete about your own life? Complete the ones you can.

53 Daily routines

A Sleep

During the week I usually **wake up** at 6.30 am. I sometimes **lie in bed** (= stay in bed) for 5–10 minutes but then I have to **get up** (= get out of bed and put on clothes). Most evenings I **go to bed** about 11.30 pm, and usually **go to sleep/fall asleep** very quickly. If I **have a late night** (= go to bed very late; *opp* an **early night**), it's easy to **oversleep** (= sleep too long) the next morning, then I may be late for work. If I can, I **have a sleep** (= for a short period, e.g. half an hour) in the afternoon. At weekends I often **have a lie-in** (= stay in bed until later, e.g. 9.30 am).

B Food

NOTE
Usually there is no definite article (*the*) with **breakfast**, **lunch** or **dinner**.

In the week I **have breakfast** at 7.00 am, lunch at 1.00, and dinner around 7 pm. I also have one or two **snacks** (= food eaten between meals, e.g. a cake or biscuits) during the day. As I live **alone/on my own** (= without other people), I have to **make my own breakfast and dinner** (= prepare breakfast and dinner for myself), but during the week I **don't bother** (= don't make an effort) to cook very much. I also have to **feed** (= give food to) my cats twice a day.

C Keeping clean

In the summer I **have a shower** in the morning, but in the winter I often **have a bath instead** (= in place of a shower). Sometimes I **have a shave** at the same time, or I shave when I **have a wash** and **clean/brush my teeth** after breakfast. I **wash my hair** two or three times a week.

English often uses a verb + noun construction, where other languages may use a verb or reflexive verb, e.g. **I had a wash** (NOT ~~I washed~~ or ~~I washed myself~~); **I had a rest** (NOT ~~I rested~~ or ~~I rested myself~~).

D Work

In the morning I **leave home** about 8.15 am and **get to work** (= arrive at work) by 9 am. I **have a lunch break** (= period when I stop work for lunch) from 1–2 pm, and usually a couple of short **breaks** (= periods to relax) during the day. I **leave work** around 5.30 and **get home** about 6.15.

E Spare time (= free time)

In the week I usually **stay in** (= stay at home) and watch TV or read in the evening. At the weekend I **go out** (= leave the house for social reasons, e.g. go to a cinema or disco), but I also **have friends for dinner** (= invite friends to my house and cook dinner for them), or friends **come round** (= visit me at the house) to **play cards**, e.g. poker or bridge.

F Housework

I **do the shopping** (= buy the food and household goods) on Saturday. **Fortunately/Luckily** (= it is lucky for me) I have a **cleaner** (= a person who cleans) and she does most of the housework: she **does my washing** (= washes my clothes), she **does the washing-up** (= washes the dishes) and most of **the ironing**.

Exercises

53.1 How many expressions with 'have + noun' from the opposite page can you remember?

have ...*breakfast*...........   have ...*a shower*...........   have ....

have ....   have ....   have ....

53.2 Match the verbs on the left with the correct word on the right to form common partnerships.

```
1  do           a rest
2  fall         my teeth
3  have         the dog
4  play         asleep
5  go           cards
6  clean        the ironing
7  feed         early
8  get up       to bed
```

53.3 Complete this dialogue with a suitable word or phrase from the opposite page.

A: Don't (1) ...*bother*............... to cook a meal this evening.

B: Why not?

A: We could (2) .... instead.

B: Yeah. Where?

A: Well, I'd like to go to that Korean restaurant. We could ask Karen and Mike to come.

B: That's miles away. No, I think I'd rather (3) .... and have an

(4) .... night.

A: But it's Friday. You can have a (5) .... tomorrow if we have a late night.

B: Yes, I know, but I'm tired. Look, why don't you ask Karen and Mike to

(6) .... for a meal? I can order some pizzas from the takeaway and we'll

have a nice evening here. We can (7) .... cards or watch a few videos.

A: Sorry, but if you don't want to come with me, I'll go (8) ....

53.4 Correct the mistakes in these sentences.

1 What time do you have the breakfast?   4 I live by my own.

2 In the morning I always let home at 8 o'clock.   5 I usually wash the hair every day.

3 I didn't shave me this morning.   6 I went to bed and slept very quickly.

53.5 Complete the phrasal verb in these sentences.

1 I usually wake .... around 7.30, and then get .... about 8.

2 During the week I usually stay .... , but at the weekend I always go ....

3 Sometimes friends come .... to the house and we play cards.

53.6 Find three facts from the opposite page which are similar to your routine, and three that are different. Complete the table below.

similar	different
1 *I go to bed around 11.30 pm.*	*I don't stay in during the week.*
2	....
3	....
4	....

54 The place where you live

A Location

NOTE
Right is often used for emphasis, e.g. I live **right** next to the park.

I live **on the outskirts of town**. (= on the edge of town, near the country)
I live **in the suburbs**. (= areas where people live outside the centre of town)
I live **in a residential area**. (= a nice area of houses/flats, with no factories)
I live **quite close to** the station. (= near the station)
I live **right in the centre**. (= exactly in the centre)

B Houses

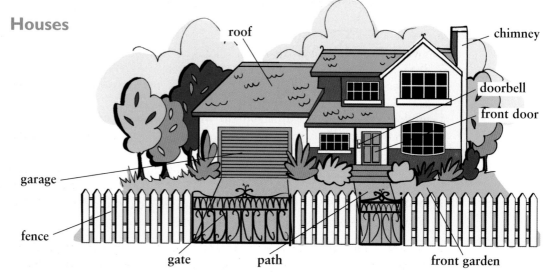

roof
chimney
doorbell
front door
garage
fence
gate
path
front garden

C Flats

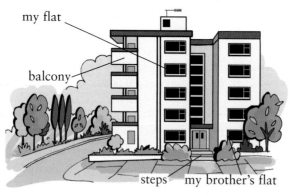

my flat
balcony
steps
my brother's flat

I live in **a block of flats**. My brother lives **on the ground floor**, and I have a flat **on the third floor**. Unfortunately there is no **lift**, so I have to **climb** (= go up/ walk up) three **flights of stairs** to reach my flat. But I have a **balcony** with a great **view** of the park opposite the building.

Steps are outside a house or inside a public building. **Stairs** connect floors inside a house or building and are often covered with a carpet.

D Describing the place where you live

My parents **own** their house (= they bought it/it **belongs to** them), but I **rent** a flat near my university (= I don't own it; I pay money every week to the owner). The rooms are **tiny** (= very small, *opp* **huge/enormous**), but they're **light** (*opp* **dark**) because they're on the top floor and get lots of sun. The flats on the ground floor are dark and also **noisy** (*opp* **quiet**) because they're nearer the traffic. Some rooms are **draughty** (= cold air comes in through windows and under doors), and are expensive to **heat** (= keep warm); but I've got **central heating** (= system of heating every room in a building) and the flat is **in good condition**.

Exercises

54.1 What can you remember about the house and block of flats on the opposite page? Answer these questions without looking.

1 Does the house have a garage?
2 Does it have a fence at the front?
3 Is the gate open or shut?
4 Does each flat have a balcony?
5 Does the brother live on the first floor?
6 Do the flats have a view of a school and offices?

54.2 Complete these sentences with a suitable word.

1 I walked up to the house and rang the ....
2 She lives .... the second floor.
3 We had to .... six flights of stairs to get to her flat because the .... wasn't working.
4 I've got a great .... from my balcony.
5 You have to walk up some .... to reach the entrance to the building.
6 Do you own the flat or do you .... it?
7 I'm living in the house now but it actually .... to my brother. He bought it two years ago. It was in very bad .... then, but he spent a lot of money on it.
8 It costs a lot of money to .... a house when you live in a cold climate. Central .... is usually quite expensive.

54.3 Write down four more positive things and four more negative things about a house or flat. When you have finished, compare your answers with section D opposite.

positive	negative
1 It's very light.	1 It's very dark.
2	2
3	3
4	4
5	5

Now think about your answers again. Which positive features are the most important for you? Which negative features do you dislike the most?

54.4 What about your home? Answer these questions.

1 Do you live in a house or flat?
2 If you live in a flat, what floor is it on?
3 If you live in a house, do you have a garden?
4 Does the house/flat belong to you (or your family), or do you rent it?
5 Do you have your own garage or personal parking space?
6 Would you describe your house/flat as dark or light?
7 Is it noisy or quiet?
8 Do you have central heating?
9 Is it near the centre, in the suburbs, or on the outskirts?
10 Is it in a quiet residential area?

55 Around the home (1)

A Rooms

The **living room** or **lounge** (= where you sit, relax and watch TV); the **dining room**; the **kitchen**; the **bedroom(s)**; and the **bathroom(s)**. Some people have **a study** (= room with a desk where you work) and a **spare room** (= room you don't use every day, and where guests can sleep). The entrance area in a house or flat is called the **hall**.

B The living room

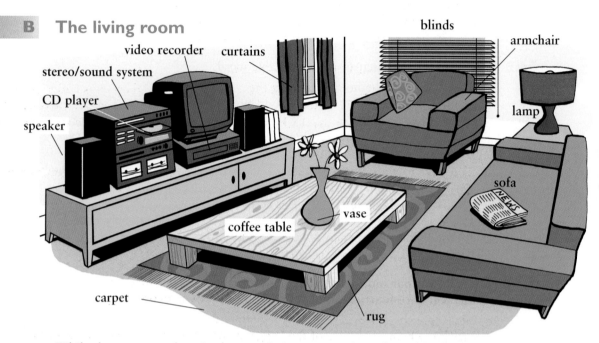

While the cat was asleep **in the armchair**, I sat **on the sofa** and **had a look** at the paper. Then I **turned on the TV** to watch the news.

C The kitchen

I **put** the meat **in the oven**, then I **made** myself a **coffee** and **put** the milk **back** in the fridge. After that, I put some **cups and saucers** in the dishwasher.

Exercises

55.1 Complete the descriptions. (There may be more than one possible answer.)

1 The bedroom, that's where you ....*sleep.*.................
2 The kitchen, that's where you do the ....
3 The bathroom, that's where you have a .... and ....
4 The living room, that's where you .... and ....
5 The dining room, that's where you ....
6 A spare room, that's often where ....
7 A study, that's usually where you ....

55.2 You are in the kitchen. Where would you put:

1 biscuits and a packet of spaghetti? *in a cupboard*
2 milk?
3 meat that you are going to cook?
4 dirty clothes?
5 dirty cups and saucers?
6 clean cups and saucers?
7 frozen food that you want to keep?

55.3 Here are some things you may find in the living room or kitchen but the letters are jumbled. What are they, and which room do you usually find them in?

Example sekd *desk (living room)*

| skin | nacitusr | rapcet | shadriswhe | teklet |
| faos | veon | digref | hiamcrar | acepasnu |

55.4 Complete these sentences with the correct adverb or preposition.

1 Shall I put the plates .... the cupboard?
2 I took the ham .... of the fridge, made a sandwich, then put the rest of it .... in the fridge.
3 We tend to sit in the same places – me .... the sofa and my husband .... the armchair.
4 I didn't have anything to do, so I turned .... the TV.
5 You normally cook the meat .... the oven for 45 minutes.
6 I took a few things .... of the cupboard and put them .... the table.

55.5 You have just moved into a new flat. For the first six months you can only have six of the following. Which would you choose, and why? Compare with someone else if possible.

Example *I would certainly choose a cooker – I can't eat cold food all the time.*

sofa	carpets	dishwasher	TV
cooker	curtains	fridge	desk
CD player	bed	dining table	washing machine
kettle	saucepans	food processor	armchair

55.6 Write down:

- three things in the lounge or kitchen you can turn on/off
- three things in the kitchen you wash regularly
- two things in the lounge or kitchen you can sit on
- two things you can use to boil water

56 Around the home (2)

A The bedroom

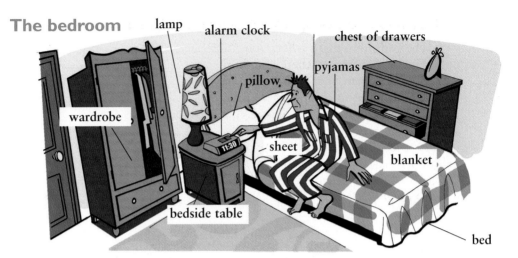

I **put on** my **pyjamas, got into bed,** and read a book for half an hour. Then I **set** the **alarm clock, switched off the light** and **went to sleep.**

B The bathroom

I didn't have time for a bath, but I **had a wash, cleaned my teeth,** and then I **went to work.**

C Housework

My room is very **tidy** (= everything in order), but my brother is very **untidy** – he leaves his clothes **all over the floor** (= everywhere) and never **makes his bed.** The room is **a complete mess.** (= very untidy)

I **do the washing-up** (= wash the dishes) every evening, and I normally **do some washing and ironing** (= wash and iron clothes) at the weekend. I **hoover** the carpets once a week.

washing machine   iron   hoover/vacuum cleaner

Exercises

56.1 Find the correct ending on the right for each of the sentence beginnings on the left, then put the sentences in the most logical order.

1	I cleaned	the light
2	I went	into bed
3	I set	a wash
4	I switched off	my teeth
5	I had	to sleep
6	I put on	the alarm clock
7	I got	my pyjamas

56.2 The pictures show six things the man did this morning. Complete the sentences below.

1 _He did the shopping._ .... 4 He ....
2 He .... 5 He ....
3 He .... 6 He ....

56.3 How often do you do the things in 56.2? Complete these sentences about yourself.

1 I often/sometimes/never .... 4 I ....
2 I .... 5 I ....
3 I .... 6 I ....

56.4 Test your memory. Cover the opposite page and answer these questions about the pictures.

1 Does the alarm clock show 11.30?
2 Does the bed have one pillow or two?
3 Is the wardrobe open?
4 How many drawers does the chest of drawers have?
5 Is the woman in the bathroom holding a towel?
6 Is the shower above the bath?

56.5 How well do you know your own home? Answer these questions as quickly as possible.

1 Have you got a mirror above the washbasin in the bathroom?
2 Have you got a towel rail on the same wall as the washbasin?
3 Is the toilet next to the bath/shower?
4 Have you got a wardrobe and chest of drawers in your bedroom?
5 Have you got a lamp on your bedside table?
6 Have you got an alarm clock?

57 Everyday problems

A There's something wrong with …

We use these expressions when there is a problem with machines and other things we use.

There's something wrong with the TV. (= there is a problem with it)
The light **isn't working**. (= not functioning/there is no light)
The light's **not working properly**. (= it is functioning but not very well)
The telephone is **out of order**. (= not in use/not functioning)

You often see a notice saying **out of order** on a public machine or piece of equipment that isn't working, e.g. pay phone, public toilet, etc. At home we usually say **it isn't working**.

B In the home

Paul had a lot of problems yesterday.

He **dropped** a cup

and it **broke**.

He got another cup, made some coffee, and then **spilt** it.

His shirt now has a large **stain** on it [see picture], and it is **ruined**. (= he can't wear it again, it has no use)

Then he decided to make some toast. He **burnt** the first piece (if you **burn** something, you damage it with heat or fire), then he realised he'd **run out of** bread (= the bread was finished/there was no more bread). He left home hungry and **in a bad mood**. (= angry and unhappy; *opp* **in a good mood**)

C Out and about

NOTE

You can say, 'I **forgot** my book', but if you say where this happened, you must use the verb 'leave', e.g. I **left** my homework **on the bus**. (NOT ~~I forgot my books on the bus.~~)

After Paul went out, **things got worse** (= his situation became worse/there were more problems). He was late, and he **missed the bus** (= the bus came and went before he got to the bus stop), so he had to walk. That made him even later. He started running, but he **fell over** and **cut himself** (see picture). Later, when he got to school, he realised he'd **lost some money** and **left** his English book **at home**. (= forgotten his books)

Exercises

57.1 Complete the past tense and past participle of these verbs.

infinitive	past tense	past participle
leave	*left*	*left*
break		
fall		
spill		
forget		
lose		
burn		
cut		

57.2 Match the sentence beginnings on the left with the correct endings on the right.

1 I lost my credit card
2 I'm afraid I've run out
3 I'm afraid I left
4 I dropped my radio on the floor
5 I spilt my coffee
6 I missed the bus
7 I burnt myself
8 I forgot

a when I lit that cigarette.
b and had to wait ages for another.
c and it has stained the carpet.
d and all my money.
e to bring my money.
f my money at home.
g and now it doesn't work properly.
h of coffee. Would you like tea?

57.3 This is what happened when Anna had a party at her house. Write a description of the damage.

57.4 Write a logical explanation for each question, using vocabulary from the opposite page.

1 Why can't we watch TV? *It isn't working.*
2 How did you break that wine glass?
3 How did you cut your knee like that?
4 I'm cold. What's wrong with the central heating?
5 What happened to the money I gave you?
6 Where's your homework?
7 What's wrong with this radio?
8 Why can't you use the public phone in the station?

57.5 Answer the questions using 'often/occasionally/hardly ever/never'. How often do you:

drop things?	break things?	burn things?
spill things?	lose things?	forget things?
fall over?	leave things somewhere?	run out of things?

58 Money

Notes and coins

In the UK the **currency** (= type of money used) is **sterling**; in America it is **the dollar**; in much of Europe it's **the euro**.

notes	coins
e.g. ten pounds, twenty euros **a ten-pound note**	e.g. fifty pence, a pound **a 50p coin, a one-pound coin**

Common verbs

spend £££ on (sth)	Last week I **spent** £100 **on** food, and £20 **on** books.
pay £££ (for sth)	I **paid** £200 **for** my new desk. (= it cost me £200)
cost	My new desk **cost** (me) £200. (= I paid £200 for it)
charge	They **charged** me (= told me to pay) £10 to repair my watch.
lend and borrow	Could **you lend me** some money? *or* Could **I borrow** some money?
waste £££ (on sth)	Parents often think that children **waste** their money (= use it badly) **on** sweets and other things they don't need.
save (up) (for sth)	I'm **saving** (up) (= keeping some of my money when I receive it) **for** my holiday – I'm hoping to go to Greece.

Adjectives

These are all used to describe the **price** of something (= the amount of money you have to pay for sth), e.g. This watch was **cheap**; the hotel was **reasonable**; my suit was **quite expensive**, etc.

free	cheap	reasonable	quite expensive	very expensive	incredibly expensive
–	£	£	£	£	£

Talking money

I **can't afford** (= don't have enough money) to go on holiday this year.

A: How much is that watch **worth**? (= What is its **value**?)   B: It's **worth** about £50.

The **cost of living** (= how much people pay for things) is high in Sweden and Norway, but people still have a good **standard of living**. (= the level of money and comfort people have)

His car **cost a fortune** (= was very expensive), but he can afford it; he's **well-off**. (= rich)

Exercises

58.1 Fill the gaps using the past tense of verbs from the box. Be careful, most of them are irregular.

buy	spend	lose	pay	cost
sell	win	waste	find	give

1 My car was five years old, so I .... it and .... a new one.
2 I was very sad when I .... my watch because it was a present from my wife and it .... her a lot of money. Fortunately, somebody .... it a few days later and took it to a police station.
3 I .... over £2,000 for my computer, but it isn't worth very much now.
4 My father .... me £50 last week but I .... most of it on Friday when I went to the concert.
5 Last week somebody .... £1 million in a game show on television. It was quite exciting.
6 I'm afraid I .... my money on those computer games – I don't think I've played them more than once.

58.2 Complete the sentences without using the <u>underlined</u> words and phrases. Don't change the meaning.

Example You want to tell a friend that your uncle is very <u>rich</u>.
My uncle is *very well-off*.

1 You want to know the <u>value</u> of your friend's gold ring. You ask:
How much is your ....?
2 A friend wants to go to a restaurant but you <u>don't have enough money</u>. You say:
I'm afraid I ....
3 You want to <u>borrow</u> some money from a friend. You ask:
Could you ....?
4 You want to know how much a friend <u>paid</u> for her dictionary. You ask:
How much ....?
5 You want to explain to someone that a disco is <u>incredibly expensive</u>. You say:
That disco ....

58.3 How quickly can you answer these questions, YES or NO? Write down answers to all of them, then go back and check. If possible, ask someone else the same questions.

1 Is the currency in America called the dollar?
2 Is a five-pound note worth less than a 50p coin?
3 If you lend something to someone, do they borrow it?
4 If you waste money, do you use it well?
5 Is the 'euro' a currency?
6 If you 'can't afford' something, do you have enough money for it?
7 Does 'cost of living' mean the same as 'standard of living'?
8 If someone tells you a hotel is reasonable, is it very expensive?

58.4 Write down the approximate price of six things in your country, e.g. a daily newspaper, a short bus journey, a cup of coffee in a bar/café, a ticket for the cinema, a takeaway burger, a pair of jeans, etc. Do you think the price is expensive, reasonable, cheap? Compare with someone else if possible.

59 Health: illness

A Common problems

A: I **don't feel well.**
B: What's the matter?
A: I've got a **sore throat** and I **keep sneezing.**
B: Oh, you've probably got **a cold** or **flu.**
   You should go to bed.
A: Yes, I think I will.

She's **sneezing.**   She's **coughing.**   She's got a **sore throat.**

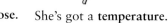

She's **blowing her nose.**   She's got a **temperature.**

What's the matter?	How do you know? (**the symptoms**)	cause of illness
I've got a **cold.**	sneezing, a sore throat, a cough	a **virus**
I've got **flu.** (= like a cold but more serious)	same as for a cold + high temperature, e.g. 40°	a virus
I've got **diarrhoea.**	I keep going to the toilet.	often food, or a virus
I feel **sick.**	I want to **vomit.** (= be sick)	many, e.g. food, illness
I've got a **hangover.**	headache, feel sick	too much alcohol

For these **illnesses,** you can go to a doctor or a **chemist** (= pharmacy). The doctor may give you a **prescription** (= paper with an order for medicine) that you get from the chemist.

B Aches and pains

We use the noun **ache** for **toothache, stomachache, backache, earache** and **a headache.**
For other parts of the body we use **pain.** With both nouns, we often use the verb **get.**
I've got a **terrible headache.** (= a bad headache)   I often **get backache.**
I woke up with **a terrible pain** in my chest.   I **get** a **pain** in my leg when I run.

Ache is also a verb, describing a pain which continues for a long time but is not strong.
By the end of the day, my feet were **aching.**

Hurt is common as a verb, used to describe a pain which is stronger or more sudden.
My throat **hurts** when I speak.   Where does it **hurt?** (= Where is the pain?)

The most common adjective is **painful.**
A: Did it hurt when you had the **fillings?** (= when the
   dentist fills a hole/cavity in the tooth)
B: It was quite **painful** when she gave me the **injection.**

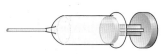

C Serious illnesses

Smoking is a major cause of **lung cancer.**
He had a **heart attack** and died almost immediately.
Hepatitis is a **disease** affecting the **liver.**
Many people **suffer from** (= have the illness of) **asthma.**
(= chest illness causing breathing problems)

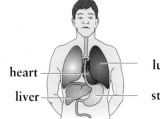

heart   lungs
liver   stomach

Exercises

59.1 Write down the main symptom or symptoms for these conditions.

1 A cold: sneezing, ...
2 Flu: ....
3 A hangover: ....
4 Diarrhoea: ....

59.2 Look at the <u>underlined</u> letters in these pairs of words. Is the pronunciation the same or different? Look at the examples first and use the pronunciation guide in the Index to help you.

Examples <u>a</u>che p<u>ai</u>n same
c<u>o</u>ld st<u>o</u>mach different

1 d<u>i</u>sease d<u>i</u>arrhoea
2 <u>ch</u>emist a<u>ch</u>e
3 l<u>u</u>ng s<u>u</u>ffer

4 v<u>i</u>rus <u>i</u>llness
5 fl<u>u</u> v<u>i</u>rus
6 c<u>ou</u>gh en<u>ou</u>gh

59.3 Complete the sentences with 'a' or nothing (–).

1 I think I'm getting .... cold.
2 Mary's got .... flu.
3 I've got .... backache.

4 I've got .... terrible headache.
5 He's got .... diarrhoea.
6 She's got .... cancer.

59.4 Look at the pictures and write what happened in the space below. Try to use at least three or four words or phrases from the opposite page.

I had ....
....

59.5 Fill the gaps with a suitable word.

1 I don't .... well. I think I'll go to bed early.
2 I hit my hand on the desk and now it really ....
3 Do you often .... backache?
4 They say she died of a heart ....
5 She had some apples that weren't ready to eat; now she's got stomach.....................
6 I've got this terrible .... in my neck from sleeping in the wrong position.
7 He died of .... cancer but he never smoked a cigarette in his life.
8 I went to the doctor, and she gave me a .... for some antibiotics.
9 There are different forms of hepatitis; one is a more serious .... than the other.
10 My back .... from sitting at that computer all day.

Health: injuries

A Common injuries

An **injury** is damage to part of your body. These are common **injuries.**

1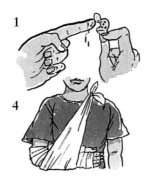

2

3

4

5

NOTE
Cut, **bruise**, **burn** and **bandage** can all be used as nouns or verbs with the same form.

What's the problem?	How did it happen?	result	solution
1 She **cut** her finger	using a knife	it's **bleeding**	**put a plaster on** it
2 He **twisted his ankle**	running for a bus	he can't walk	**put a bandage on** it
3 She's got **a bruise**	she hit her ankle when she fell over	it's **swollen** black and blue	ice pack
4 He **broke** his arm	he fell off his bike	he can't use it	**a sling**
5 She **burnt** her hand	on the kettle	it's very **painful**	**put cream on** it

The verb **hurt** is often used to describe the pain from injuries. It has different structures:
I **hurt** my back in the garden.   She **hurt herself** when she fell over.
I hit my leg against the table and it **really hurts**. (= it's a bad pain)

B Hospital treatment

John **fell out of** the window and **hit his head** on the ground. His wife called an **ambulance** but John was still **unconscious** when it arrived. He was **rushed to hospital** (= taken to hospital very quickly) and when he **came round** (= became **conscious**), he didn't know where he was.

Two players jumped for the ball and **bumped into each other** (= hit each other but it was an accident). One **cut** his head and had to **go to hospital**. He needed ten **stitches**.

C Wounds and injuries

Wound and **injury** describe damage to the body, but a **wound** is usually caused by a **weapon** (e.g. gun or knife) and happens in fights and wars. The verbs are **wound** and **injure**.

He was **seriously** (= badly) **injured** in a car crash.
Two of the soldiers were **wounded**.
Someone **shot** him (with a gun).
He **got into a fight** and he **was beaten up**.

Exercises

60.1 Check the pronunciation of these words in the Index (especially the <u>underlined</u> letters). Practise saying them.

in<u>ju</u>ry	bl<u>oo</u>d	band<u>age</u>	unconsci<u>ou</u>s
w<u>ou</u>nd	sw<u>o</u>llen	br<u>ui</u>se	w<u>ea</u>pon

60.2 Complete the table. Use a dictionary to help you.

noun	verb	noun	verb
cut	*cuted*	blood	*bleeding*
injury	*injory*	bruise	*bruesed*
shot	*shoted*	treatment	*terted*

60.3 Look at the pictures and write the story.

Now compare your story with the story about John on the opposite page.

60.4 Match the wounds/injuries on the left with the results on the right.

1 He hit his head on the door.
2 He bruised his leg.
3 He broke his leg.
4 He cut his finger.
5 He burnt himself.
6 He got into a fight.

a It's swollen and it hurts when he walks.
b He was beaten up quite badly.
c It's very painful.
d He's got a big bruise on it.
e It's still bleeding.
f He won't be able to walk for six weeks.

60.5 Answer these questions about yourself. If the answer is 'yes', when did it happen? How? How did you feel? If possible, ask another person the same questions.

1 Have you ever broken your arm or leg? *yes yes*
2 Have you ever needed stitches? *no*
3 Have you ever been unconscious? *yes*
4 Have you ever been in an ambulance? *yes*
5 Have you ever got into a fight? *yes*

61 Clothes

A **Pockets, buttons, collar, sleeves**

For 'buttons' and 'zips', we usually use the verbs **do up** and **undo**.
Do up your jacket before you go out. I can't **undo** these buttons – my hands are too cold.

B **Verbs and phrases used with clothes**

> **NOTE**
> See Unit 24 for information about word order with phrasal verbs, e.g. put on, hang up, etc.

The following text shows common verbs and phrases in an everyday context.

I got up at 7.30, had a shower, **got dressed** (= put on my clothes), and had breakfast. It was a cold morning so I **put on** my coat and left home about 8.20. When I got to work I **took** my coat **off** and **hung it up** behind the door. It was hot in the office, so I **took** my jacket **off** as well. During my lunch break I had a look round the shops. I saw a nice jacket in one place and **tried it on,** but it didn't **fit** me – it was too small and they didn't have the **right size**. When I got home I took off my suit and **changed into** jeans and a T-shirt.

C **'Too' + adjective and adjective + 'enough'**

The man on the right is wearing a suit but it doesn't fit him very well – the jacket is **too small** (= **not big enough**), and the trousers are **too short.** (= **not long enough**)

Exercises

61.1 Finish this sentence with five more different items of clothing.

> I need a pair of ...*trousers*...
> *sockes*
> *boot*
> *hat*
> *socker boot*
> *suit*^(x2)

61.2 Put these sentences in a logical order. The first one has been done for you.

a He took off his jeans. *3*
b He put his shoes back on. *7*
c He tried on the trousers. *4*
d He went into the changing room. 1
e He took them off. *5*
f He paid for the trousers. *8*
g He took off his shoes. *2*
h He went back to the sales assistant. *9*
i He put his jeans on again. *6*

61.3 What's different? Find five things in the first picture that aren't in the second picture.

1 *r i n g*
2 *bottens*
3 *pucket*
4 *earing*
5 *chines*

61.4 Fill the gaps with suitable words. (More than one answer may be possible in some cases.)

1 She decided to wear a ...*caring*... and a ...*chines*... instead of a dress.
2 I tried on a ...*coat*... ; the jacket was fine but the ...*shoes*... were too short.
3 It was hot, so I took off my jacket and ...*jumpers*..., and rolled up the sleeves of my ...*shirt*...
4 It was very embarrassing because I couldn't ...*jeanes*... up the zip on my jeans.
5 I wanted to buy the jacket, but unfortunately the one I tried on wasn't big ...*enahre*... and they didn't have it in a bigger ...*it was*...
6 I tried on a jumper, but the medium size was ...*getting*... big and the small size wasn't big ...*jumply*...

61.5 Write down:
1 Five things usually worn by women only
2 Five things worn by men and women
3 Five more items of clothing you have at home

Shops and shopping

A Shop and shopping

Where's the **shop assistant**? (= person who works in a shop; also called **sales assistant**)
The shoes were in the **shop window**. (= the window at the front of the shop)
We went to the new **shopping centre**. (= a place with many shops, outside or indoors)
I just went **window shopping**. (= looking round the shops without buying anything)
Did you make a **shopping list**? (= a list of things to buy)
I **went shopping** yesterday. (= I bought things, e.g. clothes, CDs, a present for my sister)
I **did the shopping** yesterday. (= I bought food and things for the house)
You have to **shop around** for the best prices. (= go to different shops to find the best price)

B Types of shop and what they sell

NOTE
Most other shops are just '+ shop', e.g. shoe shop or record shop. Some countries have stalls/ shops in the street for newspapers. We call them **kiosks**.

name of shop	what they sell
department store	almost everything (furniture, clothes, **electrical appliances**, e.g. TV and washing machine, **toys**, e.g. dolls, games, **jewellery**, e.g. rings, earrings)
supermarket	most things, but especially food and **household goods**, e.g. cleaning products and kitchen equipment, etc. In some, you buy meat at a **meat counter** and fish at a **fish counter**. (= place where people serve you)
newsagent('s)	newspapers, cigarettes, **stationery**, e.g. writing paper, envelopes
butcher('s)	meat
chemist('s)	medicine, baby products, shampoo, soap, toothpaste, etc.
off-licence	specialist shop for wine, beer and soft drinks

C In a clothes shop

ASSISTANT: Can I help you?
CUSTOMER: Yes, I'm **looking for** (= I want) a blue jumper.   *or*
No, I'm **just looking**, thanks. (= I don't need help)   *or*
I'm **being served**, thanks. (= another assistant is already serving/helping me)

ASSISTANT: What **size** are you? (e.g. large? small? medium? 14? 16?)

CUSTOMER: Where's the { **changing room**? (= the room where you try on clothes)
{ **fitting room**?

ASSISTANT: It's down there on the right.

CUSTOMER: Yes, I'll **take** this one/these. (= Yes, I want to buy this one/these.)

CUSTOMER: No, I'll **leave it** thanks. (= No, I don't want to buy it/them.)

CUSTOMER: Excuse me. Where do I pay for these?
ASSISTANT: Over at the **cash desk** (also **till**).
CUSTOMER: And can I **pay by** credit card?

Exercises

62.1   What 'general' word on the opposite page describes each group of items below.

1 *meat* .... e.g. lamb, beef, pork
2 .... e.g. shoes, trousers, jacket
3 .... e.g. potatoes, beans, onions
4 .... e.g. sofa, armchair, table
5 .... e.g. television, washing machine, food processor
6 .... e.g. ring, earrings, necklace
7 .... e.g. teddy bear, plastic gun, Lego
8 .... e.g. writing paper, envelopes

62.2   Where would you buy these things? Choose from the shops below.

butcher   newsagent   chemist   supermarket   department store

Write down two more things you could buy in each shop.

62.3   What word or phrase is being defined in these sentences?

1 A shop where you buy meat.
2 A place with many shops, either outside or indoors.
3 A person who works in a shop.
4 The place where you can try on clothes in a shop.
5 The place where you pay for things in a shop.
6 To look round the shops without planning to buy anything.
7 A shop where you buy wine, beer and soft drinks.
8 A shop where you buy medicines, baby products, shampoo, etc.

62.4   Complete this shopping dialogue with a suitable word or phrase.

ASSISTANT A: Can I help you?
CUSTOMER: Yes, I'm (1) .... a blouse like this, but in blue.
ASSISTANT A: I see. And what (2) .... are you?
CUSTOMER: Er, 12 usually.
ASSISTANT A: OK, I'll just go and see if we've got any.
CUSTOMER: Fine.
ASSISTANT B: Can I help you?
CUSTOMER: No, it's OK, I'm (3) .... thanks.
ASSISTANT A: Here we are. The last one in stock.
CUSTOMER: Great. Can I try it on?
ASSISTANT A: Yes, of course. The (4) .... is just over there. *[pause]*
             How was it?
CUSTOMER: Yeah, fine. I'll (5) ....

63 Food

A Fruit

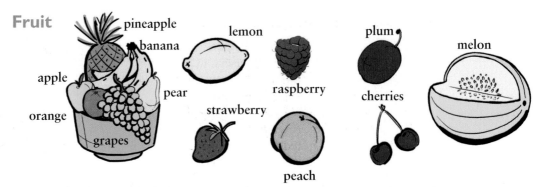

apple, pineapple, banana, lemon, plum, melon, pear, raspberry, cherries, orange, strawberry, peach, grapes

You normally **peel** oranges and bananas (= remove the skin) before you eat them.

B Vegetables

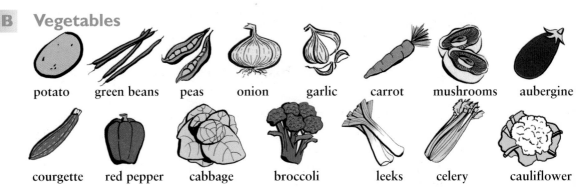

potato   green beans   peas   onion   garlic   carrot   mushrooms   aubergine

courgette   red pepper   cabbage   broccoli   leeks   celery   cauliflower

I peeled the potatoes and **chopped** the carrots. (= cut into small pieces)

C Salad

A **salad** is usually a mixture of uncooked vegetables. In Britain it often contains **lettuce**, but may also contain **tomato**, **cucumber**, and other things. We often put **salad dressing** (usually a mixture of **oil** and **vinegar**, or oil and lemon juice) on salad.

lettuce   tomato   cucumber   vinegar oil

D Meat (animals), fish and seafood

animal:	cow	**calf** (= young cow)	**lamb** (= young sheep)	pig	chicken
meat:	beef	veal	lamb	pork	chicken

NOTE
A person who does not eat meat is a **vegetarian**.

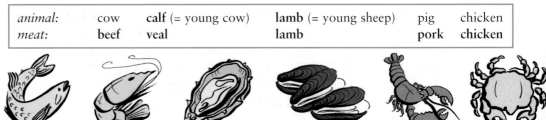

salmon   prawn   oyster   mussels   lobster   crab

Exercises

63.1 Write down at least one vegetable and fruit:

	vegetable	fruit
1 beginning with the letter 'p'	potato, peas	
2 beginning with the letter 'b'	broccoli	banana
3 beginning with the letter 'm'	mushrooms	melon
4 beginning with the letter 'c'	cabbage, carrot	cherries
5 beginning with the letter 'a'	aubergine	apple

63.2 Match words in the two boxes where the <u>underlined</u> letters are pronounced the same.

Example b<u>a</u>nana   mel<u>o</u>n

lett<u>u</u>ce	<u>o</u>nion	tomat<u>o</u>	~~mel<u>o</u>n~~
<u>o</u>range	~~banana~~	p<u>o</u>rk	chi<u>c</u>ken
<u>au</u>bergine	sa<u>l</u>mon	ca<u>l</u>f	la<u>m</u>b
r<u>a</u>spberry	pr<u>aw</u>n	br<u>o</u>ccoli	m<u>u</u>shroom

63.3 Which is the odd one out in each group, and why?

1	pork	veal	<u>salmon</u>	beef	Salmon is a fish, the others are meat.
2	lettuce	leek	tomato	cucumber	
3	peach	onion	mushroom	courgette	
4	chicken	lamb	beef	crab	
5	grape	cherry	aubergine	melon	

63.4 Do you eat the skin (= the outside) of these fruits *always*, *sometimes* or *never*? Make three lists.

apple	orange	banana	cherries	melon
strawberries	pear	pineapple	peach	grapes

63.5 What do we call:

1 the meat from a cow?
2 the meat from a calf?
3 the meat from a pig?
4 the main vegetable in a green salad?
5 the two things we often put on salad? Oil and .... or ....

63.6 Using words from the opposite page, complete these sentences about yourself and your country. If possible, compare your answers with someone else.

1 In my country .... is/are more common than ....
2 In my country .... is/are more expensive than ....
3 In my country a mixed salad usually contains ....
4 In my country we don't grow ....
5 And we don't often eat ....
6 Personally, I prefer .... to ....

64 Cooking and restaurants

fry   boil

grill

roast/bake

A Ways of cooking food

NOTE
Food which is not cooked is **raw**.

boil: in water, e.g. potatoes or rice
fry: in oil or butter above the heat, e.g. sausages
grill: under the heat, e.g. toast or meat
roast: in the oven using oil, e.g. meat
bake: in the oven without oil, e.g. cakes

B How would you like your steak?

Rare (= cooked quickly and red inside); **medium-rare** (= cooked longer but still red in the middle); **medium** (= cooked more and pink); or **well-done**. (= cooked longer and not pink)

C What does it taste like?

Taste the sauce (= try a bit to see if it's good) and add salt if necessary.
You can really taste the garlic in this.   It's very **tasty**. (= lots of flavour; a positive word)

D Describing food and drink

salty: lots of salt   **hot/spicy**: lots of spices, e.g. curry, chilli
sweet: lots of sugar (*opp* **bitter**, e.g. very strong coffee, or **sour**, e.g. lemons)
fresh: recently produced or picked, e.g. **fresh bread**, **fresh fruit**
fattening: food which makes you **put on weight**/get fat, e.g. cream, cakes, etc.
healthy: good for your health/fitness, e.g. salad or fruit
chilled (= very cold), e.g. white wine is usually chilled
still: describes water without gas; **sparkling** is water with gas (also called **fizzy** water)

E A typical menu

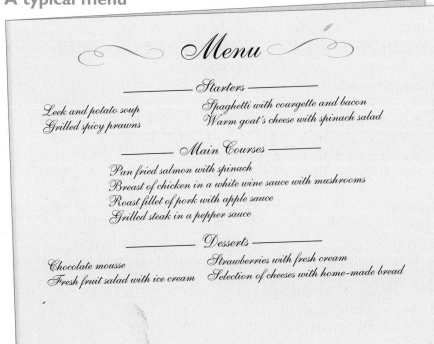

Menu

——— *Starters* ———
Leek and potato soup   *Spaghetti with courgette and bacon*
Grilled spicy prawns   *Warm goat's cheese with spinach salad*

——— *Main Courses* ———
Pan fried salmon with spinach
Breast of chicken in a white wine sauce with mushrooms
Roast fillet of pork with apple sauce
Grilled steak in a pepper sauce

——— *Desserts* ———
Chocolate mousse   *Strawberries with fresh cream*
Fresh fruit salad with ice cream   *Selection of cheeses with home-made bread*

salt and pepper

napkins

toothpicks

vinegar oil

Exercises

64.1 Do you often eat the following food in your country? If so, do you eat it in the same way?

Example In Britain, we often eat 'fish' but not usually 'raw fish'.

raw fish	fried rice
fried eggs	baked potatoes
roast beef	raw spinach
roast peppers	boiled eggs
grilled cheese	baked bananas

64.2 Look at the menu on the opposite page again, and answer these questions.

1 Which starter doesn't contain vegetables? Grilled spicy prawns
2 Which dish contains pasta?
3 Which main course may be rare or well-done?
4 Which main course is definitely cooked in the oven?
5 Which main course will probably be quite spicy?
6 Which main course contains alcohol?
7 Which dessert(s) will be quite sweet?
8 If you don't want to put on weight, which would probably be the best dish for the main course?

64.3 Choose an adjective from the opposite page which could describe these things.

	adjective		*adjective*
honey	sweet	bacon	
lemon	....	fillet steak	....
bread	....	mineral water	....
cakes	....	coffee	....

64.4 Answer these questions about the food you like, and eating in your country. If possible, ask another person the same questions.

1 Do you eat steak? If so, how do you like it cooked?
2 Do you like hot spicy food?
3 In restaurants, do you normally drink still or sparkling water?
4 Do waiters normally leave fresh bread on the table?
5 Do you normally eat a starter, main course and dessert when you eat out?
6 How many of these do you normally find on the table in a café or restaurant in your country?

salt	YES/NO	pepper	YES/NO	oil	YES/NO
vinegar	YES/NO	toothpicks	YES/NO	napkins	YES/NO

7 Generally, do you add more salt to your food when you eat in cafés or restaurants?
8 Do you think that food in your country is generally quite fattening?

City life

A Buildings and places

Here are some of the things you will find in most towns and cities.

commercial centre (= area with lots of banks and company offices)
shopping centre (= place with many shops, either indoors or outdoors)
car parks (= places to leave many cars)
factories (= buildings where you make/manufacture things, e.g. cars)
skyscrapers/high-rise buildings (= buildings with many floors)
libraries (= places where you can borrow books)
suburbs (= areas outside the centre of town where people live)

B People on the move

For many people, the worst time of day is the **rush hour** (= the time when people travel to and from work, e.g. 7–9 in the morning). At this time of day the **public transport system** (= trains and buses) has to **cope with** (= manage something which is difficult) the people who live in the city, and also **commuters** (= people who live in the country but travel into the city for work). The roads get **congested** (= busy and full of cars) and people are always **in a hurry** (= want to get to another place very quickly). For many, this is very **stressful**. (= makes you nervous and anxious)

C Going out (= going to places for social reasons)

I live and work in the suburbs, but I usually **go into town** (= the town centre) two or three times a week. In the evening, it is pretty **lively** (= lots of people and lots of things happening), and **there's plenty to do** (= lots of possibilities, e.g. bars, discos, etc.). One problem is that **there's nowhere to park** in the centre, so I usually **get/take a bus** into town and **take/get a taxi** home if I'm late.

There are many common phrases using this construction: **there's plenty to do; there's nothing to do; there's plenty to see; there's nowhere to go; there's nowhere to park**, etc.

D Advantages and disadvantages

'**The best thing about living in a city is that:**'
There's good **nightlife**. (= places to go at night, e.g. bars, discos, cinemas)
There's a **wide range of shops**. (= many shops selling different things)
You can **get whatever you want**. (= buy everything and anything you want)
There are lots of **cultural activities**. (e.g. museums, concerts, films)
It's **cosmopolitan**. (= full of people from many different countries and cultures)
There are **more job opportunities**. (= easier to find work)

'**The worst thing about living in a city is that:**'
It's very **crowded**. (= full of people)
People are more **aggressive**. (= seem angry and very unfriendly)
It can be **noisy** (*opp* **quiet**) and **dangerous**. (*opp* **safe**)
The streets are often **dirty** (*opp* clean) and it's **polluted**. (= dirty air)
There's **traffic congestion** (= too many cars) and **parking** is difficult.
There's a high **crime rate**. (= number of crimes)
You have a higher **cost of living**. (e.g. houses are more expensive, so is transport)

Exercises

65.1 Combine words from the left and right to form common compound words and phrases.

1	rush	a	building
2	traffic	b	life
3	night	c	rate
4	cost	d	hour
5	crime	e	park
6	shopping	f	of living
7	high-rise	g	congestion
8	car	h	centre

65.2 Complete the dialogues in a suitable way. Each gap is one word.

1 A: The town is full of people from different countries and cultures.
   B: Yes, it's very ....._cosmopolitan._......

2 A: There are cinemas, theatres, museums, art galleries and everything.
   B: Yes, I know, there are lots of ....

3 A: There's a .... of shops.
   B: Oh yes. You can buy .... you want.

4 A: There's plenty to do in the evening.
   B: Yes, the .... is great.

5 A: There's a better chance of finding work.
   B: Yes, there are more job ....

6 A: The transport system has to .... with the people who live in the country but work in town.
   B: Yes, I know, there are too many ....

65.3 Complete this table of opposites.

towns and cities	villages in the countryside
.....noisy..............	quiet and peaceful
....	clean air
....	safe
....	not much traffic
....	nothing to do in the evening

Put a tick ✓ beside each answer you agree with, and a ✗ beside each answer you don't.

65.4 Think of your journey to school, college or work. How many of these do you see or pass?

a car park	a factory	a museum	commuters	skyscrapers
a library	suburbs	a railway station	lots of traffic	a shopping centre

65.5 Do you live in a big town or city? If so, answer questions 1a-b. If not, answer 2a-b.

1a For me, the best thing about living in a big town/city is that ....
1b The worst thing about living in a big town/city is that ....
2a For me, the best thing about not living in a big town/city is that ....
2b The worst thing about not living in a big town/city is that ....

66 Life in the country

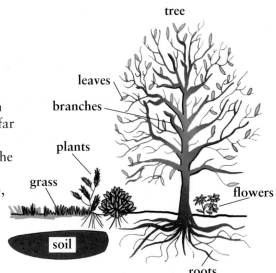

A Surrounded by nature

I **grew up** (= spent my childhood) in a **rural area** (= an area in the country; *opp* an **urban area**). It was quite a **remote area** (= an area far from towns), and we lived in an old **cottage** (= a type of house, often small, you find in the country). My sister and I played a lot in the **woods** (= an area of trees like a small forest), not far from the nearest **village** (= a place smaller than a town). I **loved being in the country.** (NOT I loved to be in the nature.)

B Working in the country

A lot of land **in the country/countryside** (both words are used) is used for **agriculture/farming**. Some farms **grow crops** (e.g. wheat, apples and potatoes) and some **keep animals** (e.g. cows, sheep and pigs). When I was younger, I worked **on a farm** during my school holidays.

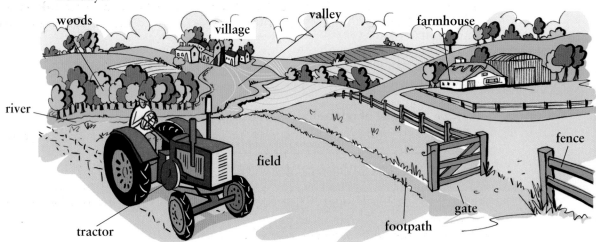

C Advantages and disadvantages

NOTE

The phrase **you get** (= there exists/you find) is very common (*opp* **you don't get**).

'The best thing about living in the country is that:'
  You get **peace and quiet.** (a common phrase to describe a place that is quiet and calm)
  You get **fresh air.** (= air outside a building or town which is clean)
  You're **surrounded by** lovely scenery and you can walk **in the countryside.**
  The pace of life (= the amount of activity in life) is slower and more relaxed.

'The worst thing about living in the country is that:'
  There isn't much **nightlife.**
  Public transport (= buses and trains) is **hopeless.** (= terrible)
  You don't get many shops.
  There isn't much **privacy** (= private life) because everyone knows what you are doing.

Exercises

66.1 You find these things in nature and they all grow, but the words are jumbled. What are they?

1 seret *trees*
2 sargs
3 velase

4 tnpsal
5 toros
6 woserlf

66.2 Fill the gaps with the correct adverb or preposition.

1 Have you ever lived .... the country?
2 I grew .... in a small village.
3 Have you ever worked .... a farm?
4 It's wonderful to be surrounded .... nature.
5 I love the pace .... life in a small village.
6 The best thing .... the countryside is that people are very friendly.

66.3 Study the picture in 66B on the opposite page for one minute, then cover it and complete this text.

We opened the (1) .... , said 'hello' to the man on the (2) .... , and then followed the (3) .... across the (4) .... and down into the (5) .... We stopped and had a picnic by the river. Afterwards we walked up through the (6) .... and came to a (7) .... where we stopped and bought some bread.

66.4 Fill the gaps with a suitable word.

1 Another word for the 'country' is the ....
2 Another word for 'farming' is ....
3 Wheat, rice and potatoes are all examples of .... that farmers grow.
4 The opposite of an 'urban area' is a .... area.
5 A place smaller than a town is called a ....
6 An area where trees grow, smaller than a forest, is called a ....
7 A .... is often quite small, and it's the type of house you find in the country.
8 Buses and trains are examples of public ....

66.5 Fill the gaps with a suitable word.

The best (1) .... about living in the country is that:
- there's peace and (2) ....
- you get (3) .... air
- you are (4) .... by nature
- the (5) .... of life is slower and more relaxed

The (6) .... thing about living in the country is that:
- there are no cinemas and discos, so there isn't much (7) ....
- everyone knows what you are doing, so there isn't much (8) ....

Can you add more things to each list?

67 On the road

A Road features

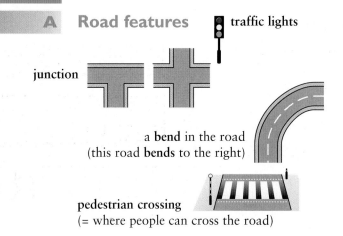

junction

traffic lights

a **bend** in the road
(this road **bends** to the right)

pedestrian crossing
(= where people can cross the road)

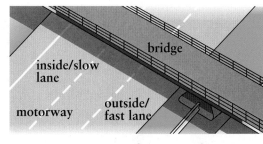

bridge

inside/slow lane

motorway

outside/fast lane

road signs (school, **roadworks**)

B An accident

There was an **accident** on one of the **main roads** into town this morning. A **lorry** [see picture] **broke down** (= stopped because of a problem) in the middle of the road. It was eight o'clock, a busy time, and with the lorry **blocking** the road (= stopping things from moving in the road), there was soon a long **tailback** (= long line of cars that cannot move). One man in a Mercedes **pulled out** (= moved out to the centre of the road) to go round the lorry, but another car **was coming in the opposite direction**. The driver **braked** (= put his foot on the brake to stop the car), but he couldn't **prevent** the accident (= stop it happening) – the Mercedes **crashed into** the front of his car. The driver of the Mercedes was OK, but the other driver was **badly injured** and both cars were **badly damaged**.

lorry

C Giving directions

Go **along** here, **turn** right **into** the main road, then **take the first turning on your left**. **Keep going** (= continue in this direction), then turn left again when you **get to** (= reach/arrive at) the bank.

Bank

You are here

X

D Common words and phrases

Cars and buses use the road; **pedestrians** (= people who walk) use the **pavement**. Cars mustn't **park** on the pavement.
The **speed limit** on motorways in Great Britain is 70 mph (120 kph). The police use **speed cameras** to catch people who are **speeding/breaking the speed limit**. (= going too fast)
Most **petrol stations** (= places where you buy petrol) in Great Britain are **self-service**. (= there are no people to put the petrol in your car; you serve yourself and then pay)
The other car was going very slowly, so I decided to **overtake** it. (= pass it on the outside)

Exercises

67.1 Complete the text using the map on the right.

Go (1) *along this road* and turn left at the
(2) .... Then you
(3) .... and
(4) .... right when you
(5) .... to the (6) ....
Then (7) ....
again into (8) .... Road, and the
bank is (9) .... the left just
(10) .... the cinema.

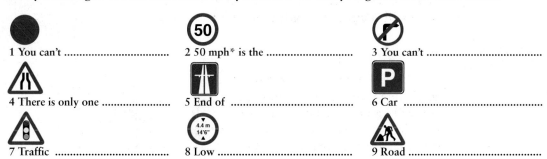

67.2 Fill the gaps with the correct word.

1 It was quite a serious .... ; both drivers were taken to hospital.
2 Almost all the petrol stations round here are self-................................
3 One driver was badly .... in the crash, and both cars were badly
   ....
4 There were four or five cars involved in the accident and it .... the road
   for about half an hour. When I got there, the .... was already about two
   miles long, and drivers were getting very frustrated.
5 The bicycle hit me just as I stepped off the .... to cross the road.
6 My car .... on the motorway and I had to phone a
   garage to come and fix it.
7 I was doing about 120 kph and then this car .... me doing about 160.
8 I couldn't stop quickly enough, and I .... into the back of the car in front.
9 Cars, motorbikes and bikes can't go down there – it's only for ....

67.3 Many road signs are international. Do you know or can you guess what these mean?

1 You can't ....   2 50 mph* is the ....   3 You can't ....

4 There is only one ....   5 End of ....   6 Car ....

7 Traffic ....   8 Low ....   9 Road ....

*mph = miles per hour (50 mph = 80 kph approximately)

67.4 Answer these questions about your own country. If possible, compare with someone else.

1 Do you have a speed limit on motorways? If so, what is it?
2 How many lanes do motorways usually have?
3 Do drivers usually stop for pedestrians at pedestrian crossings?
4 Are most petrol stations self-service, or do people serve you?
5 Do many people park their cars on the pavement?
6 Do you have speed cameras at the side of the road?

68 Transport

bus

coach

A Vehicles

Vehicle is the general word for all types of road transport.

A: How did you get here?
B: I came **by bus**.
A: And the others?
B: Sue and John came **by car**.
A: And Paul?
B: He missed the bus, so he had to **get a taxi**.

bicycle

motorbike

van   lorry

B Get a bus, take a taxi

NOTE

We can say:
I **go** to work
on my bike
(= bicycle), or I
cycle to work.

bus	train	plane	taxi	bicycle	car
driver	driver	pilot	driver	cyclist	driver
drive	drive	fly	drive	ride	drive
(£) fare	fare	air fare	fare	–	–
get/catch/take	get/catch/take	get/take	get/take	go on (my)	go in (my)
get on/off	get on/off	get on/off	get in/out (of)	get on/off	get in/out
journey	journey	flight/journey	–	ride	journey
bus station	railway station	airport	taxi rank	–	–

C Trains

These are things **train passengers** (= people who travel by train) often say or ask:

Single to Edinburgh, please. (= a ticket to Edinburgh)
Return to Bath, please. (= a ticket to Bath <u>and back</u>)
Does this train **go to** (= take me to) Oxford?
Do I have to **change**? (= change to another train)
Is it a **fast train** or a **stopping train**?

A: Which **platform** for Liverpool?
B: Number three.
A: And when is the train **due to arrive**? (= timetabled to arrive)

D Buses

Sometimes buses are **punctual** (= arrive at the correct time), but not always. Where I live, buses should **run** (= travel/operate) every ten minutes, but sometimes I wait at the **bus stop** for half an hour **in a queue** (= line of people), and then three buses come together, and they're all **full up**. (= full of people) Other times the bus is early and I **miss** it. (= I don't catch it)

E Taxis

Taxis show what you have to pay on the **meter**. When you want the driver to stop, you can say this: Could you **drop me** here? (= Could you stop here?) People often give taxi drivers a **tip** (= extra money as well as the fare). For example, if the **fare** is £8.40, you can give the driver £9.

Exercises

68.1 <u>Underline</u> the correct word in brackets in these sentences.

1 You mustn't (ride/drive) a motorbike without a crash helmet in the UK.
2 She told him to (get in/get on) the car and fasten his seat belt.
3 The bus (fare/ticket) is cheaper than the train.
4 Trains to the airport (travel/run) every half hour.
5 The pilot couldn't (drive/fly) the plane in such bad weather.
6 Have a look at the train (schedule/timetable) to see when the next one is due.
7 We were late, so we had to (get/catch) a taxi.
8 They left a bit late and (lost/missed) the bus.

68.2 Write down two different words that can combine with each of the words below.

Example miss the bus the train

1 .... fare   3 .... station   5 get in ....
  ....

2 get on ....   4 .... driver   6 .... journey
         ....

68.3 Write the names of these vehicles without looking at the opposite page.

1 .... 2 .... 3 .... 4 .... 5 ....

68.4 Fill the gaps with the correct word.

1 Our train leaves from .... seven in ten minutes.
2 I waited at the .... for ten minutes, and then two buses arrived at the same time.
3 I couldn't get on the first bus because it was ....
4 After we took off, the .... told us a bit about the plane and the journey.
5 Buses are not very .... Sometimes they come every five minutes, then other times you have to wait for 40 minutes.
6 When I got to the bus stop there was a long .... of people.
7 The flight was fine but we had a terrible .... from the airport to our hotel.
8 I think the next train is .... to arrive in about ten minutes.

68.5 Are these statements true or false in your country?

1 Trains are more punctual than buses.
2 Train fares are more expensive than bus fares.
3 Train journeys are more interesting than bus journeys.
4 Railway stations are nicer places than bus stations.
5 In city centres, taxis are quicker than going in your own car.

69 Work: duties, pay and conditions

A What do you do?

People may ask you about your job. They can ask and you can answer in different ways:

What do you do? **What's your job?** **What do you do for a living?**	**I'm** a banker/an engineer/a builder. (**I'm** + 'a(n)' + job) **I work in** a bank/marketing. (**work in** + place or type of work) **I work for** UnionBank/Fiat. (**work for** + name of company) (= **I'm employed by** Union Bank/Fiat, etc.) I'm **self-employed.** (= I work for myself.)

B What does that involve?

When people ask you to explain your job, they want to know your **responsibilities** (= your duties/what you have to do), or something about your **daily routine** (= what you do every day). They can ask like this: **What does that involve?** (= What do you do in your job?)

General duties/responsibilities
I'm **in charge of/responsible for** security in the **factory**. (= the place where a product is made)
I **deal with/handle** customer **complaints**. (= take all necessary action when customers are unhappy)
I **run** the coffee bar in the museum. (= I am in control of it/I manage it)

Daily duties/routines
I have to **go to/attend** (*fml*) a lot of **meetings**.
I visit/see/meet **clients**. (= people I do business with, who pay for my service)
I **advise** clients. (= give them help and my opinion)
My job **involves** travelling. [Notice the *-ing* form after **involve**.]

C Working hours

For many people in Britain, **working hours** are 8.30–9.00am to 5.00–5.30pm, so people often talk about a **nine-to-five job** (= regular working hours). Some people **do flexitime** (= they can start work earlier or finish later); and some **do shiftwork** (= work at different times, e.g. during the day one week, at night the next). Some people **work/do overtime.** (= work extra hours for more money)

D Pay and conditions

Most workers are **paid** (= receive money) every month. This is called a **salary**. We can also use the verbs **earn/make**, e.g. I **earn/make** $60,000 a year. (= My **salary** is $60,000 a year.)

Some people are paid for the hours they work. The lowest amount for one hour's work is called the **minimum wage**. This amount is decided by the government.

With most jobs you **get 4–6 weeks' paid holiday**; you also **get sick pay.** (= pay when you are ill)

The total amount of money you receive in a year is called your **income**. This could be your salary from one job, or the salary from two different jobs. You have to **pay** part of your income to the government; this is called **income tax**.

Exercises

69.1 Match words on the left and right to form compound nouns or phrases.

1 nine-to-	a time
2 working	b tax
3 flexi-	c wage
4 income	d five
5 minimum	e hours

69.2 Match the verbs on the left with the nouns on the right. Use each verb once only.

1 earn	a overtime
2 work	b meetings
3 deal with	c a shop
4 attend	d complaints
5 run	e £2,000 a month

69.3 Rewrite these sentences starting with the words given. The meaning must stay the same.

Example I'm a banker.
         I work in *banking*.

1 What do you do?
   What's ....
2 I'm employed by the government.
   I work ....
3 I earn $50,000.
   My ....
4 I get £20,000 from my teaching job and another £10,000 from writing.
   My total ....
5 In my job I look after all the computers in the building.
   My job involves ....
6 I'm responsible for one of the departments.
   I'm in ....

69.4 This is part of a conversation with a teacher about her job. Write the missing questions.

A: .... ? B: I start at nine and finish at four.
A: .... ? B: Yes, a bit. On certain courses I work until 5.30.
A: .... ? B: 12 weeks. That's one of the good things.
A: .... ? B: Yes, we do, but we have to have a doctor's note.

69.5 What about working conditions in your country?

1 What are normal working hours for most office jobs in your country?
2 How much income tax do most people pay, e.g. 10% or 20% of what they earn?
3 Do workers normally get paid holidays? If so, how many days do they usually get?
4 Is there a minimum wage decided by the government? If so, how much is it?
5 What jobs often involve shiftwork in your country? (Give at least two examples.)

69.6 Think about your own job or the job of someone you know well. How many of the things on the opposite page are true in your country? How is the work different? Can you explain your/their responsibilities and daily duties in English?

70 Jobs

A Manual jobs

These are jobs where you work with your hands, and these are all **skilled**. (= need a lot of training)

bricklayer
(**builds** walls
with bricks)

carpenter
(makes things
using wood)

plumber
(**installs** and
repairs water
pipes, etc.)

electrician
(**installs** and **repairs**
electrical things)

mechanic
(**repairs** cars)

B Professional people

job	definition
architect	**designs** buildings
lawyer	**represents** people with legal problems
engineer	**plans** the building of roads, bridges, machines, etc.
accountant	**controls** the financial situation of people and companies
university lecturer	teaches in a university
stockbroker (on the stock market)	**buys and sells** stocks and shares (e.g. on Wall Street)
sales/personnel manager	**responsible for** sales or personnel staff

C The medical profession

Doctors, **nurses** and **surgeons** (= specialist doctors who **operate on** people) work **in hospitals**. **GPs** (= general practitioners – doctors who treat people with general problems), **dentists** and **vets** (= animal doctors) work in places we call **surgeries**. All of these people **treat** (= give medical help, e.g. advice, medicines) and **look after** (= care for/take care of) people or animals.

D The armed forces and the emergency services

My cousin **joined/went into** the army when he was 18.

soldier
(in the **army**)

sailor
(in the **navy**)

pilot
(in the **air
force**)

**police officer/
policeman/policewoman**
(in the **police force**)

firefighter/fireman
(in the **fire brigade**)

Exercises

70.1 Write down one job from the opposite page that would probably be impossible for these people.

1 Someone who didn't go to university   *doctor*
2 Someone with very bad eyesight (= cannot see very well)
3 Someone who is always seasick on a boat
4 Someone who understands nothing about cars
5 Someone who will not work in the evening or at weekends
6 Someone who is afraid of dogs
7 Someone who is afraid of heights and high places
8 Someone who is terrible at numbers and maths
9 Someone who doesn't like to see blood (= the red liquid in your body)
10 Someone who is a pacifist (= is anti-war)

70.2 Complete these definitions.

1 A university lecturer ....*teaches in a university.*....................
2 An architect ....
3 An accountant ....
4 A vet ....
5 A lawyer ....
6 An engineer ....
7 A bricklayer ....
8 A stockbroker ....
9 A mechanic ....
10 A surgeon ....

70.3 Respond to the statements below, as in the example.

Example   A: She's a police officer.
            B: *Really? When did she join the police force?*

1 A: She's a soldier.
  B: .... ?
2 A: He's a sailor.
  B: .... ?
3 A: He's a fighter pilot.
  B: .... ?
4 A: He's a fireman.
  B: .... ?

70.4 You have just bought a piece of land and you are planning to build a house on it. Write down at least six people from the opposite page that you may need to help you. What would you need their help for?

Example   A bricklayer to build the walls

70.5 Write a list of friends, relatives and neighbours who have jobs. What does each person do?

Example   My uncle Jim's an engineer. His wife is an accountant.

71 The career ladder

A Getting a job

When Paula left school, she **applied for** (= wrote an official request for) a job in a local company. They gave her a job as a **trainee** (= a very junior person in a company). She didn't **earn** much (= didn't get much money/she had a **low salary**), but they gave her **in-house training** (= the company gave her help and advice to become better), and she **went on/did** several **training courses.**

B Moving up

Paula worked hard and her **prospects** (= future possibilities in the job) looked good. Her **manager/boss** (*infml*) was very pleased with her progress and she soon got a good **pay rise** (= more money every week/month). After two years she **was promoted** (= was given a higher position with more money and responsibility). After five years she was **in charge of** (= the boss of) a department with five **employees** (= workers) **under her.** (= under her control)

> **employer** (= person who employs); **employee** (= worker)
> **trainer** (= person who gives training); **trainee** (= person who receives training)

C Leaving the company

By the time Paula was 30, she decided she wanted a **fresh challenge** (= a new exciting situation) and a **career change** (= to work in a different kind of job). She wanted to **work abroad** (= work in another country), so she **resigned** (= officially told the company she was **leaving her job**; also **quit** *infml*) and started **looking for** another job. After a month she got a job with an international company which **involved** (= included) a lot of foreign travel. She was very excited about this and at first she really enjoyed it, but …

D Hard times

NOTE
Paula didn't **have a job** for nine months. (NOT She didn't have ~~a work.~~)

After six months, Paula started to dislike the travelling and living in hotels. She didn't do well in the job either. After a year the company **dismissed/sacked** her (= told her to leave), and Paula found life difficult. She was **unemployed/out of work** (= without a job) for nine months until she got a **part-time job** (= working only part of the day or week) in the kitchen of a restaurant.

E Happier times

Paula loved the restaurant. She enjoyed learning to cook, and two years later she **took over** (= took control of) the restaurant. After a year, she opened a second one, and after 20 years she had 10 restaurants. Last year Paula **retired** (= stopped working completely) at the age of 50, a rich woman.

Exercises

71.1 Write a synonym (= word with a similar meaning) for each of these phrases.

1 sack someone = ...dismiss............. someone
2 out of work = ...
3 leave a company = ...
4 be given a better position in a company = be ....
5 future possibilities in a job = ...
6 stop working (often at 60 or 65) = ...
7 workers in a company = ...
8 take control of something (e.g. a company) = ...

71.2 Find the logical answer on the right for each of the questions on the left.

1 Why did they sack her?   a Because she was 60.
2 Why did they promote her?   b Because she was late for work every day.
3 Why did she apply for the job? c Because she needed more training.
4 Why did she retire?   d Because she was out of work.
5 Why did she resign?   e Because she was the best person in the department.
6 Why did she go on the course? f Because she didn't like her boss.

71.3 Complete these sentences with a suitable word.

1 He's not happy in his own country. He wants to work ....
2 I don't want a full-time job. I'd prefer to work ....
3 She'd like to go on another training ....
4 I'm bored in my job. I need a fresh ....
5 At the end of this year we should get a good pay ....
6 She's got more than a hundred workers under ....
7 I didn't know he was the new manager. When did he take .... ?
8 I know it's not a great job. How much does she .... ?

71.4 Complete the table. Use a dictionary to help you.

verb	general noun	person
manage	....management....	....
promote	....	–
employ	....	.........................../...........................
resign	....	–
retire	....	–
train	....	.........................../...........................

71.5 Have you got a job in a company? If so, answer these questions as quickly as you can. If possible, ask another person the same questions.

1 Are you responsible for anything or anyone?
2 Have you had much training from the company?
3 Have you been on any training courses?
4 Have you been promoted from the time you started your job?
5 Do you normally get a good pay rise at the end of each year?
6 What do you think about your future prospects in the company?

A Office equipment

files — drawers — wastepaper basket — briefcase — calculator — diary — desk — noticeboard — calendar — keyboard — monitor — filing cabinet — computer

B Office work

Brian works for a company which **produces** (= **makes/ manufactures** *fml*) furniture. He works in an office, opposite the **factory** where the furniture is made. This is how he spends his day:

He **works at a computer** most of the time, where he **types** [see picture] letters and reports, and **sends** lots of **e-mails**.

He sends **invoices** (= paper showing products sold and the money to pay) to customers, and **does** quite a lot of **paperwork**, e.g. **filing reports** (= putting them in a file/ filing cabinet), etc.

Occasionally he **shows people round the factory**.

He has to **make appointments** for his boss and put them in the diary. He also **arranges meetings** for managers from different departments and types the **agenda** (= list of things to discuss at a meeting). Sometimes he has to **attend** (= go to *fml*) meetings and **take the minutes**. (= write down everything that is said during the meeting)

C Office problems

Like most people who work in an office, Brian has his problems. This is how he explains them.

The **photocopier** is **broken**.
The printer **isn't working**.
We've **run out of** paper. (= the paper is finished) The computer's **down** (= not working) at the moment.
One of my **colleagues** (= people you work with) is **off** (= not at work) today and we've got **loads of work** (= a lot of work *infml*) to do.

Exercises

72.1 Find the best noun in the box to complete each of the sentences.

e-mail	~~work~~	letter	minutes	visitors
appointment	computer	meeting	reports	drawer

1 I've got loads of ...*work*............... to do today.
2 I made an .... to see their managing director next week.
3 The pens are in the top .... of my desk.
4 Could we arrange the .... for next Thursday?
5 The .... was down this morning, so I couldn't do anything.
6 I sent her an .... yesterday but she hasn't replied.
7 Have you filed those .... yet?
8 Could you type a .... for me to send to the bank?
9 I'm busy tomorrow. I have to show some .... round the factory.
10 Who took the .... of yesterday's meeting?

72.2 Complete the compound noun in each sentence.

1 I told him to put the details on the **notice**...............................
2 He put most of the stuff in the **filing** ....
3 I'm sure I put those reports in my **brief**...............................
4 It's a very boring job and I spend most of my time doing general **paper**...............................
5 I threw all that stuff in the **wastepaper** ....

72.3 Rewrite these sentences. Replace the <u>underlined</u> words with the correct form of the word on the right. Add any other words that are necessary, but the meaning must stay the same.

1 My secretary <u>isn't here</u> today.   is *off*   OFF
2 The photocopier <u>is broken</u>.   WORK
3 We <u>are very busy</u> today.   LOADS
4 <u>There's a problem with</u> the computer.   DOWN
5 We <u>don't have any more</u> paper for the photocopier. RUN OUT

72.4 What words from the opposite page are being defined here?

1 People you work with.   *colleagues*
2 Something you put on a wall which tells you the date.
3 A book where you often write down all your appointments and things you have to do.
4 A piece of paper which shows the products a customer bought and the money to pay.
5 A building where things (e.g. cars or computers) are made.
6 A list of things to discuss at a meeting.

72.5 Have you got a job? If so, are these statements true for you at work? If you haven't got a job, answer the questions about someone you know well. Compare your answers with a partner if possible.

I work at a computer a lot of the time.	I have to do a lot of paperwork.
I use e-mail a lot.	I show people round my workplace.
I arrange meetings.	I attend quite a lot of meetings.

73 Business and finance

A Banks and business

Companies often borrow money from banks to **finance** (= pay for) **investments** (= things they need to buy to help the company in future, e.g. machines). This money is called **a loan**, and companies have to **pay interest** on it, e.g. if you borrow £1,000 for a year, and the **interest rate** is 10%, then you have to **pay back** £1,000 + £100 **in interest**.

B Profit and loss

The **main aim/objective** of a company (= most important thing for a company to do) is to **make a profit** (= receive more money than it spends; *opp* **make a loss**). If a company does not make a profit or a loss, it **breaks even**. For example:
Most new companies are happy if they **break even** in their first year of business.

Companies receive money from selling their products (this money is called the **turnover**), and they spend money (called the **expenditure**) on these things: **raw materials** (= materials in their natural state, e.g. coal and oil are important **raw materials** used to make plastics), and **overheads** (= things a company must always spend money on, e.g. rent, electricity, etc.). For many companies, **labour costs** (= money paid to workers) are very expensive.

C Rise and fall

NOTE
Rise, **increase** and **fall** are also used as nouns. For example: **a rise of** 10% ('of' introduces the amount); **a fall of** $3.5 million; an **increase in** sales ('in' introduces the thing that is changing); **a fall in** profits.

These verbs describe **trends** (= movements) in sales, prices, profit and loss, etc.

rise/go up/increase   e.g. **rise slowly**   **go up steadily**   **rise sharply**
(also **gradually**)

fall/go down/drop   e.g. **fall slowly**   **fall steadily**   **drop sharply**

Notice the different uses of prepositions with these verbs:
by + size of change   Pre-tax profits rose **by** 11% (**to** £120 million).
from + previous level   Prices dropped **from** $594 **to** $386.
to + new level

D Businesses and the economy

Most companies want:
to grow/expand (= get bigger) and **be successful** (= do well and make a lot of profit); **low inflation**, so prices do not go up; **low interest rates** to borrow money; **economic** and **political stability** (= no quick changes in the economic/political situation); **a healthy/strong economy** (= an economy in good condition; *opp* an economy **in recession**); **tax cuts** (= tax reductions/lower taxes), so they can keep more of their profit.

Exercises

73.1 What single word or phrase is being defined in each of these sentences?

1 Money you borrow from a bank for your business.
2 What you must pay the bank if you borrow money.
3 The continuous increase in the price of things.
4 Total amount of money a company receives from selling its products.
5 When a company does not make a profit or a loss.
6 Money that a company spends on rent, electricity, paper, etc.

73.2 Complete the missing preposition in these sentences.

1 Sales rose .... 10% last year.
2 The stock market value fell .... 240 .... 225 in the space of two days.
3 There was a rise .... 5% in the value of the shares.
4 The shares were £2.50 last week, but the value has just gone up 20p .... £2.70.
5 There has been a steady increase .... the profit.
6 We had to pay over £5,000 .... interest.

73.3 Replace the <u>underlined</u> word(s) with another word or phrase that has the same meaning.

After last year when sales (1) <u>dropped</u> by 5%, I am pleased to say there has been a (2) <u>slow</u> rise in sales in the first quarter of this year, and we are optimistic that the company will continue to (3) <u>do well</u> in the next quarter. In the longer term, our (4) <u>objective</u> for the company is to (5) <u>grow</u> by at least 10% over the next two years, and of course, to make sure that our profit (6) <u>increases</u> by a similar amount.

73.4 Look at the graph and complete the sentences on the left. Each gap is one word.

1 In 1998 sales ....
2 In the following year they
   ....
3 In 2000 there was a ....
   .... in sales.
4 In 2001 business improved and there
   was a ....
5 And in 2002 sales ....
   ....
6 In the five-year period sales
   .... by ....

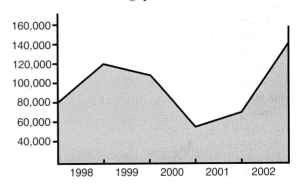

73.5 Complete the compound words or common phrases. There may be more than one answer.

1 profit and ....
2 .... rate
3 tax ....
4 raw ....
5 a healthy ....
6 .... stability

73.6 Can you answer these questions about your own country?

1 What is the inflation rate at the moment?
2 If you borrow money from the bank, what is the interest rate approximately?
3 What is the state of the economy at the moment? Is it strong? Is it in recession?

74 Sport: ball games

A Ball games

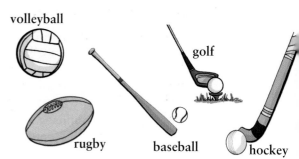

football
basketball
volleyball
golf
tennis
table tennis
rugby
baseball
hockey

B Equipment (= what you need to play the games)

For most ball games you need **boots** or **training shoes**. (also **trainers** *infml*)

You need a **racket** for tennis, a **bat** for baseball/table tennis; a **stick** for hockey; and **clubs** for golf [see picture].

In tennis and volleyball and there is a **net** across the middle of the **court**. There is also a **net** around each **goal** in football.

C Things you can do with a ball

throw it   head it   pass it   hit it   catch it   kick it

D Places and people

Places

The playing area for football and rugby is called a **pitch**. Around the pitch there is an area for **spectators/the crowd** (= people who watch the game). The total area is the **stadium**. The playing area for tennis, volleyball and basketball is a **court**; for golf it is a **course**.

Officials

Football and rugby have a **referee**; tennis and baseball have an **umpire**. In football the referee uses a **whistle** to control the game.

E Winning and losing

NOTE
We write **2–2**, but say **two-all**.

Spain **beat** Switzerland 3–2. (= Switzerland **lost to** Spain 3–2) In other words: Spain **won** the match. (= Switzerland **lost** the match) Spain were the **winners**. (= Switzerland were the **losers**)

If two teams/players have the same **score** (= number of goals or points) at **full-time** (= the end of the game), it is a **draw**. We can also use **draw** as a verb, e.g. We **drew** 2–2.

When a game is in progress, we use **lead** to describe the position of the teams or player with the most goals/points, and **latest** to describe the **score**:

At half-time, Brazil **are leading** Chile 2–1. (= the **latest score** is 2–1 to Brazil)

Exercises

74.1 Complete the table with the correct forms.

infinitive	past tense	past participle
win	won	....
lose	....	....
beat	....	....
catch	....	....
draw	....	....

74.2 Write down six things you can do with a ball. Cover the opposite page first.

.... it   .... it   .... it

.... it   .... it   .... it

74.3 Write down:

1 Five games where you can hit the ball (with various kinds of equipment)
2 Four games where you can pass the ball (with hands or feet)
3 Three games where you can catch the ball
4 Two games where you can kick the ball
5 One game where you can head the ball

74.4 Complete these sentences with a suitable word.

1 I think the final .... was 3–1.
2 The Czech Republic .... Holland 2–1, so they are in the semi-final.
3 Bayern Munich .... 1–1 with AC Milan last night.
4 The Maracana .... in Brazil is the biggest in the world. It holds over 100,000 people.
5 Many of the .... ran onto the pitch after the game.
6 Paris St Germain will play the .... of the game between Barcelona and Roma.
7 United scored first and they are still .... 1–0 with five minutes to go until half-time.
8 With 20 minutes to go, the .... score we have is 2–1 to Real Madrid.

74.5 Organise these words and put them in the correct columns below.

football	racket	course	pitch	tennis	boots
golf	net	court	clubs	training shoes	whistle

sport	place	equipment
football	booty	coppee
tenis	clubs	
golf		

Sport and leisure

A Sports

sport	place	equipment
athletics	track	vest, shorts, running shoes
motor racing	circuit	crash helmet
swimming	pool	swimming costume (women); trunks (men)
boxing	ring	vest, shorts, gloves, boots
ice hockey	rink	sticks, skates, puck
skiing	ski slopes	skis, sticks, ski suit, ski boots

B Outdoor leisure activities

| hiking | camping | rock climbing | jogging |

I often **go camping** in the summer.
I really **enjoy** hiking.

I **do** a bit of/a lot of **rock climbing** in Wales.
Jogging **keeps me fit**. (= keeps my body healthy)

C What do you do?

Notice the common verb + noun combinations here, e.g. **do exercise** or **play a game**.

Do you **do** much **sport**?
I **go skiing** in the winter.
I **play** a lot of **ice hockey**.
I **go to the gym** (= gymnasium) twice a week,
where I **do aerobics** and a bit of **weight training**.
Is it expensive to **join** (= become a member of) a sports **club**?
I plan to **take up** (= start) golf when I get older.
I had to **give up** (= stop) athletics after I injured my back.
Swimming is **good for you**. (= helps people to stay healthy)
You need to **do/take** more **exercise** if you want to **get fit**.
(= become fit/get in good condition)
A: Which **team** do you **support**? (= like and follow)
B: Real Madrid. I've **supported** them all my life.

D Do you take it seriously?

A: I **take** sport **very seriously** (= sport is very important to me) and when I play team games I'm very **competitive** (= I try hard and always want to win). What about you?
B: No. **I'm the complete opposite** (= I'm completely different: *opp* **I'm exactly the same**). I only play **for fun**. (= for pleasure/enjoyment)

Exercises

75.1 Organise these words and put them in the correct columns below.

swimming	costume	motor racing	crash helmet	trunks	circuit
pool	skates	ice hockey	rink	puck	sticks

sport	place	equipment
Swimming		

75.2 Fill the gaps with the correct verb.

1 Do you .... much exercise?
2 I only .... volleyball in the summer.
3 If possible, I'd like to .... a fitness club.
4 A: I love football.
   B: Do you? Which team do you .... ?
   A: Liverpool.
5 My Dad played football but he .... last year. He said he was too old.
6 We used to .... camping in the mountains.
7 Why don't you .... hiking or swimming, or something? You need more exercise.
8 If you want to .... fit, you need to run three or four miles every other day.

75.3 Complete these sentences with a suitable word.

1 Do you still do a lot of weight .....training...... ?
2 I enjoy jogging and it keeps me ....
3 Liz doesn't have much opportunity now to go rock ....
4 Nigel loves dangerous sports; I'm the complete ....
5 He has played for several good teams and he takes it very ....
6 I used to play a lot of ice ....
7 We still like watching motor ....
8 I played for years, then I injured my ankle and I had to give ....
9 In the summer I go jogging in the park. In the winter I exercise indoors and go to the ....
10 I love swimming, and it's really good for ....

75.4 Answer these questions. If possible, discuss your answers with someone else.

1 What sport do you do?
2 Do you take sport seriously or do you do it just for fun?
3 Are you very competitive?
4 Are you good at any sports?
5 Have you taken up a new sport recently?
6 Have you ever had to give up a sport for any reason?

76 Cinema and theatre

A Inside a theatre

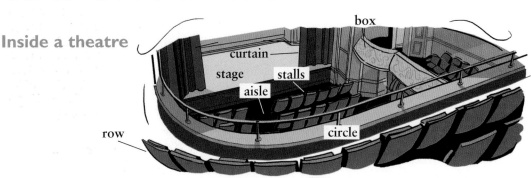

B Plays and musicals

At the theatre you can see **plays**, e.g. *Hamlet*, written by Shakespeare; or **musicals**, e.g. *Phantom of the Opera*, written by Andrew Lloyd Webber. You usually **book** (= reserve) tickets **in advance** (= some time before you see the play). When you see the play (or film), it is called a **performance**, e.g. The evening performance usually starts at 8 pm.

C Cinema

Films **are shown** on a **screen**. In your country, films made in English may have **subtitles** (= a written translation at the bottom of the screen), or they **are dubbed**. (= the English is replaced by actors speaking the words in your own language)

The person who makes the film is the **director**, e.g. Steven Spielberg, and the people in the film are **actors**. Famous actors are often called **film stars** (or **stars**), e.g. Julia Roberts.

D Types of film

war film, e.g. *Apocalypse Now*; *Platoon*
romance (= a love story/about a relationship)
thriller (= interesting and exciting; often about crime)
disaster movie, e.g. *Titanic*

action film, e.g. *Indiana Jones*
horror film, e.g. *Dracula*
comedy (= funny film; makes you laugh)
romantic comedy (= love story and funny)

E Describing plays and films

Journalists who write about films and plays are called **critics**, and their articles are called **reviews**. These are some common words they use.

brilliant/superb acting (= fantastic acting)
very **moving** (= has a big effect on our emotions; often sad)
violent scenes (= scenes including fighting and death)

an **awful/dreadful** film (= terrible)
a **slow** film (= boring)
a **gripping** story (= exciting/interesting)
good fun (= enjoyable but not serious)
a **complex plot** (= story with many ideas)

F Telling the story

The film **is set** (= happens) in the 1920s. **It's about** (= the subject/story is) a young man from a poor **background** (= family history and situation), who meets a girl and they **fall in love**. But her family don't accept him, so they **run away** (= go to another place to be away from the parents). **At first** (= in the beginning) everything is fine, but then **things go wrong** (= problems appear in their situation) and she has to leave him or they will be unhappy.

Exercises

STAGE

76.1 Look at the picture and answer the questions.

1 Did you sit in the stalls or circle?
2 Which row were you in?
3 Were you next to an aisle?
4 Did you have a good view of the stage?

76.2 Match the words on the left with the best definition on the right.

1	violent	a	very exciting
2	moving	b	terrible
3	complex	c	fantastic
4	gripping	d	lots of fighting
5	funny	e	very enjoyable
6	good fun	f	lots of different ideas
7	dreadful	g	sad and emotional
8	superb	h	it makes you laugh

76.3 What word or phrase is being defined?

1 A play or film, and part of the story is sung to music.
2 The people who watch a play at the theatre.
3 The person who makes a film.
4 Journalists who write articles about films and plays.
5 The name of the articles they write.
6 The translation of the words of a film across the bottom of the screen.
7 To reserve tickets before the performance.
8 The most important actors in a film.

76.4 Complete these sentences describing parts of the story of different books and films.

1 The film is .... in the 1940s, during the Second World War.
2 At the beginning, Paul meets Jennifer in a bookshop and they fall in ....
3 The film is .... two women who drive across America.
4 The main character is young, clever and comes from a very rich ....
5 The couple are too young to marry, and their parents are very unhappy about the relationship, so they run ....
6 In this film the husband loses money gambling, but .... first his wife knows nothing about it.
7 At the beginning, the company is successful, but then things start going ....
8 There's a love story in it, and it's very funny. I suppose you'd call it a ....
....

76.5 Test your general knowledge of cinema. What kinds of films are these?

1	*Pearl Harbor*	4	*Frankenstein*
2	*Four Weddings and a Funeral*	5	*Silence of the Lambs*
3	*Die Hard*	6	*Basic Instinct*

Have you seen any of these films? If so, what words or phrases would you use to describe them?

77 Music

A Types of music

Classical music, e.g. Beethoven, Mozart (NOT ~~classic~~ music)
Opera (= a play in which the words are sung), e.g. *La Boheme* by Puccini, *Carmen* by Bizet
Rock and **pop music**, e.g. U2, Madonna, Robbie Williams, Alicia Keys
Jazz, e.g. Duke Ellington, Miles Davis

There are many types of rock and pop music. Some are popular for long periods, others have a short history. Examples in the last 25 years are: punk, reggae, rap, garage and hip-hop.

B Musical instruments and musicians

C People

Rock and pop music are usually **performed** (= played to an audience) by a **group/band**, e.g. Bon Jovi or Travis. Most groups have a **lead singer**, a **lead guitarist** (guitar with six strings), a **bass guitarist** (four strings) and a **drummer**.

Solo artists (= people who perform alone, e.g. Robbie Williams or Madonna) play with a **backing group,** and some of them are **songwriters.** (= they write their music/songs)

Classical music is written by a **composer**, e.g. Bach, and performed by an **orchestra** (= a large group of musicians including violins and cellos) with a **conductor** (= person at the front who directs the musicians). Some music also has a **choir.** (= a large group of singers)

D A hit record

A **hit record** is a song that is very popular and bought by many people, e.g. 'Bohemian Rhapsody' was a **hit single** for Queen, and 'Angel' was a **hit single** for Robbie Williams. Groups and solo artists also **produce albums** (= make a collection of songs, usually 8–12, on one CD). 'Sergeant Pepper' by the Beatles is one of the most famous albums ever made.

These are also common phrases we use to talk about popular music.

Craig David's **new album is out** next week. (= you can buy his new album next week)
They plan to **release a new record** (= put it in the shops for people to buy) for Christmas.
Have you heard **the latest album** by Stereophonics? (= the most recent/newest album)
Kylie Minogue's new single is **number one.** (= the most popular record in the shops this week)
Which is your **favourite track** on the album? (= the song on the album you like the most)
Has your **taste in music** (= the type of music you like) changed in the last ten years?

Exercises

77.1 **What do you call the people who play the following instruments?**

1 piano *pianist*   3 guitar   5 drums
2 violin   4 cello

77.2 **Fill the gaps with the correct word.**

1 Do you play a musical .... ?
2 A: Do you like .... music?
  B: Yes, very much.
  A: Who's your favourite .... ?
  B: It's hard to say, but I love Bach.
3 I sang in a .... for years. We performed in churches all over the country.
4 Their new CD is .... next week. I'm sure it'll go to number ....
5 Their first single was very popular, but they haven't .... an album yet.
6 I think their .... album is brilliant, and much better than their last one.

77.3 **Now use the context and your own knowledge to fill the gaps with a suitable word.**

1 He used to be conductor of the Berlin Philharmonic ....
2 Robbie Williams was in a .... called Take That before he became a
  .... artist.
3 Elton John .... piano, and writes and .... all his own songs.
4 I think 'Hey Jude' or 'I want to hold your hand' is the Beatles' biggest selling hit
  .... , but 'Sergeant Pepper' is probably their most famous ....
  That or 'Abbey Road'.
5 I haven't been to the .... since I saw *The Marriage of Figaro* last year.
6 Keith Richard has been .... guitarist of the Rolling Stones for over
  30 years.
7 Duke Ellington is one of the greatest .... pianists ever.
8 'Waterloo' was one of Abba's most famous hit ....
9 Eric Clapton sings on his albums, but he first became famous as a ....
10 Before he became a solo artist, Sting was the .... singer with Police.

77.4 **Complete this story of Craig David's early years.**

Craig David was born and grew up in
Southampton, on the south coast of England.
As a teenager he used to write his own
(1) .... on a dictaphone, and his
(2) .... in music at that time ranged
from Terence Trent D'Arby to Michael Jackson
and Stevie Wonder. His first (3) ....
was 'Human', a version of the song that was
a (4) .... for the 'Human League'.
After that David became better known, and
his first album was (5) .... in
summer 2000.

77.5 **Answer these questions. If possible, ask someone else the same questions.**

1 What sort of music do you like best?
2 Who's your favourite singer/group/composer?
3 What was the last record or album you bought?
4 Has your musical taste changed in the last few years?

78 Newspapers

A Background

Most newspapers are **daily** (= they **come out/are published** every day). Some are national, some are local. Magazines are **weekly** or **monthly** (= published every week/month).

Some newspapers are **tabloids** (= small in size). These are usually the **popular press** (= short articles and lots of pictures), and they often have a larger **circulation** (= number of readers). The more serious newspapers are bigger in size. People often refer to newspapers as **the press**.

B Contents

Reports (= pieces of writing about news items, e.g. **a report in** *The Times*)
Articles (= pieces of writing about an important subject, e.g. **an article about** drugs)
Headlines (= title in large letters above the report/article, e.g. **a front-page headline**)
Reviews (= articles giving an opinion of new films, books, etc., e.g. **a review of** …)
Adverts (= words and pictures about a product, to make people buy it, e.g. **an ad for** …)

C People

Editor (= person in control of the daily production)
Reporters/journalists (= people who report news and write articles)
Photographers (= people who take the pictures in the papers)

D Headlines

Certain words (usually short) are common in newspaper headlines. Verb grammar is also different in headlines: the present simple can be used for present or past events; an infinitive often refers to the future. Articles (*the/a*) and the verb *be* are often not included.

row (= an argument)	Government in new row over schools
back (= support)	Bush backs new law (= Bush has backed a new law)
quit (= leave a job)	British Rail chairman to quit (= the chairman is going to quit)
hit (= have a bad effect on)	Bad weather hits farmers
bid (= try/attempt)	UN in bid to end war
talks (= discussions)	Government and IRA in new talks
cut (= reduce/make less)	Bank of England cuts rate again
key (= very important)	Zidane could be key player

E 'It said in the paper that …'

When we refer to something written in a newspaper we use these phrases:

It said in *The Times* that they've found the missing girl. (NOT ~~it's written~~ in …)
According to *The Guardian*, the missing girl was found last night.

Exercises

78.1 These words can be difficult to pronounce. Check the pronunciation in the Index and practise saying them. Remember, you must stress the second syllable of 'advertisement' and 'photographer'.

publish	article	ad'vertisement
journalist	pho'tographer	row (= argument)

78.2 Fill the gaps with the correct preposition.

1 There was a report .... *The Independent* .... this new law.
2 Have you read any reviews .... his new film?
3 It's an advert .... a type of mobile phone, I think.
4 I read it .... the paper.
5 High unemployment won't last according .... the paper.

78.3 Fill the gaps with a suitable word.

1 A: Is the paper ....*published*.......... every day?
  B: No, it .... out once a week.
2 There are more than ten national .... newspapers in Britain.
3 I haven't read 'Hello' magazine. Is it a weekly or a .... ?
4 The manager was interviewed for the paper by their best known ....
5 Do you understand this _____ ? '200 WOMEN GIVEN WRONG DIAGNOSIS'
6 The picture on the front page was taken by one of their youngest ....
7 There was a fantastic .... in the paper yesterday about 'Space'. Did you read it?
8 I read a .... of his latest film. It doesn't sound very good.
9 You often see .... in the paper which promise that you can learn a language in ten hours with this method. It's nonsense.
10 .... to *The Times*, the government is starting to panic.

78.4 Rewrite these headlines in your own words. Don't repeat the <u>underlined</u> words. Remember that small words like articles (*the/a*) and pronouns (*his/my*) are often not included in headlines, but they will need to be in your answers.

1 MINISTER TO <u>QUIT</u>

    A minister is going to leave his/her job

2 Japan and US start fresh <u>talks</u>

3 GERMANY <u>BACKS</u> US PLAN

4 POLICE DISCOVER <u>KEY</u> WITNESS

5 Government to <u>cut</u> spending on new hospitals

6 Bad weather <u>hits</u> rail service

7 MINISTERS IN NEW <u>ROW</u> OVER TAX

8 *New <u>bid</u> to <u>cut</u> teenage smoking*

78.5 Think about newspapers in your own country. Answer these questions.

1 How many daily national newspapers are there?
2 How many are tabloids?
3 How many newspapers <u>only</u> come out on Sunday in your country?
4 Which newspaper has the largest circulation?
5 Can you name two or three famous journalists who write for daily newspapers?

79 Television

remote control

A Using a television/telly/TV

plug it in

turn it on (*opp* turn it off)

You can also **turn it up** (= increase the volume; *opp* **turn it down**) and **turn over** (= change to a different **channel**; e.g. from 1 to 3). You can use **switch on, switch off,** or **switch over** in place of **turn**. (NOT ~~switch it up/down~~)

B Types of programme

Soap opera: a programme often on two or three times a week, which follows the lives of a group/community of people. The stories are often exciting, dramatic and hard to believe.
Quiz show or **Game show**: individuals or teams (called **contestants**) answer questions or play different games against each other. The winner gets a **prize**, e.g. money or a holiday.
Chat show: a programme where a presenter talks to famous people about their lives.
Documentary: a film with factual information, often about a problem in society.
Series: a number of programmes about the same situation or the same characters in different situations. This may be a **comedy series** (= programmes that try to be funny), or a **drama series**. (= programmes with interesting characters and exciting situations)
Current affairs: programmes about a social or political problem. **Current** means happening 'now/at the present time'.

C TV in Great Britain

At the moment there are five 'terrestrial' **channels** (or **stations**) on TV (BBC 1, BBC 2, ITV1, Channel 4 and Channel 5). If you pay extra, you can have a **satellite dish** and receive **satellite TV**; or pay to have **cable TV** (TV sent through wire cables underground). There are many channels available.

D Talking TV

What's on TV tonight? (= what programmes are showing on TV tonight?)
Is there anything on TV tonight?
What time's the film **on**? (= what time is the film showing?)

I quite like **television commercials**. (= the advertisements between programmes)
Are they showing the game **live** (= as it happens) or just **recorded highlights**? (= parts of the game after it has been played, e.g. later in the day/evening)
'Friends' is on tonight, but it's a **repeat** (= the programme has been on TV before). I've seen it.
What's your **favourite** programme? (= the programme you like most/best)

Exercises

79.1 You are watching TV with a friend. What could you say in each of the situations below?

1 You want to watch a programme on TV. _Could you turn the TV on?_
2 You can't hear the programme very well. Could you .... ?
3 You want to watch a different programme. Could you .... ?
4 Now it's too loud for you. Could you .... ?
5 You don't want to watch any more. Could you .... ?

79.2 Here are the evening programmes on three British TV channels. Find one example of: a documentary; a quiz show; a game show; a drama series; a current affairs programme.

7.00 Telly Addicts
Noel Edmonds hosts the quiz in which teams have their television knowledge put to the test.

7.30 Watchdog
Anne Robinson presents the stories that affect consumers. With Alice Beer and reporters Chris Choi and Jonathan Maitland.

8.00 EastEnders
Kathy tries to come to terms with Ted's revelations. Michelle receives a letter that could change her life. For cast see Tuesday.
Stereo Subtitled 5500

8.30 2 Point 4 Children
The Deep. There's something fishy going on when Bill and Ben are asked to look after their neighbour's house.

9.00 Nine O'Clock News
With Peter Sissons.
Subtitled
Regional News
Weather Rob McElwee 3245

7.00 The Krypton Factor
Four new contestants compete for a place in the November final.
Director Tony Prescott; Producer Wayne Garvie
Stereo Subtitled 9448

7.30 Coronation Street
It's farewell time at the Rovers. Episode written by Stephen Mallatratt. For cast see Wednesday. *Repeated on Wednesday at 1.25 pm Subtitled* 239

8.00 Bruce's Price is Right
Game show testing knowledge of the price of consumer goods.
Director Bill Morton; Producer Howard Huntridge
Stereo Subtitled 2968

8.30 World in Action
In a classroom fitted with cameras, World in Action reveals what is really going on in Britain's overcrowded schools and asks who is to blame.

9.00 New series
Cracker
CHOICE Brotherly Love (part 1). In the first of this three-part thriller, a prostitute is found raped and murdered, opening old wounds at the station.

7.00 Channel 4 News
Presented by Jon Snow and Cathy Smith. Including Weather
Subtitled 829535

7.55 The Slot
The daily soapbox offering viewers the chance to air their opinions.
Stereo 141603

8.00 New series
Desperately Seeking Something
A four-part series in which Pete McCarthy explores the strange universe of alternative beliefs.

8.30 Baby It's You
Continuing the six-part series which uses natural history filming techniques to observe the first two years of a baby's life.

9.00 Cutting Edge
The Trouble with Money
CHOICE Strange though it seems to some, not everyone enjoys winning the lottery. This documentary explores the joys and pitfalls of getting rich quick.

There is also one comedy series, and two soap operas. Can you guess what they are?

79.3 Complete these dialogues in a suitable way.

1 A: What's .... TV tonight?
   B: Oh, the usual soap .... and stuff like that.
2 A: Did you see the game live?
   B: No, they just showed the recorded ....
3 A: Ally McBeal is .... tonight.
   B: Yes, it's a good programme, but I've seen it before: it's a ....

79.4 Answer these questions about TV in your own country.

1 How many channels approximately can you watch?
2 Do you watch a lot of satellite TV and/or cable TV?
3 In total, how much TV do you watch every week?
4 What are your favourite programmes on TV at the moment? When are they on?
5 Do you enjoy watching the commercials?

80 On the phone

A ## Phone and telephone

mobile phone   telephone directory   answerphone   phone box   phone number   phone card

0208 969 7612

B Starting a phone conversation

NOTE

When British people answer the phone at home, they usually just say 'hello' and occasionally they give their number. Usually they do not give their name.

The first conversation is informal between friends; the second is a formal business call.

MARY: Hello?

RUTH: **Is that** Mary? (NOT ~~Are you Mary?~~ or ~~Is it Mary?~~)

MARY: Yeah.

RUTH: Hi. **It's** Ruth. (NOT ~~I am Ruth~~ or ~~Here is Ruth~~)

RECEPTIONIST: Good morning. Chalfont Electronics.

PAUL SCHOLES: Oh, good morning. **Could I speak to** Jane Gordon, please?

RECEPTIONIST: Yes. **Who's calling**, please?

PAUL SCHOLES: **My name is** Paul Scholes from 'Bexel Plastics'. (= a typical formal introduction)

RECEPTIONIST: Right, Mr Scholes. **I'm putting you through** (= I'm connecting you)
... *pause* ...

JANE GORDON: Hello?

PAUL SCHOLES: Mrs Gordon?

JANE GORDON: **Speaking.** (= yes, this is Mrs Gordon)

C Telephone problems

4.20 pm You phone your sister Susan, but **it's engaged** (= the phone line is busy). In other words, Susan is already **on the phone** (= using the phone) talking to someone else.

4.30 pm You phone again but a stranger answers and says: '**I think you've got the wrong number.**' (= you have **dialled** another number, e.g. 637424 and not 627424)

4.35 pm You **get through to** (= make contact with) your sister's number, but she's **out** (= not at home). Her husband answers and says: 'Susan **won't be back** (= will not return) for an hour', so you **leave a message**: 'Could you ask Susan to ring me when she **gets back** (= returns)?' The husband agrees to **give** Susan **the message**: '**I'll tell her you called.**'

6.00 pm Susan **phones** you **back** but you're out. She leaves a message on the answerphone. Her message is: 'Jean, this is Susan. I'm just returning your **call**. I'll **give you a ring** (= phone you) tomorrow. Bye.'

D Useful vocabulary

To phone another city/country, you need the (**dialling**) **code,** e.g. the code for Cambridge is 01223.

Phone calls in a town are **local calls**; calls to another country are **international calls**.

Text messages are short written messages you can send from one mobile phone to another.

Exercises

80.1 Write four more words or expressions that include 'phone'.

phone ....*number*....   phone ....   phone ....

.... phone   .... phone

80.2 Complete these phone conversations with suitable words or phrases.

A: Hello?
B: Good morning. Could I (1) .... Alicia James?
A: (2) ....
B: Oh, good morning, Mrs James. My name is …

A: Good morning. Boulding Limited. Can I help you?
B: Yes. (3) .... Paul Mathews and I'm trying to contact Mr Patterson. He left a (4) .... on my answerphone yesterday afternoon.
A: I see. Well, I'm afraid Mr Patterson's (5) .... at the moment. Can I ask him to phone you (6) .... later?
B: Yes, please. I shall be here until lunchtime. My (7) .... is 748 7267.

A: Hello?
B: Hi. (8) .... Sandra?
A: No, sorry. Sandra's not (9) .... at the moment.
B: Oh. Do you know when she'll (10) .... back?
A: No, I've no idea.
B: OK. Well, in that case, could I (11) .... a (12) .... for her?
A: Yes, of course.
B: Could you ask her to (13) .... me a (14) .... this evening?
A: Sure. What's your name?
B: Catherine. I'm a colleague from work. She's got my (15) ....
A: Right. I'll tell her.

A: Hello?
B: (16) .... Carlos?
A: Yeah, speaking.
B: Hi, Carlos. (17) .... Serena.
A: Oh, hello. I was expecting you to ring yesterday.
B: I did – I tried. I rang about six times last night but I couldn't get (18) .... It was (19) .... all the time.
A: Oh, yes, I'm sorry about that. I was (20) .... the phone to my brother for about an hour and then someone rang me about the table tennis next week.

80.3 Answer these questions. If possible, discuss your answers with someone else.

1 Have you got a mobile phone? How often do you use it? What do you use it for? Do you send many text messages?
2 In your country, what is the emergency number for the police?
3 From your country, what's the dialling code for the United Kingdom?
4 How much does it cost to make a local call?
5 What's the phone number of your English school?

81 Computers and the Internet

A Hardware and software

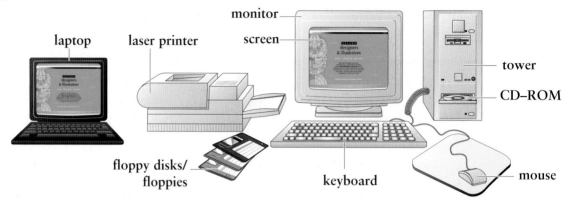

laptop   laser printer   monitor   screen   tower   CD–ROM

floppy disks/floppies   keyboard   mouse

There is **hardware** (= the machines), and **software** (= the programs needed to work the machines). These programs are **stored** (= kept) on **disks: hard disk** (inside the tower), **floppy disks, CD-ROMs** or **DVDs**.

B Operating a computer

open a new document   **open** an existing document   **save** the data in this document   **print**   **cut**   **copy**   **paste**

You can **print** it **out** later.   Have you **saved** it in a new file?

C The Internet

The Internet/the Net is a system **connecting** (= linking) millions of computers **worldwide** (= around the world). In order to **get online** (= become connected) you must **connect** your computer to a phone line using a **modem**. You also need an **Internet Service Provider (ISP)**, e.g. aol, freeserve. On the Internet, there are different **search engines** you can use such as 'Yahoo' or 'Excite' to find what you are looking for.

When you **go online** (= use the Internet), you can **browse** (= look at) different **websites** and **download** stuff **from** the Internet. (= move data from one computer to another)

D E-mail

I **sent** you an **e-mail** yesterday.   What's your **e-mail address**?
Did you **check** your **e-mail** today? (= look to see if you received any e-mails)
You can **e-mail** me at pd@freeserve.co.uk. (spoken as: pd **at** freeserve **dot** co **dot** uk)

E Important vocabulary

Some computers and programs are more **user-friendly** (= easy to use) than others.
If your computer has **a virus** (= a software problem), it may **crash** (= stop working).
Because of this you should make **a back-up copy**. (= a second copy on a floppy disk)

Exercises

81.1 Complete the words and phrases below with words from the box.

Provider	copy	~~computer~~	disk	sites
board	address	printer	user	top

1 *computer* .... program
2 floppy ....
3 ....-friendly
4 Internet Service ....
5 key...............................

6 e-mail ....
7 laser ....
8 lap ....
9 back-up ....
10 web...............................

81.2 Can you remember what these symbols mean?

1 ....
....

2 ....
....

3 ....
....

4 ....
....

5 ....
....

6 ....
....

7 ....
....

81.3 Fill each gap with a suitable word.

1 I wrote a report on the computer this morning, then I .... out two copies –
one for me and one for my boss. Then, without any warning, the computer
.... , and I'm afraid I lost the whole document.
2 If you want to get online, you have to .... your computer to a phone line
using a modem.
3 You can .... a lot of information from the Internet onto your own
computer, but it can take a lot of time.
4 There was a warning on the news this morning about a new computer ....
that attacks e-mail. If you open a message called 'April Showers', it destroys all your
e-mail contacts.
5 A: Have you .... your e-mail today?
   B: No, I haven't.
   A: Well, I .... you an e-mail this morning. You'd better have a look.
6 I spend ages just .... different websites.
7 It may depend on the .... engine you are using.
8 My new e-mail address is: janebriggs .... aol .... com.

81.4 Answer these questions. If possible, ask someone else the same questions.

1 Do you have a computer at home? If so, what is it (e.g. PC, Mac, etc.)?
2 Do you use computers at school/college/university or work?
3 What do you use them for?
4 What software are you familiar with?
5 Do you use e-mail? If so, what's your e-mail address?
6 Do you use the Internet? If so, what are some of your favourite websites?

82 Education: school

A The state system (= free education)

Age of 3	most go to **nursery school**
5	everyone starts **primary school**
11	**pupils** (= the name for students at this age) go to **secondary** school
16	go to a college for **vocational** (= job) **training**, e.g. hotel management, secretarial courses; or **stay at school** for two more years; **leave school** and **get a job**
18	leave school and **go to university**; **go to a college** for further education/training, e.g. teaching, business studies; get a job

You **go to school** and **go to university** (NOT go to ~~the~~ school/university). Other examples are: **go to church** (= to pray), **go into hospital** (= as a patient because you are ill), **go to bed** (= to sleep), **go to prison** (= as a criminal). There are also **public/independent/private schools** and parents pay to send their children to these schools. The **school fees** are expensive. About 7–10% of the population go to private schools in the UK.

B Subjects (= topics you study)

arts	sciences
English	maths (= mathematics)
French, German, Spanish	physics
history	chemistry
geography	biology
art, music	information technology (= about computers and communication)

Some words look plural, but in fact they are singular and need a singular verb, e.g. Maths **isn't** my favourite subject. Other examples are: physics, politics and economics.

C Timetable

The school day is **divided into** 6–7 lessons in different subjects, with a **break** (= period of rest between work) in the morning and afternoon. There is also a one-hour **lunch break**. The school year is usually **divided into** three **terms** (= periods of study). Each term is about 13 weeks, and each week pupils **do** (= study) about ten **subjects**. At the end of the school year they **do/take an exam** in each subject. After the holidays, pupils **go back** (= return) **to school**.

D Success and failure

success	failure
I **passed** my **exam**.	I **failed** my **exam**.
I **did** very **well**.	I **did** very **badly**.
I **got nine out of ten** for my homework. (= 9/10)	I **got three out of ten** for my homework.
I **got a very high mark**. (e.g. 18/20)	I **got a very low mark**. (e.g. 5/20)
I **got a good grade**. (e.g. B+)	I **didn't get a very good grade**. (e.g. D–)
I'm **good at** English.	I'm **hopeless at** (= very bad at) maths.

Exercises

82.1 Here are some school subjects but the letters are mixed up. What are the subjects?

1 tahms ....maths...............   6 irthosy ....
2 cnecsei ....   7 nisgehl ....
3 hogtceynlo ....   8 ehgoragpy ....
4 rat ....   9 simcu ....
5 ehnfcr ....   10 srheyictm ....

82.2 How much can you remember? Answer these questions without looking at the opposite page.

1 At what age do English children go to nursery school?
2 When do they start primary school?
3 When do they go to secondary school?
4 At what age can children leave school?
5 What can they do if they pass all their exams at the age of 18?

82.3 Complete this text about the timetable of a typical secondary school in Britain.

The school day is normally (1) .... into six or seven (2) .... ,
with (3) .... during the morning, at lunch and in the afternoon. Over the
whole week, (4) .... usually do about ten different (5) .... The
school year normally has three (6) .... , with exams at the end of the year.

82.4 Complete these sentences with a suitable phrase.

1 When she was a child she went .....to school............ in a small village.
2 He didn't go to school last term. He was very ill and he had to go ....
3 I was very tired, so after I finished my homework I went ....
4 When I left school I went .... and studied medicine.
5 It was a religious school, so we had to go .... quite a lot.
6 The police caught him and he went .... for six months.

82.5 Write the opposites.

1 I passed my exam.
2 I did very well.
3 I'm very good at English.
4 I got a very high mark.

82.6 What about you and your country? Answer these questions.

1 Did you go to nursery school?
2 Do most children start primary school at the age of five?
3 Is the secondary school system similar or different to the English system?
4 How many subjects do/did you study at secondary school?
5 Do/Did you study any subjects which are not included on the opposite page?
6 What is/was your favourite subject?
7 How many lessons do/did you have every day?
8 Is/Was your school a state school or private school?
9 At what age can you leave school?
10 How many terms are there in a school year?

83 Education: university

A Subjects

You can normally **do/study** these **subjects** at university but not always at school. (The underlining shows the syllable you must stress in each word.)

m<u>e</u>dicine	law	phil<u>o</u>sophy
engin<u>ee</u>ring	psych<u>o</u>logy	soci<u>o</u>logy
architecture	p<u>o</u>litics	business studies
agriculture	h<u>i</u>story of <u>a</u>rt	econ<u>o</u>mics

B Studying at (a British) university

If you want to **go to** (= **enter** *fml*) university, you must first **pass examinations** that most students take at the age of 18 (called 'A' levels). Students usually take three or four 'A' levels (examinations in three or four subjects), and they must do well to **get a place** at university.

If you get a place, most students have to pay part of their **tuition fees** (= money for teaching). Some students also **get** a government **grant** (= money to pay for living expenses, e.g. food and somewhere to live), but most students need **a loan** (= money you borrow from a bank) to **cover the cost of** (= pay for) university life. Students at university are called **undergraduates** while they are studying for their first degree.

Most university courses **last** (= continue for) three years, some courses last four years, and one or two courses, e.g. medicine, are five years. During this period students can say they are **doing a degree**, and when they finish and pass their exams, they can say they **have a degree**. This can be a **BA** (= bachelor of arts) or a **BSc** (= bachelor of science). For example:

He hopes to **get a place** at Oxford.   She's **at university** in Glasgow.
She's **doing a degree** in physics.   I've **got a degree** in German from York University.
She's **got a BA** in French.   He's **got a BSc** in computer science.

C Postgraduate courses

When you complete your first degree, you are a **graduate**. Some students then **go on** (= continue) to do a second course or degree, called a **postgraduate course/degree** (or **postgrad course**). These students are then **postgraduates** and they often study for:

an **MA** (Master of Arts), e.g. I'm **doing a Masters** in English *or*
an **MSc** (Master of Science), e.g. She **did a Masters** in biology *or*
a **PhD** (Doctor of Philosophy) [minimum three years], e.g. He's **got a PhD** in computer science.

When people study one subject in great detail (often to find new information), we say they are **doing research**, e.g. My sister is **doing research into/on** the effects of stress at work.

D School vs university

School has **teachers** and **lessons**; at university you have **lecturers** and **lectures**. The head of **department** (also called a 'faculty', but less common in spoken English) at a university is usually called a **professor**. (An ordinary teacher or lecturer is <u>not</u> a professor.)

Exercises

83.1 Read these sentences spoken by university students. What is each person studying?

1 I'm concentrating on Le Corbusier and Frank Lloyd Wright. *architecture*
2 We have to know every bone in a person's body.
3 The way we use fertilisers is much more precise than 20 years ago.
4 We're going to concentrate on Freud and Jung this term.
5 I've been reading some books on time management.
6 Expressionism was really a reaction to the work of the Impressionists.
7 We've spent a lot of time on American foreign policy.
8 You must know this case; it's one of the most famous in legal history.

Now mark the stress on each of your answers, check with the pronunciation in the Index, and practise saying the subjects.

83.2 What do you call:

1 the money some students receive if they get a place at university?
2 the qualification you get at the end of university?
3 the name we give students during this period at university?
4 teachers at university?
5 students when they have completed their first degree?
6 students studying for a second, higher degree?
7 the study of one subject in great depth and detail, often to get new information?
8 the talks/lessons that students go to while they are at university?

83.3 Replace the <u>underlined</u> verbs with less formal verbs that have the same meaning in the context.

1 Is it very difficult to <u>obtain</u> a place at university?
2 You have to pass exams before you can <u>enter</u> university.
3 He's <u>studying</u> physics, I think.
4 Did she <u>receive</u> a grant for her course?
5 The course <u>continues for</u> three years.

83.4 Fill the gaps with a suitable word.

1 My brother is 20. He's still .... university in York.
2 She's got a degree .... economics.
3 He's .... research .... various types of nervous disorder.
4 She's already got a BA. She's doing a .... degree now.
5 Who is the professor in your .... ?

83.5 Answer these questions. If possible, compare your answers with someone else from your own country and/or someone from a different country.

1 Do you need to pass examinations before you can go to university?
2 Do some students get a grant to study at university?
3 Is the tuition free if you go to university?
4 Do most degree courses last three years?
5 What is your equivalent of the British BA or BSc?
6 Do you have similar postgraduate degrees in your country?

Law and order

A The police

When someone **commits a crime** (= **breaks the law** and does something **illegal/against the law**/wrong), the police do a number of things.

They **investigate** the crime. (= try to find out what happened and who is responsible)
If they **catch** (= find) the person they believe is responsible for the crime, they will **arrest** them. (= take them to the police station because they think the person has committed the crime)
At the police station, they **question** them. (= ask them questions)
If they are sure that the person committed the crime, the person is **charged with** the crime. (= the police make an official statement that they believe the person committed the crime)
For a serious crime (e.g. murder), the person must then **go to court for trial**. [see section B]

B In court

In **court**, the **defendant** must try to **prove** (= provide facts to show something is true) that they did not commit the crime. In other words, they must try to prove that they are **innocent** (*opp* **guilty**). Twelve members of the public (called the **jury**) listen to the **evidence** (= information about the crime, for and against) and then make their decision. People who see a crime are **witnesses**, and they usually give evidence at a trial.

C Punishment (= what a person must suffer if they do something wrong)

If someone is guilty of a crime, the judge will give the **sentence** (= the punishment). If a person is guilty of murder, the sentence may be 10–20 years **in prison**. The person then becomes a **prisoner**.

For crimes that are not serious (called **minor offences**, e.g. illegal parking), the punishment is usually **a fine**. (= money you have to pay)

Exercises

84.1 **Put this story in the correct order. The first event has been given.**

a they found both men guilty.
b and charged them with the robbery.
c £10,000 was stolen from a bank in the High Street.   1
d After the jury had listened to all the evidence
e The judge gave the men a prison sentence of five years.
f The trial took place two months later.
g and they finally arrested two men.
h They questioned them at the police station
i The police interviewed a number of witnesses about the crime

84.2 **Answer the questions.**

1 Who investigate(s) crimes?   *the police*
2 Who sentence(s) people?
3 Who live(s) in prison?
4 Who decide(s) if someone is innocent or guilty?
5 Who defend(s) people and present(s) evidence?
6 Who commit(s) crimes?

84.3 **Fill the gaps with the correct word.**

1 A: Have you ever .... the law?
   B: No, never.
2 A: Does anyone know why she .... the crime?
   B: I think she needed the money.
3 A: Is it legal to ride a motorbike without a licence?
   B: No, it's .... the law.
4 In Britain it is .... to drive a car without insurance.
5 If you drive through a red light, you will have to pay a ....
6 The defendant must try to .... he or she is innocent.
7 The jury must decide if the defendant is innocent or ....
8 Before they reach a decision, the jury must look at the .... carefully.
9 If someone is guilty of murder, the .... will be at least ten years in prison.
10 He has been in trouble before, but it was only a minor ....

84.4 **Read the text, then write your answers to the questions below, based on your knowledge of the law in your own country. If possible, discuss your answers with someone else.**

> Two 15-year-old boys broke into a house when the owner was out, and took money and jewellery worth about £900. The owner reported the crime when she got home at 6 pm.

1 Will the police investigate this crime?
2 How will they investigate? What will they do?
3 Do you think the police will catch the two boys?
4 If they do, what crime will they be charged with?
5 Can boys of this age go to prison?
6 What do you think the sentence would be? Do you think this is the correct sentence?

85 Crime

A The law

If you do something **illegal/against the law** (= wrong), you have **committed a crime**. Most people commit a crime at some time in their lives, e.g. driving above the speed limit or parking illegally, etc. If you **break the law** (= do something wrong/illegal) and commit a crime, you could **get into trouble** (= be in a bad situation) with the police.

B Crimes

crime	criminal (= person)	verb
theft (= general word for stealing)	**thief**	**steal** (also **take**)
robbery (= steal from people or places, e.g. banks)	**robber**	**rob**
burglary (= **break into** a shop/house and steal things)	**burglar**	**break in**
shoplifting (= steal from shops when they're open)	**shoplifter**	**shoplift**
murder (= kill someone by intention)	**murderer**	**murder**
manslaughter (= kill someone but without intention)	–	–

C Scene of the crime

Two men **robbed** a jeweller's in west London early this morning. They **broke in** (= forced their way into the building, e.g. they broke a window) around 7 am and **took/stole** rings and necklaces valued at over £10,000. Several **witnesses** (= people who see a crime) saw them leave the shop and **get away/escape** (= go away from a dangerous situation) in a blue car. The police believe both men **are armed** (= have guns) and extremely dangerous.

D Crime prevention

What can governments do to **prevent crime** (= stop crime happening) or **reduce** it (= make it less)? These things happen in some countries.

The police **carry guns**. (= have guns)
The police **are allowed to** (= are permitted to/can) stop anyone in the street and ask them questions.
Criminals receive **tough** (= hard) **punishments**, e.g. go to prison for long periods.
There is **capital punishment** (= death, e.g. by injection or electric chair) for some crimes.

What can people do to **protect themselves** (= keep themselves safe) and their **property** (= home and land)? They can do these things.

Avoid (= keep away from) dark streets **late at night** (e.g. midnight).
Avoid wearing (= try not to wear) expensive rings or watches. [Note the *-ing* form after 'avoid'.]

Have a **burglar alarm**.
Put money and **valuables** (= things worth a lot of money) in **a safe**.
Leave lights **on** at home when they go out.
Lock doors and windows when they go out.

safe   burglar alarm   lock

Exercises

85.1 Complete this table.

crime	person
bank robbery	...bank robber...
murder	....
burglary	....
theft	....
shoplifting	....

85.2 Respond to these statements or questions confirming the crime in each one.

1 A: He broke into the house, didn't he?
   B: Yes, he's been charged with ....burglary...............
2 A: He killed his wife?
   B: Yes, he's been charged with ....
3 A: She stole clothes from that department store, didn't she?
   B: Yes, and she's been charged ....
4 A: The man on the motorbike didn't mean to kill the boy.
   B: No, but he's been ....
5 A: He took the money from her bag?
   B: Yes, but they caught him and he's ....

85.3 Find the best noun on the right to follow each verb on the left.

1 lock   a a gun
2 commit   b a house
3 go   c the door
4 carry   d a crime
5 break into   e the law
6 break   f to prison

85.4 How safe and secure are you? Answer these questions with YES or NO.

1 Do you often walk in areas which are not very safe?	YES = 1 NO = 0
2 Do you often walk on your own in these areas late at night?	YES = 2 NO = 0
3 Do you wear an expensive watch or expensive jewellery?	YES = 1 NO = 0
4 Do you lock doors and windows before you leave the house?	YES = 0 NO = 2
5 Do you have a burglar alarm?	YES = 0 NO = 1
6 Do you leave lights on when you go out?	YES = 0 NO = 1
7 Is there someone who protects the building when you are out?	YES = 0 NO = 2
8 Do you have a safe in your home?	YES = 0 NO = 1

Add up your score. Less than 3 = very safe; 3–5 = quite safe; 6–8 = you could take more care; more than 8 = you are a dangerous person to know!

85.5 Fill the gaps in these questions with a suitable word. What's your opinion?

1 Do you think the police should .... guns?
2 Do you think the police should be .... to stop people without a reason?
3 Do you agree with capital .... for certain crimes such as murder?
4 Do you think tougher punishments will help to .... crime?

Politics

A Types of government

Monarchy: a state **ruled by** a king or queen (= the king or queen has power and control). Some countries, e.g. the UK, have a monarchy, but the monarch is not the **ruler**.

Republic: a state governed by **representatives** (= men or women chosen by the people) and a president, e.g. the USA or France. People who believe in this system are **republicans**.

Democracy: a system of government in which leaders are chosen by the people, e.g. France or the United Kingdom. People who believe in this system are **democrats**.

Dictatorship: a system of government in which one person **rules** the country (= one person has total power). This person is called a **dictator**.

B Political beliefs

noun politics	*person* politician	*adjective* political
conservatism	conservative	conservative
socialism	socialist	socialist
social democracy	social democrat	democratic
liberalism	liberal	liberal
communism	communist	communist

People who **believe in** social democracy are social democrats.
It is a **democratic** government, with liberal **beliefs**.

C Political positions

The government is very **reactionary** (= they don't want any changes). **The opposition** (= the main political party which is not in government) is more **radical** (= they want to make changes to the system). The Prime Minister is quite **right-wing** (= conservative/ capitalist), and the leader of the opposition is more **left-wing** (= socialist).

D Elections

In a democracy, people **vote for** (= they choose in a formal way) the **political party** (e.g. social democrats) they want to form the government. They do this in an **election** (= when everyone votes). Quite often elections **take place/are held** (= happen) every five years.

42% **voted for** the socialists in the **election**. (= The socialist party got 42% of the **votes**.)
They **elected** a new **president** last year. (= The new president **was elected** last year.)
The **election takes place** next week, and the Liberals hope to **form** the next government.

E Government

Political systems are different **all over the world** (= in every part of the world). In the UK, when a political party wins a **majority** (= 51% or more) of **seats** (= official places in parliament) in an election, they are **in power** (= the government of the country), and their **leader** (= person in control of the party) becomes **Prime Minister**.

The government must have **policies** (= programmes of action) to **run** (= manage and control) the country. This means, for example, an **economic policy** (for the economy), and a **foreign policy** (for actions by the country in other parts of the world).

Exercises

86.1 **What kind of political system is being described?**

1 The country is ruled by a king or queen.
2 The country is governed by men and women who are chosen by the people.
3 The country is ruled by one person.

86.2 **Complete the tables. Use a dictionary to help you if necessary.**

general noun	person
socialism	...socialist...
democracy	....
politics	....
conservatism	....

verb	general noun
believe	...belief...
elect	....
govern	....
vote	....

86.3 **Rewrite the sentences using the words on the right. The meaning must stay the same. Make any necessary changes.**

Example It's in every part of the world.   ALL
It's *all over the world.*

1 Elections take place every five years.   HELD
Elections ....
2 The government is socialist.   WING
The government is ....
3 I'm a democrat.   BELIEVE
I ....
4 Who controls the country at the moment?   POWER
Who ....

86.4 **Fill the gaps in this text about the political system in the United Kingdom.**

In the UK (1) .... take place every five years. The (2) .... Minister may decide to have one after four years, but five years is the maximum. The country is divided into 652 areas and people in each area can only (3) .... for one person from one political (4) .... The person with the most (5) .... is the winner, and that person becomes one of the 652 members of parliament.
The political party with a (6) .... of the seats in parliament then forms the government, and the (7) .... of that party becomes Prime Minister. His or her job is then to decide on a number of different (8) .... to run the country.

86.5 **Answer these questions about your own country. If possible, ask someone else.**

1 Which are the main political parties in your country?
2 Which party is in power at the moment?
3 When were they elected?
4 Did you vote in this election?
5 Who is the leader of this party?
6 Is this person the President or Prime Minister of your country?
7 Do you think you are left-wing, right-wing, or in the centre?
8 Do you think your political beliefs have changed/will change during your life?

Bureaucracy

A What is it?

Bureaucracy is the rules used by **officials** (or **bureaucrats**) to control an organisation or country. It is often used in a negative way to mean unnecessary rules, e.g. **filling in** (= completing) forms, and waiting for **documents**. (= pieces of paper with official information)

B Important documents (e.g. passport)

identity card (= card with your name, date of birth and photo to show who you are. The United Kingdom is one of the few countries where people do not have identity cards.)
driving licence (= the official document which permits you to drive on public roads)
visa (= document which gives you permission to enter, pass through or leave a country)

Officials often **check** (= look at and examine) your documents, e.g. customs officials check your passport or identity card, and the police may check your driving licence.

We also use the word **certificates** for official pieces of paper stating certain facts: a **birth certificate** gives the important facts about your birth, **exam certificates** state you have passed certain exams, and a **marriage certificate** states you have married.

Some documents are for a fixed period of time, e.g. a visa may be for six months. At the end of that period, the visa **runs out** (*infml*)/**expires** (*fml*) (= it finishes/comes to an end). If you want to stay in the country, you must **renew** it (= get a new one for a further period of time). You can normally **renew** a visa, a passport, a membership card for a club, etc.

C Forms

There are situations where you need to **fill in** (= complete) forms.

landing card: a form you may have to fill in when you enter another country
enrolment form (sometimes called a **registration form**): a form you often have to fill in when you join a school or course
application form: a form where you write details about yourself, often when applying for a job

With many forms, you will need to **sign** them (= write your **signature**) and **print** your full name **underneath**. (= under it)

Signature	*Julia Gonzales*
Name (in capitals)	JULIA GONZALES

D Language of forms

Forms often contain formal expressions. In spoken English, this may be different.

written		*spoken*
date of birth	=	When were you born?
place of birth	=	Where were you born?
country of origin	=	Where do you come from?
marital status	=	Are you single or married?
date of arrival	=	When did you arrive?
date of departure	=	When are you leaving? (*or* When did you leave?)

Exercises

87.1 Check the pronunciation of these phrases in the Index (you will find them at the <u>underlined</u> words). Repeat them until you can say them fluently.

<u>identity</u> card   important <u>document</u>   exam <u>certificate</u>   <u>registration</u> form

87.2 Write down a word that can be used before these nouns, but <u>not</u> including words in 87.1.

.... card   .... licence
.... certificate   .... form

87.3 Complete these sentences with a suitable word.

1 Will you need to ...*get*............... a visa if you go to the United States?
2 I was surprised that nobody .... my passport when we arrived in France.
3 Could you .... in this form for me, please?
4 They sent the form back to me because I forgot to .... it at the bottom.
5 A: Do I have to put my .... at the bottom of this form?
   B: Yes, please – and then print your full name underneath.
6 A: I only had a visa for six months and it .... next week.
   B: Are you going to .... it?
   A: Yes, if I can. I don't think it'll be a problem.
7 Write your first name here and your .... underneath.
8 I want to do a course, so I wrote to the school and asked them to send a(n)
   .... form.

87.4 How many of these documents do you have?

passport	identity card
driving licence	birth certificate
exam certificates	marriage certificate

87.5 Rewrite these sentences in more informal English.

1 What's your date of birth? ..*When were you born?*......
2 What's your country of origin? .... ?
3 What's your marital status? .... ?
4 What was your date of arrival? .... ?
5 When's your date of departure? .... ?

87.6 I asked some British people about problems they had had with bureaucracy. What about you? Have you had any problems? If so, write them down and compare them with the replies in the Answer key on page 236.

1 ....
2 ....
3 ....

Global problems

A **The environment** (= air, water and land around us)

Many people believe we are **destroying** the environment. (If you 'destroy' something, you damage it so badly it does not exist any more.) For example:

Cars and factories **pollute** the air. (= make the air dirty)

We continue to **cut down rainforests** and increase the dangers of **global warming**. (= an increase in temperature because of increased carbon dioxide around the earth)

How can the **planet** (earth) **survive**? (= continue to exist)

• We must **save/conserve** (= use less and use well) **natural resources** (e.g. water, oil and gas). We mustn't **waste** them. (= use them badly)
• We must **protect** animals and plants. (= keep them safe from human damage)
• We mustn't **throw away** bottles and cans. We must **recycle** them. (= use them again)

Many of the verbs above form common nouns:

verb	noun	verb	noun
destroy	destruction	pollute	pollution
survive	survival	protect	protection
waste	waste	recycle	recycling

B **Natural disasters**

A **disaster** is when something terrible happens and people often die. A **natural disaster** is caused by nature. For example:

famine (= situation where people die because there isn't enough food)
drought (= no rain for a long period of time; this often causes famine)
floods (= too much rain in a short period of time, causing damage to houses and land)
earthquakes (= violent movement of the earth; buildings are often destroyed)

C **War and peace**

A **war** is a long period of fighting between two or more countries. Some countries have been **at war** (= fighting a war) for years. There are also **civil wars** (= fighting between two or more groups in the same country). These are some of the most violent – **soldiers** (= the people in the army) are killed, but many **civilians** (= people not in the army or navy, etc.) also die. Wars often end with a **peace settlement**. (= both sides agree to stop fighting)

D **Terrorism**

NOTE
Assassinate = to kill a famous person, often for a political reason.

This is violent action for political reasons. People who do this are **terrorists**. A common terrorist crime is **planting bombs** (= putting bombs in public places) often to **kill/assassinate** important people. Terrorists also **hijack** planes and buses (= take control of them by force). The people on board then become prisoners (called **hostages**). The terrorists may agree to **release** the hostages (= permit the hostages to go free) if governments agree to their **demands** (= what they ask for), perhaps giving them money or releasing other terrorists from prison.

Exercises

88.1 Many words in this unit are difficult to pronounce. Check the pronunciation in the Index at the back of the book and practise saying the words.

pollution	survive	resources	disaster	civilian	terrorists
famine	drought	flood	earthquake	soldiers	hostage

88.2 Complete the tables.

noun	*verb*
waste	....
pollution	....
damage	....

noun	*verb*
....	protect
....	destroy
....	survive

88.3 If we want to look after the environment, there are certain things we shouldn't do and certain things we should do. Complete these sentences with suitable verbs.

We shouldn't:

1 ....*throw away*...... paper, bottles and cans; we should .... them.
2 .... water and energy; we should .... them.
3 .... rainforests; we should .... them from human damage.

88.4 Match words from the left and right to form compound words or phrases.

1 peace   a resources
2 civil   b settlement
3 natural   c warming
4 global   d war

88.5 Complete these definitions with a word or phrase.

1 Global warming is an increase in temperature caused by an increase in ....
2 A disaster is when something ....
3 A famine is a long period of time when people may die because there isn't enough
    ....
4 A flood is the result of too much ....
5 A drought occurs when there is a long period without ....
6 A war is a long period of ....
7 A civil war is a war between two or more groups from ....
8 To assassinate means to ....
9 Soldiers are people who fight in an ....
10 Civilians are people who are not ....

88.6 Complete these sentences with a suitable word.

1 Terrorists have hijacked a ....
2 Two men attempted to assassinate the ....
3 One of the terrorists planted a ....
4 The terrorists have agreed to release all the ....
5 During the fighting a number of civilians were ....
6 The two sides have agreed to a peace ....

89 Air travel

A Departures

When you arrive at the airport, you can look at the **departures board** which shows the **flight numbers** (e.g. BA735), **departure times** (e.g. 0840) and **destinations** (e.g. Venice). At the **check-in desk** they **weigh your luggage**. Usually you can take about 20 kilos. If it is more, you may have to **pay excess baggage** (= you pay extra). They also check your ticket and give you a **boarding card** for the plane with your seat number on it. Then you go through **passport control** where an official **checks your passport**, and into the **departure lounge**. Here, you can also buy things in the **duty free,** e.g. perfume or alcohol. About half an hour before **take-off,** you go to a **gate** number, e.g. gate 14, where you wait before you **get on** the plane. When you **board** (= get on) the plane, you find your seat. If you have **hand luggage,** you can put it under your seat or in the **overhead locker** above your seat. If there are no **delays** (= when you have to wait until a later time for some reason), the plane moves towards the **runway.** (= the area where planes take off and land)

Delay can be used as a noun and verb. It is a common word at airports.
There's **a** two-hour **delay** on our flight.   Why **is** the flight **delayed?**
What's the reason for **the delay?**   We **were delayed** at Athens airport.

B The flight

NOTE

The cabin crew are both men (**stewards**) and women (**stewardesses**). They are also called **flight attendants**.

The **captain** (= the pilot) or **cabin crew** (= people who look after passengers) may say these things:

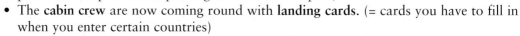

- Please **fasten your seat belt** and put your seat in the **upright position**.
- **May we remind passengers** (= to passengers: please remember) that there is no smoking now until you are inside the **terminal building**. (= the part of the airport where passengers arrive and depart)
- The **cabin crew** are now coming round with **landing cards**. (= cards you have to fill in when you enter certain countries)

C Arrival

NOTE

You **hire** something for a short period, and **rent** something for a long period, e.g. a flat. For a car you can use both.

When the plane **lands** (= arrives on the ground), you have to wait for it to stop. When the doors are open, you **get off** the plane and walk through the **terminal building** and go to the **baggage reclaim** (= place where you collect your luggage). You **go through customs** (GREEN = nothing to declare; RED = goods to declare). At most airports, you can **hire** a car. (= **rent** a car)

luggage trolley

Exercises

89.1 Complete the words or phrases below using words from the box.

control	number	desk	card	baggage
lounge	luggage	reclaim	locker	

1 boarding ....
2 excess ....
3 check-in ....
4 flight ....
5 overhead ....
6 departure ....
7 baggage ....
8 passport ....
9 hand ....

89.2 What do you call these?

1 The place where you go when you arrive at the airport with your luggage.
2 The card they give you with the seat number on it.
3 What you have to pay if your luggage is very heavy.
4 The bags you carry onto the plane with you.
5 The place above your head where you can put these bags.
6 The part of the airport where the plane accelerates and takes off.
7 The people who look after you on the plane.
8 Another verb used to say 'rent' a car.

89.3 Complete these sentences with a suitable word.

1 There was a mechanical problem, and we ended up with a two-hour ....
2 Several passengers had to fill in landing ....
3 I went through passport control and sat in the departure ....
4 If you have nothing to declare, you follow the green sign when you go through

....
5 A woman at the check-in desk weighed my ....
6 I looked for our flight number on the departures ....

89.4 Fill the gaps in this letter.

Dear Tom,

I've just arrived in Rome but I'm still recovering from a really terrible flight. We
(1) .... two hours late because of bad weather, and then over the channel
we had more bad weather. The (2) .... told us to (3) ....
our seat belts, which worried me a bit, and for half an hour we (4) ....
through a terrible storm. I was almost sick, but the cabin (5) .... were
really nice. It was still raining and very windy when we (6) .... in Rome
and I was really glad to (7) .... the plane and get into the airport
building. I really hope the return (8) .... is a lot better ...

89.5 Answer these questions. If you don't fly very much, try to ask someone who does.

1 What is the most interesting part of the flight, and what is the most boring part?
2 Where do you often have delays, and why?
3 What do you usually do during the flight?
4 Do you always eat the food they give you? Do you ever drink alcohol on the flight?

90 Hotels and restaurants

A Types of hotel accommodation

a single room	=	room for one person with a single bed
a double room	=	room for two people with one large bed
a twin room	=	room for two people with two single beds
full board	=	includes breakfast, lunch and dinner
half board	=	includes breakfast and dinner
B&B	=	just bed (= the room) and breakfast

B Visiting a hotel or restaurant

At busy times, e.g. the weekend, you may need to **book** (= reserve) **a room** in a hotel or **a table** in a restaurant **in advance** (= before you go). When you arrive at a hotel you **check in at reception** (= tell the receptionist you have arrived); at a restaurant you ask for a table (e.g. Could we have a table for two? *or* I booked a table for two. The name is Carter.)
In restaurants you can **tip** the **waiter/waitress** (= give money for good service) if service is not included; in a hotel you may also give the **porter** (= person who carries luggage) **a tip**.
At the end of a **meal** in a restaurant or the end of your **stay** in a hotel, you **pay the bill**.

C In a restaurant

You can see the food available **on the menu**, and choose wine (and other drinks) from the **wine list**. There are usually three parts to a meal: a **starter** (e.g. soup), a **main course** (e.g. meat or fish) and a **dessert** (e.g. fruit or ice cream). A drink before the meal is often called an **aperitif**.

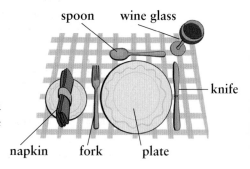

D Useful words and expressions

In a hotel

GUEST: Are you **fully booked** (= completely full) next week?
Do you have any **rooms available** (= free rooms) this weekend?
Is breakfast/dinner included? (= Does the price include breakfast/dinner?)
Where's the **lift**? (= the machine which takes you up or down a floor)
Excuse me. **How do I get to** (the underground station) from here?
There's something wrong with (= there's a problem with) the heating in my room.
What time do we have to **check out**? (= leave the room on our last day)

In a restaurant

WAITER: **Are you ready to order?** (= Have you decided what you want?)
Would you like to **try the wine**? (= taste the wine to see if it is OK)
Is everything all right with your meal?

CUSTOMER: Are you **fully booked?**
What's *vichysoisse* exactly?
I'll have the (soup) **to start**. (= as a starter)
Excuse me. Where's the toilet?

Exercises

90.1 Put the sentences in each column in a logical order.

Hotel

a I paid my bill.
b I checked in at reception.
c I left the hotel.
d I went up to my room.
e I spent the night in the hotel.
f I had an early morning call.
g I booked the hotel.   1
h I went out to a local restaurant for dinner.
i I arrived at the hotel.
j I got up and had breakfast.
k I tipped the porter who took my bag to the room.

Restaurant

a I had the starter.
b I paid the bill.
c I left the restaurant.
d I looked at the menu.
e I gave the waiter a tip.
f I booked a table.   1
g I had a dessert.
h I ordered my meal.
i I arrived at the restaurant.
j I had my main course.
k I looked at the wine list.

90.2 Finish these questions or statements with a suitable word.

HOTEL GUEST

1 I'm leaving in a few minutes. Could I pay my .... ?
2 Is that just bed and breakfast or full .... ?
3 Could I book a twin .... ?
4 I'm interested in next weekend. Do you still have rooms .... ?
5 [Your room is on the tenth floor.] Excuse me. Where's the .... ?

WAITER

6 Right, madam. Are you ready to .... ?
7 Would you like to try the .... ?
8 Is everything all right with your .... ?

RESTAURANT CUSTOMER

9 I'll .... the soup to start.
10 Excuse me. Is service .... ?

90.3 What would you ask the hotel receptionist in these situations?

1 You think a hotel is busy next weekend, but you're not sure. What could you ask?
   Are you fully booked next weekend?

2 You want to stay in a hotel for two nights next weekend with your husband/wife. You phone the hotel. What do you say?

   ....

3 You are planning to leave in about 15 minutes. What could you ask?

   ....

4 You want to go to the nearest bank but you don't know where it is. What do you ask?

   ....

90.4 You are staying in quite a good hotel (e.g. two-star or three-star) in your country. Would you expect to have the following? Compare your answers with someone else if possible.

1 Colour television
2 Satellite TV
3 Hair dryer

4 Mini-bar (= fridge with drinks)
5 Tea- and coffee-making facilities
6 Air-conditioning

91 A sightseeing holiday in the city

Famous places

1 palace   2 market   3 temple   4 statue   5 castle   6 cathedral

Many people **go on a sightseeing tour** of a town (usually in a bus); they can also **go on a tour of a castle, cathedral**, etc. When you are sightseeing, it helps to buy a **guidebook** (= a book of information for tourists) and a **map** of the town you are visiting.

B **Tourist activities**

go sightseeing	We **went sightseeing** almost every day.
do a bit of/a lot of sightseeing	I didn't **do** a lot of **sightseeing** in Warsaw.
have a look round (= visit somewhere casually)	We **had** a quick **look round** the shops.
	I wanted to **have a look round** the **art galleries**.
take pictures (= photos)	I **took** hundreds of **pictures** on holiday.
spend money	I **spent** lots of **money** – too much.
get lost (= lose one's way)	We **got lost** almost every day in London.
have a great/nice/terrible time	They **had a lovely time** in Venice.
go out (= leave home/your hotel to go to a social event, e.g. restaurant or disco)	On holiday we **went out** every night.

C **Describing 'places'**

The word **place** can describe a building, an area, a town, or country:
Bruges is a lovely **place** (= town) and we found a really nice **place** (= hotel) to stay.
The town is full of interesting **places**. (= areas/buildings)

Venice is beautiful but it's always **packed** (= very crowded) **with tourists**.
New York is very **cosmopolitan**. (= full of people from different countries and cultures)
St Petersburg has lots of **historic monuments**. (= important places built a long time ago)
Many beautiful cities are now very **touristy**. (= a negative word: 'too much tourism')
São Paolo is a really **lively** place (= full of life and activity) and the **nightlife** is fantastic.

To ask if it is 'a good idea' to visit a place, use **be worth + -ing** or noun.

A: If I go to Scotland, **is** it **worth** spending a few days in Edinburgh?
B: Yes, definitely – and Glasgow **is worth a visit** as well.

Exercises

91.1 Complete this postcard. You may need a word or phrase in each space.

Hi everyone,

I've been in Paris for over a week now and I'm having a great (1) .... In the first few days I did quite a lot of (2) .... – the Eiffel Tower, Notre Dame, and all the usual tourist attractions. Most places are absolutely (3) .... with tourists, so yesterday I decided to have a (4).......................... round the shops.

Today I've been to a couple of interesting art (5) .... I got (6) .... on my way back to the hotel, but it didn't matter because I discovered a really fascinating

(7) .... with lots of little stalls, selling just about everything from apples to antiques.

I ate in the hotel the first night but usually I (8) .... for dinner – the restaurants are great and I can get a set meal for less than 25 euros. I'm afraid I've (9) .... a lot of money, but it's a great place. You'll be able to see for yourself when I get back – I've taken lots of (10) ....

I hope you're all well. I'll write again next week.

Love, Emma

91.2 Which of these places do you usually visit or go to when you are on holiday?

museums	art galleries	churches and cathedrals	tourist shops
concerts	discos/nightclubs	castles/palaces/temples	the cinema
markets	restaurants	bars	the theatre

91.3 Agree with the information in the questions without repeating the same words and phrases. Use words and phrases from the opposite page.

Example A: You've got quite a few pictures, haven't you?
            B: Yes, I took lots of photos.

1 A: It's a fabulous city, isn't it?
   B: Yes, it's a ....
2 A: There's a big mix of people in London, isn't there?
   B: Yes, it's very ....
3 A: It was very crowded, wasn't it?
   B: Yes, it was ....
4 A: There's a lot to do in the evenings, isn't there?
   B: Yes, the .... is very good.
5 A: Did you enjoy yourselves?
   B: Yes, we had a ....
6 A: Kyoto is a good place to go to, isn't it?
   B: Yes, Kyoto is definitely ....

91.4 Think of a place in your country (a different place for each number) which is:

1 cosmopolitan
2 lively
3 very touristy
4 famous for its historic monuments
5 worth visiting
6 not worth visiting

92 Holidays by the sea

A Places to stay

When people **go on holiday** they stay in **various** places (= a number of different places): some go to hotels; some **rent an apartment** (a holiday flat); some prefer to **go camping** and sleep in a **tent**.

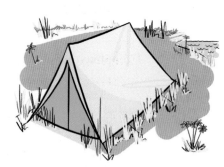

B On the beach

Many people **spend** their **holiday** in **seaside resorts** (= towns by the sea for tourists, e.g. Malaga, St Tropez, Okinawa) where they can **go to the beach** every day.

You sometimes get a **gentle breeze** (= a light pleasant wind) from the sea, which helps to **cool you down** on hot days, but it can also burn you [see section D].

C Seaside activities

I like to go for a walk **along the cliffs**.
On **sandy beaches**, I often **play volleyball**.
I sometimes **go windsurfing/snorkelling/diving**.
I don't swim much but I like to **have a paddle**. (= just put my feet in the sea)
My sister likes to **have a swim** in the sea, but not if it is very **rough** (*opp* **calm**).

diving   snorkelling   windsurfing

D In the sun

Many people go to the beach to **sunbathe** (= lie in the sun) and **get a suntan** (= when the body goes an attractive brown colour from the sun; we can also say, **be brown**). This can be dangerous, and you should always put on **suntan lotion** (= cream or oil to stop your skin burning). This will also help you to **get a tan** and **protect your skin** (= keep your skin safe). If you don't protect your skin, you may **get sunburn** (= the skin becomes red and very painful). For total protection, use **sunblock**.

Exercises

92.1 Write down four more words beginning with 'sun'.

sun*shine*................ sun......................... sun......................... sun......................... sun.........................

92.2 Match a word from the left with a word from the right to form six phrases.

1	beach	a	breeze
2	suntan	b	umbrella
3	seaside	c	sea
4	gentle	d	lotion
5	sandy	e	resort
6	rough	f	beach

92.3 Identify these seaside activities.

3 ....

1 ....

2 ....

4 ....

92.4 Can you find 11 words (including one phrasal verb) from the opposite page in this word square? All the answers are vertical or horizontal.

S	C	A	L	M	T	C
T	O	W	E	L	A	A
R	O	C	K	S	N	M
C	L	I	F	F	B	P
A	D	R	L	P	R	I
H	O	R	I	Z	O	N
S	W	I	M	O	W	G
H	N	S	K	I	N	T

92.5 Fill the gaps with a suitable verb (one word only). If possible, discuss your answers with someone else.

1 How often do you .... on holiday?
2 Where did you .... your last holiday?
3 Do you or your family often .... an apartment for your holidays?
4 Do you ever .... camping?
5 Do you enjoy .... on a beach?
6 Do you .... a suntan easily?

93 Time

A Prepositions: at, on, in

at a specific time   at 8 o'clock, at 3.30, at midnight
on a day   on Monday, on July 14, on the second day
in a period   in the morning, in April, in the summer, in 1998

> Important exceptions are: **at Christmas**, **at Easter**, **at the weekend**, **at night**.

B Prepositions often confused

I'll stay **until** she phones; I'll be here **until** 4.30. (= I'll leave <u>after</u> she phones/<u>after</u> 4.30)
I'll be in the office **by** 8.15 (= not later than 8.15); I'll be back home **by** 6.30. (= not later than 6.30)

I've worked in this office **for** six months. [For + a period of time, e.g. a week, a month]
I've worked here **since** May. [Since + a point in time in the past, e.g. last Friday, 3 March]

I worked on a farm **during** the summer/the holidays. [This tells you 'when'.]
I worked on a farm **for** two years. [This tells you 'how long'.] (NOT ~~during two years~~)

I'm going back to Brazil **in** ten days' **time**. (= ten days from now) (NOT ~~after ten days~~)

C Approximate periods of time: past, present and future

Past
I've known the two girls **for ages**. (= for a long time)
I haven't been to the dentist **recently/lately**. (e.g. in the last few months)
I saw Tom **recently**. (e.g. a few weeks ago/not long ago)
I used to go skiing, but that was **a long time ago**. (e.g. 5–10 years ago)
My sister went to the zoo **the other day**. (= a few days ago, perhaps a week)

Present
I don't see my sister much **these days**. (= a period including the past and now)

Future
This dictionary will be OK **for the time being**. (= for now/the near future – but not long)
I'm sure I'll go to America **one day**. (= in the future but I don't know when)

D Counting time

There are 60 **seconds** in a **minute**, 60 minutes in an hour, 24 hours in a day, 7 days in a week, 2 weeks in a **fortnight**, 52 weeks in a year, 10 years in a **decade**, 100 years in a **century**.

E 'Take' and 'last'

We use **take** to say how long we need to do something.
It **takes** me (= I need) half an hour to get to school.
We can walk, but it'll **take** (= we'll need) a long time.

We use **last** to talk about the duration of something, from the beginning to the end.
The cookery course **lasted for** ten weeks. (= it continued for ten weeks)
How long does the film **last**? (= How long is it from the beginning to the end?)
The battery in my camera **didn't last long**. (= didn't continue to function for a long time)

Exercises

93.1 Complete the text with *at*, *on* or *in*.

There's one bus from London which gets here (1) .... ten o'clock (2) .... the morning and then another which gets in (3) .... four o'clock (4) .... the afternoon. That's (5) .... weekdays, but (6) .... the weekend the timetable is different. (7) .... Saturday there are still two buses but the second one arrives (8) .... five thirty; (9) .... Sunday there is just the one bus (10) .... two o'clock. And (11) .... the winter, the service doesn't run at all (12) .... Sundays.

93.2 <u>Underline</u> the correct answer in (brackets).

1 The teacher told us to finish our homework (by/until) Monday.
2 We can't leave (by/until) the others get back.
3 I've been in the army (for/since) I was 18.
4 They've worked here (for/since/during) six months.
5 I visit my uncle every week (for/since/during) the winter.
6 I was at university (for/since/during) three years.
7 She's going back to France (in/after) three months' time.
8 I'll see you (in/after) ten days' time.

93.3 Replace the <u>underlined</u> words with more 'approximate' time expressions.

1 I went to Egypt with my parents but that was <u>ten years ago</u>.   *A long time ago*
2 I went to the library <u>three days ago</u>.
3 I haven't been to the cinema <u>for the last three weeks</u>.
4 I haven't been to a concert <u>for three or four years</u>.
5 This computer will be OK for me <u>now and in the next year</u>.

93.4 General Knowledge Quiz. Can you complete these sentences with the correct number?

1 The Olympic Games usually lasts about .... weeks.
2 Pablo Picasso was born in the ....th century, and died in the ....th century.
3 President Kennedy died in .... That's over .... years ago.
4 It takes approximately .... hours to fly from London to New York.
5 The best athletes can run 100 metres in less than .... seconds.

93.5 Complete these sentences about yourself and your country.

1 On weekdays I usually get up at .... and leave home at ....
2 I always clean my teeth in ....
3 I don't go to school/college/work on ....
4 I usually have a holiday in ....
5 I have been in my present school/college/job for ....
6 I have been studying English since ....
7 I haven't spoken English since ....
8 It takes me .... to get to school/college/work.
9 You can't get a driving licence until ....
10 It rains quite a lot during ....

94 Numbers

A Cardinal numbers

379 = three **hundred** <u>and</u> seventy-nine	2,860 = two **thousand** eight hundred <u>and</u> sixty
5,084 = five thousand <u>and</u> eighty-four	470,000 = four hundred <u>and</u> seventy thousand
2,000,000 = two **million**	3,000,000,000 = three **billion**

There is no plural 's' after hundred, thousand, million and billion when they are part of a number. When we are talking more generally, they can be plural, e.g. **thousands** of people; **millions** of insects.

B Ordinal numbers and dates

One problem with dates is that we write them and say them in a different way.

We write **4 January** (or 4th January), but say **the fourth of January** *or* **January the fourth**.
We write **21 May** (or 21st May), but say **the twenty-first of May** *or* **May the twenty-first**.
1997 = **nineteen ninety-seven**   2003 = **two thousand and three**

C Fractions and decimals

$1\frac{1}{4}$ = one and **a quarter**	1.25 = one **point** two five
$1\frac{1}{2}$ = one and **a half**	1.5 = one point five
$1\frac{3}{4}$ = one and **three quarters**	1.75 = one point seven five

D Percentages

26% is spoken as twenty-six **per cent**.
More than 50% of something is the **majority of** it; less than 50% is the **minority**.

E Arithmetic

There are four basic processes. Notice how they are said when we are **working out** (= calculating) the answer.

+ = **addition**	e.g. 6 + 4 = 10 (six **plus/and** four **equals/is** ten)
− = **subtraction**	e.g. 6 − 4 = 2 (six **minus** four equals/is two)
× = **multiplication**	e.g. 6 × 4 = 24 (six **times/multiplied by** four equals/is twenty-four)
÷ = **division**	e.g. 8 ÷ 2 = 4 (eight **divided by** two equals/is four)

Some people are not very good at **mental arithmetic** (= arithmetic in your mind without paper) and often **get stuck** (= have a problem) if they have to **work something out**. The easiest way is to use a **calculator**. (= small electronic machine for working out numbers)

F Saying '0'

This can be spoken in different ways in different contexts.

telephone number: 603 724 = six **oh** three, seven two four
mathematics: 0.7 = **nought** point seven; 6.02 = six point **oh** two *or* six point **nought** two
temperature: −10 degrees = ten degrees below **zero** *or* **minus** ten degrees

Exercises

94.1 How do you say these numbers in English? Write your answers after each one.

1 462 ....
2 2½ ....
3 2,345 ....
4 0.25 ....
5 1,250,000 ....
6 10.04 ....
7 47% ....
8 10 April ....
9 3 July ....
10 602 8477 (phone number) ....
11 –5° centigrade ....
12 In 1976 ....

Now repeat them until you can say them fluently.

94.2 Correct the mistakes in these sentences.

1 After the game I heard that the crowd was over twenty thousands.
2 We arrived on the four August.
3 There were two hundred twenty altogether.
4 My birthday is the thirty-one August.
5 My phone number is seven twenty three, six nought nine.

94.3 Fill the gaps with a suitable word.

1 The .... were in favour of the new plan; about 80%, I think.
2 A small .... were not happy with the idea, but it was only 5%.
3 I'm not very good at mental arithmetic. I always have to use a ....
4 When I tried to add all the numbers together, I couldn't .... it out.
5 I can do simple mental arithmetic, but I get .... if the numbers are very big.

94.4 Can you do these mental arithmetic problems? If you find it difficult, use paper or a calculator.

1 23 and 36 is ....
2 24 times 8 is ....
3 80 minus 20 is ....
4 65 divided by 13 is ....
5 Add 10 and 6, multiply by 8, then subtract 40 and divide by 11. What have you got?
6 Divide 33 by 11, multiply by 7, add 10, and subtract 16. What's your answer?

94.5 Answer these questions. Write your answers in words.

1 When were you born?
2 How much do you weigh?
3 What is the number of the flat or house where you live?
4 What is the approximate population of your town?
5 What is the approximate population of your country?
6 What is the normal temperature of a healthy person?
7 How many kilometres are there in a mile?

95 Distance, size and dimension

A Distance

These are common ways of asking about distance, with typical replies.

A: **How far is it?** B: **The nearest** one (= the shortest distance from here) is about five miles.

A: Is it **far?** B: No. **It's just round the corner.** (= very near)

A: Is it **a long way?** B: No, **not far** (= quite near) – about **ten minutes' walk.**

A: Is it **very far?** B: Yes, **quite a long way.** *or* Yes, **too far to walk.**

We can use **far** in a question or a negative, but not in a positive statement on its own (**it's a long way** NOT ~~it's far~~). But we can say: 'It's **too far** to walk.'

B Size and dimension

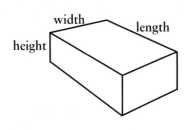
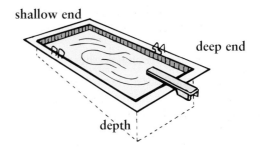

We can ask and answer about dimensions like this:

questions		answers
What's the **length** of the room? *or* **How long** is the room?		It's 5 metres (**long**).
What's the **width** of the path? **How wide** is the path?		It's 60 cm (**wide**).
What's the **height** of the wall? **How high** is the wall?		It's two metres (**high**).
What's the **depth** of the pool? **How deep** is the pool?		It's 3 metres (**deep**).

C Size in people and things

NOTE
We usually use **tall** to describe people, trees and buildings; and **high** to describe walls, mountains, etc.

We use different words to describe the size of people and things. For example:

a **tall** girl (*opp* a **short** girl) fat people (*opp* **thin** people)

a **long** book (= many pages) (*opp* a **short** book)

a **deep** lake (= many metres) (*opp* a **shallow** lake)

a **thick** book (*opp* a **thin** book) a **wide** road (*opp* a **narrow** road)

We can use **big** or **large** to describe size in English, but not **great**, which usually means 'fantastic' in spoken English. But we can use **great big** to say that something is very big, e.g. There was a **great big** dog in the garden, so I stayed outside.

Exercises

95.1 Think about the building you are in now, and answer these questions using expressions from the opposite page.

1 How far is it to the nearest shop?
2 How far is it to a bank?
3 Is it very far to the nearest bus stop?
4 Is it very far to a post office?
5 Is it a long way to the nearest swimming pool?
6 Is it a long way to the next big town?
7 How far is the nearest railway station?
8 Is it far to the centre of town?

If possible, ask someone else the same questions and compare your answers.

95.2 Write down at least six different questions you could ask about the distance, size or dimensions of: the lake, the mountain, the football pitch and the person.

Example How big is the lake?

95.3 Disagree with the speaker in the dialogues below. Look at the example first.

Example A: Is it a long film?
            B: No, it's *quite short.*

1 A: Is he very fat?
   B: No, he's quite ....
2 A: The water's deep, isn't it?
   B: No, it's ....
3 A: Is the road very wide at that point?
   B: No, ...
4 A: He's quite tall, isn't he?
   B: No, ...
5 A: They only live in a small place, don't they?
   B: No, it's ....
6 A: It's a fairly boring place, isn't it?
   B: No, ...

Shapes, colours and patterns

A Shapes

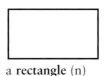

a **square** (n)
square (adj)

a **rectangle** (n)
rectangular (adj)

a **circle** (n)
round (adj)

a **semi-circle**

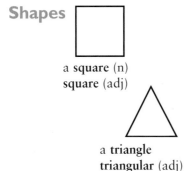

a **triangle**
triangular (adj)

a **point** (n)
pointed (adj)

a **star**

a **diamond**

The room was almost **square**.
It was like a **triangle**.

We haven't got a **round** table.
An unusual **star-shaped** candle.

We sat in a **semi-circle**.
The end was **pointed**.

B Colours

You will already know most of the common colours.
Here are some that are less common.

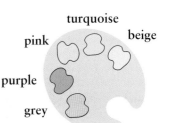

turquoise

pink

beige

purple

grey

C Shades of colour (= degrees and variation of colour)

NOTE
With some colours, we use **pale**, not **light**, e.g. pale yellow, pale pink.

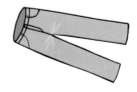

She bought a **dark** green skirt.

He's wearing **light** blue jeans.

The shirt is **pale** yellow.

D Patterns (also called 'designs')

These are common on clothes and furniture.

striped shirt

tartan skirt

check dress

E Use of the suffix -ish

When we want to say that a shape is 'almost round' or a colour is 'a sort of green', we can also express this idea with the suffix *-ish*.

She had a **roundish** face.   He wore a **greenish** tie.   The wall was a **yellowish** colour.

Exercises

96.1 Complete the table.

noun	adjective
square	....
rectangle	....
circle	....
point	....

96.2 Complete these sentences with the correct colour.

1 You mix black and white to get ....
2 You mix red and white to get ....
3 You mix brown and yellow to get ....
4 You mix red and blue to get ....
5 You mix blue and green to get ....

96.3 Describe these pictures using the correct adjective(s) and noun.

1 _a rectangular table_ ....   4 ....   7 ....

2 ....   5 ....   8 ....

3 ....   6 ....   9 ....

96.4 What object is being described in each of these sentences?

1 It's got a point at one end and that's the end you write with.
2 It's rectangular and often green. There are white lines on it, and people play on it.
3 It's a reddish-orange vegetable, quite long and usually pointed at one end.
4 For some of the month it's completely round; at other times, it's closer to a semi-circle.
5 It can look grey, pale blue, dark blue, or a greenish blue. It really depends where it is and whether the sun is shining on it.
6 It's roundish, and white, beige or brown in colour. You eat the inside when it's cooked.
7 The bottom part is triangular, and at the top there is another bit in the shape of a semi-circle. You put things on the triangular part and hang them using the semi-circular part.
8 It lives in the sea. It's quite small and greyish, but goes pink when you cook it. Then you eat it.

96.5 What are you wearing? Write a description, including the exact colour of everything.
If there is a colour or design you cannot describe, use a bilingual dictionary.

97 Notices and warnings

A Information

Out of order  No vacancies · SOLD OUT

OUT OF ORDER
for a machine that is
not working, e.g. public
phone or washing machine

NO VACANCIES
in the window of a B&B
(cheap hotel), it means
the hotel is full

SOLD OUT
outside a cinema or concert
hall – there are no tickets left;
they have all been sold

B Do this!

Please queue other side · KEEP RIGHT · **KEEP OFF THE GRASS** · SILENCE Examination in progress

PLEASE QUEUE OTHER SIDE
(= wait in a line on the other side of
this notice) e.g. in a bank or post office

KEEP RIGHT
(= stay on the right side, and continue on
the right side) e.g. in airports, on the
underground

C Don't do this!

·NO SMOKING· · **NO PARKING** · Do not lean out of the window

Do not leave bags unattended · Do not disturb · **Please do not feed the animals** · **NO EXIT**

D Be careful!

With these notices, something bad may happen if you do not pay attention to them.

·MIND YOUR HEAD· · · MIND THE STEP · · **FRAGILE** · Beware of PICKPOCKETS

MIND YOUR HEAD
(= be careful you
don't hit your head)
e.g. in front of a low
door

MIND THE STEP
(= be careful you
don't hit the step and
fall) e.g. in front of a
step

FRAGILE
(= be careful, this
will break easily)

BEWARE OF PICKPOCKETS
(= be careful, there are
people here who will
steal things from your
bag or pocket without
you knowing)

Exercises

97.1 Complete these notices and warnings in possible ways, without looking at the opposite page.

PLEASE QUEUE ....
MIND THE ....
SOLD ....
OUT OF ....
KEEP ....

BEWARE OF ....
MIND YOUR ....
PLEASE DO NOT ....
NO ....

97.2 Where could you see these notices or warnings?

1 **Nothing to declare** _at an airport_ ....

2 **No vacancies** ....

3 Beware of PICKPOCKETS ....

4 Please queue other side ....

5 *Out of order* ....

6 **SOLD OUT** ....

7 **FRAGILE** ....

8 **KEEP OFF THE GRASS** ....

97.3 What notice(s) might you see in each of these places?

1 A zoo ....
2 A waiting area in a busy airport ....
3 The door of a hotel room at 9 o'clock in the morning ....
4 In front of garage doors ....
5 Above the window of a train ....
6 Inside a theatre ....
7 On the underground ....
8 A door going into a low room ....

97.4 Now write some different notices of your own. Think of six possible notices you could put in one of these places:

- a school ....
- a university ....
- a language school ....
- a place where people work, e.g. bank, factory, hospital ....

Where would you put these notices? If possible, do this activity with another person or show it to another person.

97.5 Look for other notices (in English or your first language). Can you understand the English notices? Can you translate the ones in your own language. Try to find six more notices in the next week.

98 Vague language

Vague means 'not clear or precise or exact'. For example, we can say:
I have a **vague idea** where it is. (= I know more or less but not exactly)
In <u>spoken</u> English, we use a lot of vague words when we are not being very precise.

A Thing(s)

- To refer to actions, ideas and facts:
  The main **thing** (= fact) about John is that he always stays calm.
  That was a terrible **thing** (= action) to do.
- To refer to <u>countable</u> objects (often the speaker and listener know what the object is):
  What's that **thing** (bicycle) doing in the house?
  Put those **things** (cups and saucers) in the cupboard.
- To refer to a general situation:
  How are **things** at school?   **Things** (= life in general) **are going really well.**

B Stuff

We can use **stuff** with <u>uncountable</u> nouns (or a group of countable nouns) when we don't need to give the exact word. Often the listener knows what the speaker is talking about.
Just leave that **stuff** (= different items of clothes) on the floor. I'll clear it up.
I play guitar but not much classical **stuff.** (= music)

C A sort of ...

We often use this phrase when we cannot find the exact word to describe something.
The walls are **a sort of** yellow. (= not exactly yellow, but more or less)
It's **a sort of** horror film. (= not exactly a horror film, but more or less)

D And things like that/and that sort of thing

We use these phrases so that we don't need to continue the examples.
I don't eat chilli and garlic **and things like that.**
She wears a lot of Armani and Versace **and that sort of thing.**

E Sometime/any time

It'll be ready **sometime next week.** (= next week but I don't know when)
You can collect it **any time after** 10. (= at 10.30 or 12.30, or 3.00 in the afternoon, etc.)

F A bit

It usually means 'a little', but it can also mean 'quite a lot' in spoken English.
Could you speak up **a bit**? (= a little) I can't hear you very well.
I thought the hotel was **a bit** (= quite) expensive, actually.

G Approximately

These words are used with numbers and all mean **approximately.**
It'll take you **about/around** 40 minutes.   It's **roughly** ten miles.
We're expecting 100 people, **more or less.**   We interviewed 20 **or so**, I think.

Exercises

98.1 **What could *thing(s)* and *stuff* refer to in these sentences?**

1 I never wear that stuff; it's got such a strong smell.   *perfume/aftershave*
2 This thing has got stuck in the lock.
3 I bought a couple of bottles when I was in Scotland. It's great stuff.
4 We don't need these things on a picnic. We can eat the food with our fingers.
5 What's that white stuff called that you mix with water to make bread?
6 There was a great thing on television last night about elephants.
7 I couldn't get any more stuff in my suitcase.
8 It's a wonderful thing and keeps my young children occupied for ages.
9 I don't know why I bought that thing – it's too heavy for me to carry even when it's empty.
10 It's good stuff. My hair feels really soft, and it didn't cost a lot.

98.2 **Add a word or phrase in the spaces to make this conversation less precise and more natural.**

A: How many people were at the conference?
B: (1) .... 400.
A: Was it good?
B: Er, I (2) .... enjoyed it.
A: You don't seem very sure.
B: Well, there were some good (3) .... , but it was (4) .... too long.
A: And did you go to John's talk?
B: Naturally.
A: How did it go?
B: Well, he was (5) .... nervous at the beginning, but it went really well.
A: What was it about exactly?
B: Oh you know, changes in the family, (6) ....
A: How many people were in the audience?
B: 75 (7) ....
A: That's good, isn't it?
B: I think John was (8) .... disappointed – he wanted at least 100.

98.3 **Reply to each of these questions with a suitable 'vague' response.**

1 A: Did you get everything you wanted?
  B: Yeah, ...*more or less.*...
2 A: Did you say the walls were blue?
  B: Yeah, ...
3 A: Will there be 20 chairs in the room?
  B: Yeah, ...
4 A: Is it a very serious film?
  B: Yeah, ...
5 A: Are you tired?
  B: Yeah, ...
6 A: Can I collect it tomorrow?
  B: Yes, ...

99 Formal and informal English

A Formal English

Formal English is more common in writing than speaking, and is used in notices, business letters and legal English. You will hear some examples in spoken English, e.g. airport announcements.

Notice in café: Only food **purchased** (= bought) here may be eaten on the premises.
Police statement: I **apprehended** (= caught) the accused outside the supermarket.
Theatre announcement: The play will **commence** (= start) in two minutes.
Business meeting: The meeting will **resume** (= start again) this afternoon at 2pm.
Lawyer in court: My client had a broken ankle, **thus** (= so) he couldn't drive the car.
Business letter: I **regret to inform you** (= I'm sorry to say) that we **are unable to** … (= can't)
Notice: If you **require** (= need) **further assistance** (= more help), please contact …
Airport announcement: Will passengers for Miami please **proceed to** (= go to) gate 36.

B Informal English

Informal language is more common in spoken English. For example:
- most uses of **get** are informal (see Unit 29)
- many **phrasal verbs** are informal (see Units 23 and 24)
- many **idioms** are informal (see Unit 13)
- most **shortened words** are informal (see Unit 100)

Informal language is not suitable for formal written English, but in spoken English (and most e-mails or letters to friends) it will help you generally to sound more natural.

I had to go and **pick up** (= collect) the **kids** (= children) from school.
I **reckon** (= think) we'll **get** (= receive/obtain) the money **pretty** (= quite) soon.
I'm just going to the **loo.** (= toilet)
Do you fancy going out? (= Would you like to go out?)
I managed to **fix up** (= arrange/make) an appointment for 7.30.
My flat is very **handy** for the shops. (= near the shops and very convenient)
I thought the book was **terrific.** (= marvellous)
Most of the students are **bright** (= intelligent) but Paul is really **thick.** (= stupid)
What's up? (= What's the matter?)
We must **get in touch with** them (= contact them) very soon.
When we **get to** (= reach/arrive) the hotel, I'll **have a word with** (= speak to) them.
I offered him ten **quid** (= pounds), but the **guy** (= man) wasn't interested.
A: Here's the book I promised you.
B: Oh, **cheers.** (= thank you. It can also mean 'goodbye'.)
Did you bring your **bike?** (= bicycle)

C Slang

This is a form of <u>very</u> informal language. It includes words used by particular groups of people, e.g. young people often refer to 'drugs' as **dope**, and also words which many people think are impolite and unacceptable in most situations. You should probably not use these words, but some of them are quite common. For example, the word **piss** is a slang word meaning to urinate/go to the toilet, and it is also used in a number of other slang expressions with different meanings.

Piss off! (= go away)   He was **pissed.** (= drunk)   It's **pissing with rain.** (= raining heavily)

Exercises

99.1 Put the words on the left into the correct column on the right.

		formal	informal
handy	loo	...purchase...........	....
purchase	resume	....	....
thus	terrific	....	....
quid	commence	....	....
apprehend	reckon	....	....
guy	cheers		....
			....

99.2 Find a synonym in the box for each of the words in 99.1.

so	buy *purchase*	convenient	catch
start	man	start again	pounds
thanks	think	marvellous	toilet

99.3 Replace the underlined words and phrases in these sentences with more informal language.
1 Where did you purchase that book?
2 I'm just going to the toilet.
3 The woman on the desk told us to proceed to gate 12.
4 What's the matter?
5 Would you like to go out for a meal?
6 When are you going to collect your bicycle?
7 My flat is five minutes from where I work, thus it's very convenient.
8 The man in the market wanted twenty pounds for this ring.
9 Most of the children are very clever.
10 I think it'll commence quite soon.

99.4 Now rewrite the underlined parts of this letter in more suitable formal English.

> Dear Mr Collins,
>
> We're really sorry to say that we can't lend you the sum of £500 that you need, but it may be possible to provide you with a loan for some of the money.
>
> If you would like to contact the branch and have a word with Mrs Jenkins, she will fix up an appointment with the assistant manager. He will be happy to discuss the matter with you.
>
> Yours sincerely,

99.5 Dictionaries will tell you if a word is formal or informal/spoken. Use your dictionary to find out if these underlined words are formal or informal/spoken. What do they mean?

I thought the film was a drag.   Patrons only.   It was too much hassle to go.
Someone has pinched my pen.   He's a nice bloke.   Smoking isn't permitted.

100 Abbreviations and abbreviated words

A Letters or words?

Most abbreviations are spoken as individual letters:

BBC	British Broadcasting Corporation	**MP**	Member of Parliament
UN	United Nations	**PM**	Prime Minister
EU	European Union	**ID**	Identification, e.g. Do you have an ID card?
USA	United States of America	**PC**	Personal computer
WWW	World Wide Web	**CV**	Curriculum vitae
ISP	Internet Service Provider	**CD**	Compact Disc

A few abbreviations are spoken as words, e.g. AIDS /eɪdz/ (= Acquired Immune Deficiency Syndrome), and occasionally they can be spoken as individual letters or a word, e.g. VAT /væt/ or [V-A-T] Value Added Tax (= a tax on goods/products in EU countries)

If you don't understand an abbreviation, you can ask about its meaning like this:
A: **What does** V-A-T **stand for?**   A: **What does** EU **stand for?**
B: Value Added Tax.   B: European Union.

B Written forms only

Some abbreviations are written forms only; they are still pronounced as full words.

Mr /mɪstə/   **St** Mark (Saint Mark)
Mrs /mɪsɪs/ (= a married woman)   Dean **St** (Dean Street)
Ms /məz/ (= a woman who may be single or married)   **Dr** (Doctor)

C Abbreviations as part of the language

Some abbreviations (from Latin) are used as part of the language.

NOTE
We write 'etc'. and 'e.g.', but when we speak we usually say 'and so on' and 'for example'.

abbreviation	pronunciation	meaning	Latin
etc.	et cetera	and so on	et cetera
e.g.	E-G	for example	exempli gratia
i.e.	I-E	that's to say/in other words	id est

D Shortened words

Some common English words can be shortened, especially in spoken English. In some cases, the shorter form is more common and the full form sounds very formal/strange, e.g. refrigerator, influenza, gymnasium and veterinary surgeon.

phone (telephone)   **fridge** (refrigerator)   **bike** (bicycle)
maths (mathematics)   **exam** (examination)   **TV/telly** (television)
board (blackboard)   **plane** (aeroplane)   **a paper** (newspaper)
case (suitcase)   **photo** (photograph)   **vet** (veterinary surgeon)
ad/advert (advertisement)   **flu** (influenza) (= illness like a cold but more serious)
lab (laboratory) (= special room where scientists work)
gym (gymnasium) (= large room with equipment for physical exercise)
sales rep (sales representative)

Exercises

100.1 What do these letters stand for? Complete each one.

1 BBC = British Broadcasting ....
2 MP = Member of ....
3 WWW = World Wide ....
4 CD = ... Disc

5 PM = Prime ....
6 UN = United ....
7 PC = Personal ....
8 ID = ...

100.2 Rewrite this note, making it more informal by using short forms where possible.

> Michael
>
> Peter had a mathematics examination this afternoon and then he had to take his bicycle to the repair shop, so he'll probably be a bit late home. You can watch television while you're waiting for him, and please help yourself to anything in the refrigerator. If there's a problem (for example, Doctor Brown rings about the influenza vaccination), my telephone number is next to the photographs on the dining room table. I should be home myself by about five.
>
> Margaret (Peter's mother)

100.3 What abbreviations in written English are often used for these words or phrases?

1 for example
2 and so on
3 Street

4 in other words
5 Mister
6 Doctor

100.4 Complete these sentences with suitable words or abbreviations from the opposite page.

1 She didn't want to walk, so she went on her ...*bike.*...
2 If you go to Mediterranean islands, ... Sardinia or Corsica, it's a good idea to hire a car.
3 If you want to apply for the job, you need to send your .... with a letter of application.
4 I asked the teacher to write the word on the ....
5 In that shop on the corner you can get books, pens, writing paper, ...
6 She was away from college last week because she had .... I think she's better now, though.
7 When I sold my records, I put an .... in the paper and had three replies the same day.
8 It was a warm day, so I put the milk and butter in the ....
9 If the tickets are very expensive, ... more than £50, don't buy any.
10 What does EU .... for?

100.5 Here are some more abbreviations. What does each one stand for, and where will you see them?

| PTO | RSVP | ASAP | CC/cc |

Answer key

Unit 1

1.1 *Suggested answers:*
1 It is better to plan regular self-study.
2 No, study the units that interest you.
3 Yes.
4 Yes, it usually is necessary.
5 It is probably better to revise for short periods but do it often.

1.3 revision/revise; pronunciation/pronounce; choice/choose; interest/interest

1.4 1 Did you **do**   2 for **half an hour**   3 the left-**hand** page
4 **I spent** twenty minutes   5 the **whole** page

1.5 2 True   3 False (it means doing certain things in the same way)   4 True
5 False ('at least 50' means a minimum of 50)   6 True   7 True
8 False ('revision' means studying something a second or third time)
9 True   10 False ('a blank piece of paper' has no writing on it)

Unit 2

2.1 *Possible answers:*

CLOTHES	RAILWAYS/TRAVEL	WORDS WITH '*un-*' PREFIX
put on gloves size jumper wear tie	platform train get on late passenger	unfriendly unhappy unable unkind

2.2 1 on   2 black   3 put on   4 make   5 gave   6 finger

2.3 1 b   2 c   3 b   4 c   5 a   6 a   7 b   8 b

2.4 The answers here will depend on your first language: a translation may or may not be suitable for all of the words. Example sentences are a good idea for most words, and there is usually something else that is also useful to know. Here are some suggestions:
concentrate: the main stress is on the first syllable, and it is followed by the preposition 'on'. The noun is 'concentration'.
beard: a picture is the best way to show meaning; it is pronounced /bɪəd/; also useful to know 'moustache'.
nearly: synonym = almost. Usually goes before the main verb except the verb 'to be', e.g. we nearly lost the game; it is nearly 4 o'clock.
empty: opposite = full. Also useful to learn 'half-empty' (= 'half-full') but seems more negative.
rescue: synonym = save; noun and verb.
knife: a picture is the best way to show meaning; the letter 'k' is silent; also important to know the plural form 'knives', and the words 'fork' and 'spoon'.

2.5 *Possible answers:*

take: a picture, a bath, a decision, a bus
make: a mistake, a decision, a mess, a noise, friends, money, coffee
do: homework, research, someone a favour, an exam, sport, the shopping, the washing-up

Unit 3

3.1 1 bilingual   2 pronunciation   3 uncountable   4 opposites   5 guess; look it up

3.2 2 Wrong ('homesick' means you are unhappy living away from home and want to return)
 3 Right
 4 Right
 5 Wrong (the opposite of 'polite' is 'impolite')
 6 Wrong (the past tense of 'begin' is 'began')
 7 Right
 8 Right
 9 Right
 10 Wrong ('depend' is followed by the preposition 'on')

3.3 **k** in knife; **b** in comb; **t** in castle; **l** in salmon; **p** in receipt

3.4 1 very small
 2 /luːz/ like 'choose'
 3 win a game
 4 chose/chosen
 5 choice
 6 It's an adjective.
 7 be and feel, e.g. She's homesick; He feels homesick.
 8 law and order

3.5 1 = def. 3   2 = def. 1   3 = def. 2   4 = def. 1

Unit 4

4.1 2 <u>in</u> Seville; preposition
 3 <u>got/took/caught</u> a train; verb
 4 <u>a</u> beautiful city; indefinite article
 5 <u>expensive/good</u> hotel; adjective
 6 <u>of</u> money; preposition
 7 wonderful <u>hotel/place/location</u>; noun
 8 <u>to</u> Spain; preposition
 9 <u>never</u> stays; adverb

4.2 uncountable noun: traffic
plural noun: shorts; jeans
a phrasal verb: get in; put on
idiom: get a move on

4.3 1 transitive   2 transitive   3 intransitive   4 transitive
 5 intransitive   6 intransitive

4.4 *Syllables and main stress (underlined):*

One syllable: noun
Two syllables: <u>Eng</u>lish; dec<u>ide</u>; be<u>fore</u>, <u>ad</u>verb
Three syllables: in<u>for</u>mal; <u>a</u>djective; <u>opp</u>osite; under<u>stand</u>
Four syllables: edu<u>ca</u>tion; prepo<u>si</u>tion
Five syllables: pronunci<u>a</u>tion

4.5
1 adjectives
2 happily; luckily; dangerously; cheaply
3 happy/content/cheerful; lucky/fortunate
4 un- (unhappy; unlucky)
5 dangerous/safe; cheap/expensive

Unit 5

5.1
1 notebook   2 file   3 briefcase   4 socket   5 plug
6 tape recorder/cassette recorder

5.2
2 a cassette/tape
3 an OHT
4 notes/papers
5 notes/books/pens, etc
6 a plug
7 rub things out/erase them
8 (photo)copy things
9 because you want it louder
10 because there aren't enough books/you've forgotten your book

5.3   2d   3e   4a   5f   6g   7h   8b

5.4
1 What does 'swap' mean?
2 How do you pronounce it?
3 How do you spell it?

Unit 6

6.1
2 incorrect   5 impatient   9 impolite   13 unlock
3 illegible   6 irregular   10 invisible   14 unpack
4 impossible   7 unfriendly   11 unemployed   15 disagree
8 informal   12 dishonest   16 dislike

6.2   2 unlock the door   3 disappear   4 get undressed

6.3
2 it's very untidy   3 he got undressed   4 it's completely illegible
5 she's very impatient   6 inadequate   7 unpleasant
8 dishonest

6.4
2 misunderstood/misread/misheard   3 unpacked   4 disappeared
5 redo/rewrite   6 overslept   7 unlock   8 disliked   9 redo/retake
10 overdoing   11 reopen   12 overcharged

Unit 7

7.1
education; improvement; jogging; government; spelling; hesitation; arrangement
stupidity; happiness; weakness; similarity; activity; sadness; popularity

7.2
2 election   3 education   4 government   5 weakness
6 stupidity   7 management   8 improvement

7.3   2 translator   3 actor   4 psychologist   5 economist   6 footballer

7.4
pop singer   bus driver   shop manager   child psychologist
film director   ballet dancer   computer operator   professional footballer

7.5
2 murders someone
3 manages a bank
4 acts on TV
5 translates books and articles, etc.
6 drives a lorry
7 writes articles in newspapers and magazines
8 paints pictures

Unit 8

8.1
2 attractive   3 creative   4 cloudy   5 (un)suitable
6 useful/useless   7 careful/careless   8 thoughtful   9 political
10 enjoyable   11 painful   12 dirty   13 sunny
14 musical   15 (un)comfortable   16 famous   17 (un)reliable
18 emotional

8.2
2 famous   3 helpful   4 dangerous   5 painful
6 useful   7 reliable   8 industrial   9 economical
10 homeless   11 fashionable   12 incomprehensible

8.3
1 *opp* awful/terrible   2 *opp* useless   3 *opp* wonderful/great
4 *opp* careless   5 *opp* ugly

8.4
homeless family   famous actor
careless mistake   useful advice
comfortable bed   cloudy morning
industrial area   enjoyable party

8.5 *Possible answers:*
2 cloudy, sunny, foggy
3 careful, careless, dangerous, reliable
4 famous, dirty, attractive, industrial
5 comfortable, fashionable, reliable, unreliable, economical

Unit 9

9.1
1 guess   2 diet   3 queue   4 murder
5 ring   6 kiss   7 chat   8 dream

9.2
1 We waited a long time.
2 This apple tastes strange.
3 We queued for half an hour.
4 The holiday cost about £500.
5 I replied to his letter yesterday.
6 She smiled at me this morning.

9.3
1 I'll give him a ring this evening.
2 I'll go on a diet if necessary.
3 If you don't know, just have a guess.
4 I put on the brakes but I still couldn't stop in time.
5 I had a dream about my mother.
6 Did you have a look in the paper?

9.4
1 same meaning
2 completely different (the verb 'to book' = 'to reserve')
3 completely different ('a break' is a rest; 'to break a leg' = to fracture a leg)
4 similar (but not exactly the same because 'a run' here is not just the action of running; it is an activity that the person chooses to do)

Unit 10

10.1 *Possible answers:*

Money: credit card, cash machine, income tax, box office (where you buy tickets)
Kitchens: dishwasher, washing machine, frying pan, tin opener
Jobs: bus driver, postman, babysitter, pop star, film star, rock star
Roads/transport: traffic lights, traffic jam, bus stop, bus driver, travel agent
Things we wear: T-shirt, sunglasses, earrings, make-up

10.2

2 traffic jam	3 film star	4 traffic lights	5 waiting room
6 babysitter	7 sunglasses	8 income tax	9 hair dryer
10 bus stop	11 science fiction	12 washing machine	

10.3 *Possible answers:*

1 living room, waiting room, chat room, bedroom, bathroom, classroom
2 pop star, rock star, film actor, film director
3 birthday card, postcard, Christmas card, phone card, credit limit
4 toothbrush, toothache, toothpick
5 traffic jam, traffic warden, street lights
6 sunshine, suntan, sunshade, sunburn
7 haircut, hairdresser, hairstyle, tumble dryer
8 girlfriend, pen friend, school friend

Unit 11

11.1

easy-going	good-looking
five-star	short-sleeved
brand-new	second-hand
part-time	left-handed
well-known	

11.2

1 sleeved	2 handed	3 new	4 behaved
5 part	6 written	7 off/paid	8 hand
9 looking	10 known	11 going	12 year

11.3 *Possible answers:*

1 well-paid; well-organised; well-written, well-equipped, etc.
2 part-time; full-time
3 badly-written; badly-dressed; badly-behaved; badly-organised, etc.
4 right-handed; left-handed

11.4   1 hotel   2 delay   3 note   4 walk   5 fine

Unit 12

12.1 heavy traffic; heavy rain; heavy smoker
miss a bus; miss a person; miss a lesson
tell a joke; tell a lie; tell the truth

12.2

2 a slight accent	3 weak coffee	4 a loud voice
5 a soft drink	6 tell a lie	7 miss the bus 8 dry wine

12.3	1 missed	2 told	3 start	4 great
	5 start	6 hard	7 vitally	8 heavy
	9 strong	10 missed	11 well	12 wasted
	13 fast; wide			

12.4 1 size; large   2 wide range   3 broad shoulders   4 vast majority

Unit 13

13.1
1 hang on	6 up
2 I haven't a clue	7 keep an eye on
3 go ahead	8 make it
4 Never mind	9 make up your mind
5 if you like	10 up to you

13.2
1 term	2 turns	3 nerves	4 theory	5 place/world
6 mind	7 rid	8 like	9 early	10 tongue
11 hand	12 getting	13 changed	14 get	

13.3 1 easy
2 for ever (they are not coming back)
3 manage

Unit 14

14.1 *The correct prepositions and sample replies:*

2 at	B: French and German.
3 for	B: Her brother, I think.
4 for	B: Assistant manager.
5 to	B: I think it's a comedy programme.
6 about	B: She said the vegetables were cold.
7 for	B: The fact that she was late twice last week.
8 to	B: The man over there.
9 at	B: One of the students in her class.
10 in	B: Thrillers, I think.
11 on	B: How much it costs, I expect.
12 of	B: The fact that she can't get out; she's claustrophobic.

14.2   2j   3a   4l   5h   6b   7d   8k   9g   10i   11e   12f

14.3 *Possible answers:*

2 to my brother/sister/mother
3 with her homework/her results
4 from hay fever/sunburn
5 with this TV
6 into five languages/French
7 of flying/heights/spiders
8 in art/music
9 on sport/English food
10 from British people
11 of going to Greece
12 of tourists/holidaymakers

14.4 fond of; concentrate on; rely on

Unit 15

15.1 1 on 2 by 3 on 4 on 5 on 6 by 7 for
8 in 9 on 10 by 11 in 12 on 13 by 14 by
15 on 16 in 17 in 18 at 19 by 20 in

15.2 1 by myself/on my own 2 in time 3 on fire 4 on the phone
5 on TV 6 by mistake/accident 7 in the end 8 at the end
9 at the moment 10 by chance

15.3 1 by accident 2 by himself/on his own 3 on foot (*or* 'by bus, by taxi, by train')
4 on business 5 on the radio 6 out of work
7 by train (*or* 'by car, by bus') 8 in love

Unit 16

16.1 2 I'm; cancelled; problem 3 keep; mind 4 sort 5 lot
6 apologise; matter 7 long; worry 8 kind 9 beg; problem
10 about; up

16.2 *Possible answers:*

2 I'm sorry I'm late, but I missed the bus.
3 Oh, thank you. That's very kind of you.
4 Don't worry. It doesn't matter.
5 I'm very sorry to disturb you, but …
6 Never mind. Don't worry. I'll sort it out.
7 I must apologise for not coming to the meeting yesterday. Unfortunately, …
8 Please accept our apologies for the delay in sending the information we promised you. Unfortunately, we had a fire at the factory last month, and this …

Unit 17

17.1 A: <u>Would</u> you like to go out this evening?
B: I'm afraid I haven't got any money. (omit 'but')
A: That's OK, I'll pay. How about <u>going</u> to see a film?
B: No, I think I'd rather stay in and do my homework. (omit 'to' after 'rather')
A: Why <u>don't you</u> do your homework this afternoon?
B: I'm busy this afternoon.
A: OK. We could go tomorrow.
B: Yeah, great.
A: Right. What film shall we see?
B: <u>I don't mind</u>.

17.2 1 sure/no problem
2 wondering; love
3 fancy; don't; idea
4 shall; about; could; rather; like
5 would; mind

17.3 *Possible answers:*

1 Yeah, sure.
2 Yes, of course.
3 I'm afraid not.
4 Yes, I'd love to.

5 I'd love to, but I'm afraid I can't.
6 Yeah, great.
7 Yes, that's a good idea.
8 Yes, if you like.
9 Well, it's a bit difficult actually because I promised to help …
10 Yeah, I don't mind/if you like.

Unit 18

18.1 1 What do you think of … ?
2 What do you think about … ?
3 How do you feel about … ?

18.2 1 of; personally ('actually' would also be correct here)
2 according
3 point
4 totally ('completely' would also be possible here)
5 opinions/views

18.3 *Possible answers:*

2 In my opinion the club needs new players.
3 I don't agree with you at all.
4 According to the newspaper terrorists started the fire.
5 Yes, I see what you mean.
6 What do you think about giving … ?

18.4 1c   2a   3d   4b

18.5 *Possible answers:*

1 Yeah, possibly, but that doesn't mean all women want to be housewives. Some want to have careers.
2 Yes, I agree to some extent, but how do you know if people don't want to work? They may want to work but there are no jobs.
3 Yes, I agree with you, but of course we have to decide what the best way to help them is.

Unit 19

19.1 1 A: I love modern art.
B: Yes, so <u>do</u> I.
2 A: Do you like this?
B: Yes, I like <u>it</u> very much.
3 A: Would you like to go out?
B: No, I'd prefer <u>to</u> stay here.
4 I'm looking forward to <u>seeing</u> you next week.

5 A: Do you like tea?
B: Yes, but I prefer coffee <u>to</u> tea.
6 A: Does he like football?
B: No, he's not <u>interested</u> in sport.
7 A: I don't like his new CD.
B: No, <u>neither</u> do I.
8 I don't mind <u>helping</u> them.

19.2 1 stand   2 thing/stuff   3 on   4 like
5 forward   6 interest   7 into   8 hearing

19.3 2 I think they'd rather go home.
3 His books don't interest me.
4 I don't really like things like that.
5 I'm very interested in archaeology.
6 I don't mind the new building.

2 So do I/me too.   3 Neither do I/me neither.   4 Neither can I/me neither.
5 So am I/me too.   6 Neither am I/me neither.

Unit 20

20.1 2 single   3 special/much   4 get   5 What
6 longer   7 How   8 sort/kind

20.2 2 Have you got the time?
3 How old are you?
4 How far is it?
5 What sort/type/kind of food do you eat?
6 Excuse me. How do I get to (the national museum)?
7 What's their new flat like?
8 What are you doing this evening?
9 How long have you been here? / When did you get here?

20.3 2 How's it going? (Also 'How are things going?')   3 Whereabouts do you live …
4 What's your steak like?   5 … the first time you've been to …
6 matter

20.4 A: How **long have you been** here?
B: Just a couple of days.
A: Really? And **how long are you staying / how long are you here for / how much longer
are you here for**?
B: Until next Friday.
A: Is this **the first time you've been** to Spain?
B: No, I came last year.

Unit 21

21.2 1 so   2 so   3 not   4 it   5 so   6 not

21.3 2f   3e   4b   5d   6a

21.4 1 shame   2 If you like   3 how   4 doubt it
5 Whatever you like/want   6 that sounds awful/terrible

21.5 *Possible answers:*
1 How exciting/That sounds wonderful.
2 Oh, what a nuisance/pain.
3 If you like/I don't mind.
4 I don't mind/Wherever you like.
5 Oh, that's brilliant/How exciting.
6 Oh, what a shame/pity.
7 Really? That's dreadful/Oh, how awful.
8 Oh, what a nuisance/pain.

Unit 22

22.1 2 Happy (21st) Birthday (*or* Many happy returns)
3 Happy New Year
4 Congratulations (on passing your exams)/Well done
5 Good luck (in your driving test)
6 See you soon

22.2 1 How do you do?; How do you do?/Pleased/nice to meet you.
     2 Have a nice weekend; Yes, you too/same to you.
     3 Bless you!
     4 Cheers; cheers

22.3 2 Sorry? (with rising intonation)
     3 Goodbye. Nice to meet you/Nice to have met you.
     4 Excuse me.
     5 Goodnight. (See you in the morning/tomorrow.)
     6 Excuse me. (You would probably add something like 'I think you've dropped something.')
     7 Congratulations.
     8 Good luck.

22.4 We use 'hard luck' to someone who has just failed in something, e.g. failed an exam.
     We ask people to 'say cheese' when we are about to take a photo of them.
     We say 'watch out' as a warning, e.g. to warn someone crossing a road that a cyclist is right behind them and could hit them if they aren't careful.
     We say 'keep your fingers crossed' when we wish and hope that a situation will have a happy or good result, e.g. 'I'm taking my driving test tomorrow, so keep your fingers crossed'. (= Let's hope I pass.)

Unit 23

23.1 2 picked   3 gone   4 get   5 gets   6 put
     7 look   8 carry/get   9 get   10 run

23.2 *Possible answers:*
     2 an hour late/for Paris/from Heathrow
     3 in a dictionary
     4 my boss/my parents/the neighbours/my teacher, etc.
     5 her coat/her jacket/her gloves, etc.
     6 smoking/chocolate, etc.
     7 the cat/the children, etc.
     8 the car
     9 paper, coffee, bread, etc.
     10 by ten pounds/next week, etc.

23.3 1 def. 3   2 def. 5   3 def. 2   4 def. 4

23.4 Look at the examples on page 48.

Unit 24

24.1 1 *correct*
     2 ... I'd pick them up after school.
     3 She grew up on a farm.
     4 *correct*
     5 ... will sort it out.
     6 *correct*
     7 ... broke into the house?
     8 *correct*

24.2 1 going up; get by; carry on
2 come in/go in; take off
3 make up; leave out
4 turned down; sort out

24.3
1 down	2 out	3 on	4 out	5 up
6 away/out	7 off	8 up	9 off/out	10 down

24.4 *Possible answers:*

2 excuses/stories
3 the TV/the light/the fire
4 my flat/my house
5 the problem/the mess/the central heating
6 tonight/on Saturday evening
7 the second question/the final part
8 just outside London/on the motorway, etc.
9 in English/on your salary
10 in a small town/by the sea

24.5 *Possible answers:*

U52: grow up; go out (with sb); split up
U53: wake up; get up; stay in; go out
U61: do up; take sth off; put sth on
U79: plug sth in; turn sth off/on/over; switch sth on/off/over
U80: put sb through; get through; phone sb back; be back; get back

Unit 25

25.1 2 I haven't got a job at the moment.
3 Does he have any change for the machine?
4 She doesn't have much money.
5 We haven't got a video at school.
6 A: Have you got an English dictionary?   B: Yes, I have.

25.2 3 We've got a small garden.
4 I think I've got a cold.
5 A: Have you got a spare pen?
6 … she's got a new boyfriend.
7 *cannot change*
8 *cannot change*
9 I've got a new computer.
10 Have you got the time?

25.3
2 dream	3 rest/break	4 party	5 think	6 problem
7 time	8 lunch	9 look	10 argument/row	

25.4 2 Could I have a look at your paper?
3 Could I have a word with you?
4 Could I have a drink/something to drink?
5 Could I have a think about it?

25.5 2 Mary is having a baby/going to have a baby.
3 Mary had a problem working the video/with the video.

4 Mary had a look at my bad shoulder.
5 Mary had a great time in Ireland.

Unit 26

26.1   1 do 2 take/do 3 make 4 do 5 take
6 made 7 do 8 take/make 9 doing 10 made

26.2   1 do my/the shopping 2 making progress 3 take a break 4 do me a favour
5 makes a (big) difference 6 make (a lot of) money 7 make a decision
8 did badly 9 take a seat 10 take a week off/take a week's holiday

26.3   1 Sally did the shopping this morning. 2 Maria did her homework after dinner.
3 Simon took a picture/photo of me this morning. 4 Michael did well in his exams.

Unit 27

27.1   1 break somebody's heart; the law
2 give somebody a hand; somebody a lift
3 keep in touch; somebody waiting

27.2   2 keep 3 broken 4 see 5 gave
6 keep 7 see 8 see 9 break 10 see

27.3   2 gave her a ring
3 broken the law
4 keep in touch
5 break her heart
6 give you a hand

27.4   1 dry 2 laughing 3 awake 4 fit/healthy 5 forgetting 6 quiet

Unit 28

28.1   1 catch (also take/get) 2 leave 3 let 4 caught
5 left 6 leave 7 catch 8 let's

28.2   1 alone 2 catch 3 know 4 see
5 left 6 message 7 catch 8 cold

28.3   1b and e; 2a and f; 3c and d

28.4   *Possible answers:*
2 me help you/me do it 3 me give you a lift 4 you know

Unit 29

29.1   1 buy/find 2 fetch 3 arrive 4 became 5 find
6 receive 7 becoming 8 buy 9 receive 10 arrive

29.2   2 I'm getting hungry. 3 I'm getting hot. 4 It's getting late.
5 It's getting dark. 6 I'm getting worse at English.

29.3   2 get to know people in this country 3 get on (very) well with my boss
4 get rid of most of the furniture in this room 5 How are you getting on?
6 really get on my nerves 7 getting ready to go out 8 get up

Unit 30

30.1   2 coming   3 go   4 take   5 taking ('bringing' is also possible here if the speaker already imagines him/herself at the party)   6 bring   7 go   8 come

30.2   2 try   3 are you   4 fetch   5 together

30.3   1 shopping   2 for a meal/for something to eat   3 for a drink
4 sightseeing   5 for a drive   6 for a swim *or* swimming

30.4   2 deaf   3 bankrupt   4 grey   5 bald
6 mad   7 blind   8 together

Unit 31

31.1   2 ripe   3 horrible   4 banana   5 sore   6 fresh
7 photograph   8 brother   9 salmon   10 old socks   11 doorbell
12 silk

31.2   1 looks sad   2 feels soft   3 tastes horrible/bad

31.3   1 listening to; heard   2 heard   3 hear   4 look at   5 watch
6 listening to   7 touch   8 press   9 hold   10 watch *or* look; see

Unit 32

32.1   1 carton   2 cup   3 bowl   4 box
5 bottle   6 glass   7 tin   8 jar

32.2   1 a cup or jar of coffee   2 is possible; also a bottle or glass of wine   3 is normal
4 a tube of toothpaste   5 is possible; also a bottle/carton or glass of milk
6 a packet of cigarettes   7 is possible; also a packet of salt
8 is normal; also a bag of tomatoes (if they are fresh)

32.3   2 gang   3 slices/pieces   4 piece   5 bit/lot   6 sheet/piece/bit
7 group (also crowd)   8 pairs   9 piece/bit   10 bit/drop/(lot)
11 pair   12 bit

32.4   1 *both correct*   2 sheet is wrong   3 gang is wrong
4 *both correct*; group is wrong   5 *both correct*   6 piece is wrong
7 *both correct* (but 'bit' would be more likely)   8 piece is wrong

Unit 33

33.2   1 I need some information.
2 The teacher has (some) news about the school trip.
3 The furniture is very old.
4 I'm looking for a new pair of jeans. *or* I'm looking for (some) new jeans.
5 Your hair is getting very long.
6 Do you have any scissors? *or* Do you have a pair of scissors?
7 We had a lot of homework yesterday.
8 Do you think she's making progress with her English?
9 These trousers are too small.
10 She gave me some good advice.

33.3 Countable: cup; coin
Uncountable: housework; spaghetti; money; travel
Countable and uncountable:
coffee U e.g. I love coffee.
         C e.g. I sat down and ordered a coffee. (= cup of coffee)
work   U e.g. Most people enjoy their work.
         C e.g. The Mona Lisa is a famous work of art.

33.4 1 some scissors/a pair of scissors
2 some sunglasses/a pair of sunglasses
3 some advice/a bit of advice
4 some furniture
5 some scales
6 some headphones/a pair of headphones

33.5 Uncountable nouns: traffic, weather
Plural noun: roadworks

Unit 34

34.1 1 to work   2 to help   3 going   4 to spend   5 to go out/going out
6 eating   7 to work/working   8 going   9 to finish   10 helping

34.2 *Possible ways to complete part (c):*

1 to have a successful career; to be happy; to have children
2 doing housework; waiting at bus stops; going to the dentist
3 getting up late; walking in the country; spending money
4 walking long distances; doing sport; drinking coffee
5 to live until they are 75; to have some disappointments; to meet a person they will love
6 making their bed; cooking their dinner; cleaning their room
7 come home at a certain time; tidy their own rooms; get up at a certain time
8 get up when they like; do what they like; have parties at their home

34.3 2 He offered to lend her the money for the hotel/offered to pay for the hotel.
3 He refused to pay for the flight and her entertainment.
4 She promised to bring him back a present and pay him back in six months.
5 They decided to go to the south of France for two weeks.
6 She forgot to bring him back a present.

Unit 35

35.1 2 He told me it's impossible/He said it's impossible.
3 The teacher is going to explain what to do.
4 She suggested that we go to … /She suggested going to …
5 Can we discuss my report?
6 I want him to leave.
7 You must answer the question.
8 I apologised for my mistake.
9 She advised me to buy a dictionary.
10 I asked the waiter for a knife.

35.2 2 showed/told   3 complained   4 asked   5 tell (*also* warn)   6 persuaded
7 advised/told   8 mention   9 blamed   10 explained

35.3 *Possible answers:*

1 that we go for a meal/stop for lunch
2 them to be quiet/to turn down the music
3 it was great
4 it in class
5 me to pay/me to lend her some
6 him to go/to walk there
7 her to lock her door/ring the police
8 the manager (for the defeat)
9 them not to drink it
10 how it works

35.4 ORDER

1 + object, e.g. He ordered a meal.
2 + object + infinitive, e.g. He ordered us to leave.
3 + 2 objects, e.g. He ordered me a steak.

RECOMMEND

1 + object, e.g. She recommended the school.
2 + 'that' clause, e.g. She recommended that we stay in a hotel.
3 + preposition, e.g. What would you recommend for young children?

PREVENT

1 + object, e.g. I couldn't prevent the accident.
2 + object + preposition, e.g. They prevented us from leaving.

Unit 36

36.1 2 tiny   3 exhausted   4 astonished   5 fascinating
6 marvellous, terrific, great   7 freezing   8 enormous/huge
9 starving   10 terrified

36.2 *Possible answer:*

We're <u>delighted</u> with the hotel – our room is (absolutely) <u>huge</u> and the food is (absolutely) <u>delicious</u>. We've been lucky with the weather as well – it's been hot every day so far, so we've spent most of the time on the beach.

Tomorrow we're planning to walk to a village a couple of kilometres along the coast. In this weather, I'm sure we'll be really <u>exhausted</u> by the time we get back, but it does sound a(n) (absolutely) <u>fascinating</u> place, so I'm looking forward to it.
I'll write again in a couple of days and tell you about it.

36.3 2 terrifying   3 astonished   4 exhausted   5 starving   6 delighted

36.4 2 disappointed   3 embarrassed   4 confused   5 astonished

Unit 37

37.1 1 on   2 in   3 at   4 at   5 in   6 on   7 on   8 at   9 on   10 in

37.2 2 down the hill   3 under the fence/under it   4 out of the car/out of it
5 (in the flat) below me

37.3 1 across   2 through/across   3 into   4 in   5 near
6 along   7 between   8 at/in   9 through/around

Unit 38

38.1
1 My brother often visits us on Sundays.
2 She hardly ever phones me.
3 I have never broken my leg.
4 I hardly ever saw him during the summer.
5 I occasionally get up early. ('occasionally' could also begin or end the sentence)
6 I quite often lose my glasses. ('quite often' could also end the sentence)

38.2
1 hardly ever/rarely   2 quite/pretty   3 nearly   4 slightly
5 incredibly/really   6 often

38.3
2 No, they were rather quiet (actually).
3 No, it's rather clean (actually).
4 No, it was rather good (actually).

38.4
2 He's been getting very/really good marks in his exams.
3 It's a very/really nice house.
4 John said the flat was fairly/quite/rather small.
5 They said it was a bit/slightly boring.
6 The clothes were quite/fairly/rather expensive.

Unit 39

39.1
1 *both*   2 get   3 while   4 leaving
5 *both*   6 just as   7 while   8 *both*

39.2 *Possible answers:*

2 we went for a swim
3 I have finished here/I finish here
4 leaving/I go out
5 he was leaving the house
6 John/Maria looked up the other half
7 the others arrived
8 I don't think I have his number
9 I was coming round the corner
10 I saw her face

39.3 *Possible answers:*

1 And for another, I've got lots of work to do.
2 Then finally we came back through the Loire valley and stayed in Tours for a couple of days.
3 Secondly,/Anyway, we can't really afford it.

39.4 *Possible answer:*

Dear Sir,
I have just returned from a weekend break at The Royal Hotel, and I'm afraid it was not a very enjoyable stay. Firstly, there was very little variety in the food and sometimes no choice at all. Secondly, the service was very slow most of the time and we had to wait half an hour between courses. And finally, when we complained to the head waiter about these delays, he was very rude and the service did not improve.

I sincerely hope that action will be taken to improve the restaurant, and I shall expect a letter of apology and explanation for the very poor standard of service in a hotel with such a fine reputation.

Yours faithfully,

Unit 40

40.1 in addition; as well; also; what's more
although; whereas; however; despite

40.2 1 Although   2 in spite of   3 *both*   4 although   5 whereas
6 *both*   7 However   8 *both*   9 however   10 also

40.3 He went to school today although he didn't feel very well.
He always worked hard at school whereas most of his classmates were lazy.
He's got the right qualifications. What's more, he's the most experienced.
He didn't pass the exam in spite of the help I gave him.
He decided to take the job. However, it's not really what he wants.

40.4 1 Despite/In spite of   2 whereas   3 In addition/What's more   4 However
5 although   6 However   7 as well/too   8 though   9 whereas
10 What's more/In addition

40.5 *Possible answers:*
1 she spoke very quickly
2 the others couldn't
3 the bad weather
4 it's much cheaper
5 I think they'll probably pass
6 I wasn't bored at all

Unit 41

41.1 1 to   2 from   3 with/to   4 in
5 between   6 from   7 with; of   8 in; with

41.2 2 unlike/different from   3 in common   4 in common
5 live at home/have jobs/like sport   6 is lazy/went to university

41.3 2 Manuela is completely different from her brother.
3 Our house is very small compared with/to their houses.
4 Everyone in the class passed the exam except Carla.
5 The two girls have nothing in common.
6 It's free every day apart from Saturday.
7 Everyone liked it with the exception of William.
8 We have similar taste in clothes/We like similar clothes.

Unit 42

42.1 2 I turned up the radio in the lounge **so (that)** I could hear it in the kitchen.
3 The restaurant was full, **so** we went to the bar next door.
4 I stayed at home **because** I was expecting a phone call.
5 It's a very large city, **so** you have to use public transport a lot.
6 I learned to drive **so (that)** my mother didn't have to take me everywhere.

42.2 2 She got the job because of her excellent qualifications.
3 We couldn't eat outside because of the terrible weather.
4 She didn't go to school because of her bad cold.
5 The referee had to stop the game because of the bad light.
6 I was half an hour late because of the heavy traffic.

42.3 1 otherwise 2 unless 3 as long as 4 Unless 5 as long as 6 otherwise

42.4 1 As 2 so that 3 As a result/Therefore 4 unless

42.5 *Possible answers:*

1 I want to improve my English because I will need it in my job very soon.
2 I bought myself a personal stereo so that I could listen to English cassettes on the bus.
3 I usually study English at the weekend as I am very busy during the week.
4 I always write words down in my notebook, otherwise I'll forget them.
5 I don't get many opportunities to practise my English, and therefore I find it difficult to remember everything I study.
6 My brother has got a number of American friends. As a result, he gets a lot of opportunities to practise his English.

Unit 43

43.1 2 moon 3 stars 4 southern 5 behind; ahead 6 in

43.2 2 an ocean 3 a country 4 a desert 5 a river and a rainforest 6 a sea
7 a continent 8 islands 9 mountain in the world 10 Lakes

43.3 1 the 2 – 3 – 4 the 5 – 6 – 7 the 8 – 9 the

43.4 1 hurricane 2 flood 3 earthquake 4 volcano (volcanic eruption)

43.5 1 drowned 2 destroyed 3 diving 4 flew 5 hit 6 climb

Unit 44

44.1 1 foggy 2 snowing 3 cloudy 4 pouring with rain/raining 5 icy 6 sunny

44.2 1 fog 2 breeze 3 lightning 4 shower
5 destroyed 6 comes 7 temperature 8 zero

44.3 2 True 3 True 4 True 5 False (a shower is a short period of rain)
6 False (the air will feel wet or damp) 7 True
8 False (it hardly ever pours with rain in the desert)

44.4 1 blows 2 hot/warm 3 winds/gales 4 snows 5 humid

Unit 45

45.1 1 same 2 different /lepəd/; /mɒskiːtəʊ/ 3 different /beə/; /iːgl/
4 different /gərɪlə/; /dʒɪrɑːf/ 5 same 6 different /mʌŋki/; /mɒskiːtəʊ/
7 different /kæməl/; /sneɪk/ 8 different /lepəd/; /ʃɑːk/ 9 same 10 same

45.2 1 wild 2 danger 3 insects 4 keep 5 ground 6 protect

45.3 *Likely answers:*

FARM ANIMALS: horse, goat, pig, sheep
WILD ANIMALS: monkey, lion, zebra, elephant, tiger, camel, leopard, bear
INSECTS: fly, mosquito, bee, ant

45.4 *Possible answers:*

1 rabbit   2 pigs   3 leopards   4 spiders   5 camels

45.5 *Possible answers:*

2 whales or sharks   3 monkeys or dogs are the most probable answer
4 leopards, lions, tigers and other big cats   5 camels   6 whales
7 monkeys or giraffes   8 snakes   9 elephants   10 sheep

Unit 46

46.1 1 Britain, the United States of America, Canada, Australia   2 Portuguese
3 Swiss-German, French, Italian (A small number of people also speak a language called Romansch.)   4 Arabic   5 Polish   6 Spanish   7 Israel   8 China

46.2 2 the Middle East   3 the Caribbean (also the West Indies)   4 the Mediterranean
5 the Far East   6 South America (also Latin America)

46.3 Ja<u>pan</u>   Japan<u>ese</u>   Egyptian   <u>Arab</u>ic   <u>Ital</u>ian   <u>Austr</u>ia
Kor<u>ea</u>   <u>Chin</u>ese   Germany   Saudi A<u>rab</u>ia   <u>Egypt</u>

46.4 1 the Japanese   2 Israelis   3 Brazilians   4 the British/British people
5 The Swiss/Swiss people   6 Russians

46.5 1 Greece   2 Turkey   3 South Korea   4 Russia   5 Poland   6 Spain

46.7 British people are **generally** polite.
In general, British people are polite.
British people **tend to be** polite.

Unit 47

47.1

47.2

1 forehead
2 cheek
3 chin
4 arm
5 chest
6 hip
7 thigh
8 knee
9 foot
10 toes

11 neck
12 shoulder
13 elbow
14 waist
15 bottom
16 wrist
17 hand
18 fingers
19 heel
20 ankle

47.3   2 bite your nails   3 comb your hair   4 fold your arms
        5 blow your nose   6 nod your head

47.4   *Possible answers:*

       2 running/exercise
       3 they're happy or when someone says something funny
       4 when they're nervous
       5 when they have a cold
       6 when they want to say 'no'
       7 when they mean 'yes'
       8 when they're sad, upset, or possibly when they're very happy
       9 they're tired or bored

Unit 48

48.1   2 hair   3 skin   4 hair   5 height/build   6 shoulders
       7 moustache   8 looking

48.2   2 plain   3 overweight   4 good-looking/handsome   5 slim

48.3   1 What does he/she look like?
       2 How tall is he/she?
       3 How much does he/she weigh?

48.4   *Possible answers:*

       2 I'm roughly 75 kilos.
       3 She's around 1 metre 70.
       4 They're both thirtyish.

Unit 49

49.1

positive	negative
clever	stupid
nice	unpleasant
relaxed	tense
hard-working	lazy
generous	mean

49.2   unfriendly; unreliable; unkind; unpleasant
       inflexible; insensitive
       dishonest

49.3   2 mean   3 unreliable   4 lazy   5 shy
       6 flexible   7 sensitive   8 ambitious

49.4   1 comes; fun   2 make   3 sense   4 confident
       5 show   6 first   7 humour   8 narrow

49.5   kindness   optimism/optimist (person)   punctuality   laziness
       confidence   ambition

Unit 50

50.1 2 pride 3 anger 4 jealousy 5 happiness 6 embarrassment

50.2 2f 3e 4a 5c 6d

50.3 *Possible answers:*

1 They are strolling along a beach.
2 They are pushing a car.
3 He/she is pressing a button.
4 They are whispering.
5 He is waving goodbye (to someone).

50.4 1 glanced 2 whispered 3 strolled 4 march 5 stared 6 shouting

50.5 1 on/at 2 at 3 of 4 at 5 of 6 of

50.6 *Possible answers:*

1 upset/embarrassed 2 frightened/excited 3 angry 4 angry/embarrassed
5 – 6 – 7 mixed feelings (sad to be leaving but happy to be going home) 8 –

Unit 51

51.1 1 John is Jill's brother-in-law.
2 Timothy is Jill's nephew.
3 Eve and Ana are Timothy's cousins.
4 Eve is Sheila's niece.
5 Albert Dodds is Tom's grandfather.
6 Barry is Eve's uncle.
7 Susan is Timothy's aunt.
8 As Paul died in 2000, Jill is a widow.
9 Tom is Mary's grandson.
10 The only two people who are not related are John and Sheila.

51.2 1 first 2 after 3 parent 4 colleagues 5 old 6 ex

Unit 52

52.1 2 retired 3 (mid-) twenties 4 (late) forties (NOT ~~in her middle age~~)
5 (early) thirties 6 elderly/old 7 baby 8 teenager 9 adult
10 adolescence (NOT ~~teenage~~)

52.2 2 False: He grew up in California.
3 False: He went out with Anthea for three years.
4 False: They split up because they had lots of rows.
5 True
6 False: Marie got pregnant a year after they got married.
7 False: Marie is now expecting her second child.
8 False: Sam left Marie.

52.3 2c 3a 4f 5i 6h 7d 8b 9g

Unit 53

53.1 **have:** lunch, dinner, a sleep, a lie-in, a late/an early night, a wash, a shave, a bath/shower, a (lunch) break, a rest, have friends for dinner

53.2   2 fall asleep   3 have a rest   4 play cards   5 go to bed
  6 clean my teeth   7 feed the dog   8 get up early

53.3   2 go out   3 stay in   4 early   5 lie-in
  6 come round   7 play   8 on my own/alone (*or* by myself)

53.4   1 What time do you have breakfast?
  2 In the morning I always <u>leave</u> home at 8 o'clock.
  3 I didn't <u>have a shave</u> this morning. *or* I didn't <u>shave</u> this morning.
  4 I live <u>on my own</u>.
  5 I usually wash <u>my</u> hair every day.
  6 I went to bed and <u>fell asleep/went to sleep</u> very quickly.

53.5   1 up; up   2 in; out   3 round (*or* 'over')

Unit 54

54.1   1 yes   2 yes   3 shut   4 no (the ground floor flats don't have balconies)
  5 no (ground floor)   6 no (a park)

54.2   1 doorbell/bell   2 on   3 climb; lift   4 view   5 steps   6 rent
  7 belongs; condition   8 heat; heating

54.3   *Possible answers:*

positive	negative
2 there's a good view	there's no view
3 it's quiet	it's noisy
4 it's got large rooms	it's got small rooms
5 it's in good condition	it's in bad condition
6 it has central heating/it's warm	it's cold and draughty

Unit 55

55.1   *Likely answers:*

  2 cooking and washing-up
  3 wash and shower (and bath)
  4 sit and relax (and watch TV)
  5 eat meals
  6 guests sleep/where you keep things you don't use all the time
  7 work/study

55.2   2 in the fridge
  3 in the oven
  4 in the washing machine
  5 in the dishwasher or in the sink
  6 in a cupboard
  7 in the freezer

55.3   LIVING ROOM: curtains, carpet, sofa, armchair
  KITCHEN: sink, dishwasher, kettle, oven, fridge, saucepan

55.4   1 in   2 out; back   3 on; in   4 on   5 in   6 out; on

55.6 Turn on/off: oven, cooker, grill, hob, dishwasher, TV, sound system, washing machine, kettle, microwave
Wash: cups and saucers, saucepans, frying pan, food processor
Sit on: sofa, (arm)chair
Boil: kettle, saucepan

Unit 56

56.1 *Most likely order (the first two could be reversed):*

I cleaned my teeth.
I had a wash.
I put on my pyjamas.
I got into bed.
I set the alarm clock.
I switched off the light.
I went to sleep.

56.2 *Possible answers:*

2 He hoovered the living room. 3 He did the ironing. 4 He did the washing.
5 He did the washing-up. 6 He made the bed.

56.4 1 Yes 2 Two pillows 3 Yes 4 Three (that we can see) 5 No 6 Yes

Unit 57

57.1

infinitive	past tense	past participle
break	broke	broken
fall	fell	fallen
spill	spilt (also spilled)	spilt (*also* spilled)
forget	forgot	forgotten
lose	lost	lost
burn	burnt (also burned)	burnt (*also* burned)
cut	cut	cut

57.2 2h 3f 4g 5c 6b 7a 8e

57.3 *Possible answers:*

She broke her glasses; She had/got a stain on her trousers; She burnt the food

57.4 *Possible answers:*

2 I dropped it (on the floor).
3 I fell over/fell off my bike.
4 It's not working properly.
5 (I'm afraid) I lost it.
6 I left it at home.
7 It's not working.
8 It's out of order.

Unit 58

58.1 1 sold; bought 2 lost; cost; found 3 paid
4 gave; spent 5 won 6 wasted

58.2 1 How much is your gold ring worth?
        2 I'm afraid I can't afford it *or* can't afford to go.
        3 Could you lend me some money?
        4 How much did your dictionary cost? *or* How much did you pay for your dictionary?
        5 That disco costs a fortune.

58.3 1 yes   2 no   3 yes   4 no   5 yes   6 no   7 no   8 no

Unit 59

59.1 1 A cold: sneezing, a sore throat, a cough
        2 Flu: sneezing, a sore throat, a cough, a high temperature (aching muscles)
        3 A hangover: headache, feeling sick
        4 Diarrhoea: keep going to the toilet

59.2 1 different   2 same   3 same   4 different   5 different   6 different

59.3 1 a   2 –   3 – ('a' is possible)   4 a   5 –   6 –

59.4 *Possible answer:*

      I had terrible toothache, so I made an appointment to see the dentist. She had a look at the tooth and decided that I needed a filling. She gave me an injection, which was quite painful, but afterwards it felt much better.

59.5 1 feel   2 hurts   3 get/have   4 attack   5 ache
        6 pain   7 lung   8 prescription   9 disease   10 aches

Unit 60

60.2

noun	verb	noun	verb
cut	cut	blood	bleed
injury	injure	bruise	bruise
shot	shoot	treatment	treat

60.3 *Possible answer:*

      Paul somehow fell from the tree where he was picking apples and he knocked himself unconscious. His wife immediately rang for an ambulance and it soon arrived and he was rushed to hospital. He had to have a number of stitches for a large cut on the side of his head, but fortunately it wasn't serious.

60.4 2a   3f   4e   5c   6b

Unit 61

61.1 *Possible answers:*

      shoes, socks, jeans, gloves, tights

61.2 2g, 3a, 4c, 5e, 6i, 7b, 8h, 9f

61.3 an earring, a ring, a button, a pocket, a necklace

61.4 *Possible answers:*

      1 top or blouse; skirt   2 suit; trousers   3 tie; shirt   4 do
      5 enough; size   6 too; enough

61.5 *Possible answers:*

worn by women: dress, top, blouse, skirt, tights, necklace
worn by men and women: hat, gloves, jeans, trousers, jacket, scarf, coat

Unit 62

62.1 2 clothes   3 vegetables   4 furniture   5 electrical appliances   6 jewellery
7 toys   8 stationery

62.2 butcher: chicken
newsagent: envelopes, notebook
chemist: aspirin, toothbrush
supermarket: aspirin, envelopes, toothbrush, chicken, grapes, notebook, bananas, loaf of bread, carrots
department store: envelopes, gloves, armchair, notebook

Possible answers:

butcher: steak, sausages, bacon, lamb
newsagent: cigarettes, sweets, greeting cards
chemist: soap, shampoo, perfume, toothpaste
supermarket: coffee, wine, cakes, biscuits, cheese
department store: clothes, washing machines, saucepans

62.3 1 butcher('s)   2 shopping centre   3 shop/sales assistant
4 changing/fitting room   5 till/cash desk   6 window shopping
7 off-licence   8 chemist('s)

62.4 1 looking for   2 size   3 being served/just looking
4 changing room   5 take it

Unit 63

63.1 1 potato/peas; peach/pear   2 beans/broccoli; banana   3 mushroom; melon
4 carrot/cauliflower/cabbage/celery; cherry   5 aubergine; apple

63.2 lett<u>u</u>ce/ch<u>i</u>cken
<u>o</u>range/br<u>o</u>ccoli
<u>au</u>bergine/tomat<u>o</u>
r<u>a</u>spberry/c<u>a</u>lf
<u>o</u>nion/m<u>u</u>shroom
s<u>a</u>lmon/l<u>a</u>mb
pr<u>aw</u>n/p<u>or</u>k

63.3 2 leeks; the others are common in salad but leeks aren't
3 peach; the others are vegetables but a peach is a fruit
4 crab; the others are types of meat but crab is a type of seafood
5 aubergine; the others are types of fruit but an aubergine is a vegetable

63.4 *Most likely answers:*

always	sometimes	never
cherries grapes strawberries	apple peach pear	banana pineapple melon orange

63.5 1 beef   2 veal   3 pork   4 lettuce   5 vinegar or lemon juice

Unit 64

64.1 *Typical answers for Britain:*

raw fish (no)   fried rice (yes)
fried eggs (yes)   baked potatoes (yes)
roast beef (yes)   raw spinach (in salad, but not very common)
roast peppers (yes)   boiled eggs (yes)
grilled cheese (yes, usually on toast) baked bananas (yes, as a dessert)

64.2 2 spaghetti with courgette and bacon
3 steak
4 roast fillet of pork
5 steak in a <u>pepper sauce</u>
6 breast of chicken in a <u>white wine</u> sauce
7 ice cream and chocolate mousse
8 probably the salmon

64.3 *Possible answers:*

lemon: sour   bacon: salty/tasty
bread: fresh   fillet steak: rare/well-done
cakes: fattening/sweet   mineral water: still/sparkling
                           coffee: sweet/bitter

Unit 65

65.1 2g   3b   4f   5c   6h   7a   8e

65.2 2 cultural activities   3 wide range; whatever (*or* anything)
4 nightlife   5 opportunities   6 cope; commuters

65.3

towns and cities	villages in the countryside
dirty/polluted	clean air
dangerous	safe
traffic congestion/congested	not much traffic
lots to do/good nightlife	nothing to do in the evening

Unit 66

66.1 2 grass   3 leaves   4 plants   5 roots   6 flowers

66.2 1 in   2 up   3 on   4 by   5 of   6 about

66.3 1 gate   2 tractor   3 footpath   4 field
5 valley   6 woods   7 village

66.4 1 countryside   2 agriculture   3 crops   4 rural
5 village   6 wood   7 cottage   8 transport

66.5 1 thing   2 quiet   3 fresh   4 surrounded
5 pace   6 worst   7 nightlife   8 privacy

Unit 67

67.1   2 junction   3 keep going   4 turn   5 get (also come)   6 school
7 turn right   8 Maldon   9 on   10 after

67.2   1 accident   2 service   3 injured; damaged
4 blocked; tailback (also traffic jam)   5 pavement   6 broke down
7 overtook   8 crashed   9 pedestrians

67.3   1 You can't park/wait   2 50 mph is the speed limit   3 You can't turn right
4 There is only one lane   5 End of motorway   6 Car park
7 Traffic lights   8 Low bridge   9 Roadworks

Unit 68

68.1   1 ride   2 get in   3 fare   4 run
5 fly   6 timetable   7 get   8 missed

68.2   *Possible answers:*

1 bus fare; train fare; air fare; taxi fare
2 get on the bus; get on the coach; get on the train; get on the plane
3 bus station; railway station; coach station
4 bus driver; train driver; taxi driver; van driver; lorry driver
5 get in the car; get in the taxi; get in the van; get in the lorry (People also sometimes say 'get in the bus' or 'get in the train'.)
6 train journey; bus journey; car journey; coach journey

68.3   1 coach   2 van   3 lorry   4 motorbike   5 bike/bicycle

68.4   1 platform   2 bus stop   3 full (up)   4 pilot
5 punctual   6 queue   7 journey   8 due

Unit 69

69.1   1d   2e   3a   4b   5c

69.2   1e   2a   3d   4b   5c

69.3   1 What's your job?
2 I work for the government.
3 My salary is $50,000.
4 My total income is £30,000.
5 My job involves looking after all the computers.
6 I'm in charge of one of the departments.

69.4   A: What are your working hours?
A: Do you do/work any overtime?
A: How much holiday/how many weeks holiday do you get?
A: Do you get sick pay?

Unit 70

70.1   *Possible answers:*

2 a pilot   3 a sailor   4 a mechanic   5 a police officer
6 a vet   7 a firefighter   8 an accountant   9 a doctor, nurse, surgeon, or vet
10 someone in the army, navy or air force

70.2 2 designs buildings   3 controls the financial situation of people and companies
4 treats animals   5 represents people with legal problems
6 plans the building of roads, bridges, machines, etc.   7 builds walls
8 buys and sells shares   9 repairs cars   10 operates on people

70.3 1 Really? When did she join the army?   2 Really? When did he join the navy?
3 Really? When did he join the air force?   4 Really? When did he join the fire brigade?

70.4 *Possible answers:*

an architect to design the house
a lawyer to give legal advice
a carpenter to make cupboards and fit doors
a plumber to fit the kitchen and bathroom
an electrician to do all the electrical work
an accountant to calculate how much everything will cost

Unit 71

71.1 2 unemployed   3 resign/quit   4 promoted
5 prospects   6 retire   7 employees   8 take over

71.2 1b   2e   3d   4a   5f   6c

71.3 1 abroad   2 part-time   3 course   4 challenge
5 rise   6 her   7 over   8 earn/get

71.4

verb	general noun	person
manage	management	manager
promote	promotion	–
employ	employment	employer (boss)/employee (worker)
resign	resignation	–
retire	retirement	–
train	training	trainer (gives the training)/trainee (receives it)

Unit 72

72.1 2 appointment   3 drawer   4 meeting   5 computer
6 e-mail   7 reports   8 letter   9 visitors   10 minutes

72.2 1 noticeboard   2 filing cabinet   3 briefcase
4 paperwork   5 wastepaper basket/bin

72.3 2 The photocopier isn't working.
3 We've got loads of work today.
4 The computer is down.
5 We've run out of paper for the photocopier.

72.4 2 calendar   3 diary   4 invoice   5 factory   6 agenda

Unit 73

73.1 1 loan   2 interest   3 inflation   4 turnover   5 it breaks even   6 overheads

73.2 1 by 2 from; to 3 of 4 to 5 in 6 in

73.3 1 fell 2 gradual 3 be successful 4 aim 5 expand 6 goes up/rises

73.4 1 rose 2 fell slightly 3 sharp fall
4 steady rise 5 rose sharply 6 rose by 60,000

73.5 1 loss 2 interest/inflation 3 cut/increase
4 materials 5 economy 6 political/economic

Unit 74

74.1

infinitive	past tense	past participle
win	won	won
lose	lost	lost
beat	beat	beaten
catch	caught	caught
draw	drew	drawn

74.2 head it; pass it; catch it; throw it; hit it; kick it; drop it

74.3 *Possible answers:*

1 tennis, table tennis, baseball, hockey, squash, cricket, golf
2 football, rugby, American football, basketball, volleyball
3 rugby, American football, cricket, baseball, basketball, football (goalkeeper only)
4 football, rugby, American football
5 football

74.4 1 score/result 2 beat 3 drew 4 stadium
5 spectators/crowd 6 winner(s) 7 leading 8 latest

74.5

sport	place	equipment
football	pitch	boots, training shoes, net, whistle
tennis	court	training shoes, racket, net
golf	course	clubs

Unit 75

75.1

sport	place	equipment
swimming	pool	trunks, costume
motor racing	circuit	crash helmet
ice hockey	rink	sticks, skates, puck

75.2 1 do 2 play 3 join 4 support
5 gave up/stopped 6 go 7 take up 8 get/be/keep

75.3 2 fit 3 climbing 4 opposite 5 seriously
6 hockey 7 racing 8 up 9 gym/pool 10 you/me

Unit 76

76.1 1 stalls 2 C 3 yes 4 yes

76.2 1d 2g 3f 4a 5h 6e 7b 8c

76.3 1 musical 2 audience 3 director 4 critics
5 reviews 6 subtitles 7 to book 8 stars

76.4 1 set 2 love 3 about 4 background/family
5 away 6 at 7 wrong 8 romantic comedy

76.5 1 war film 2 romantic comedy 3 action film
4 horror film 5 horror film 6 thriller

Unit 77

77.1 2 violinist 3 guitarist 4 cellist 5 drummer

77.2 1 instrument 2 classical; composer 3 choir 4 out/released; one
5 produced (recorded or released are also possible) 6 latest (new is also possible)

77.3 1 orchestra 2 group/band; solo 3 plays; performs/sings
4 single/record; album 5 opera 6 lead 7 jazz 8 singles/records
9 guitarist 10 lead

77.4 1 songs/music 2 taste 3 record (CD)/single 4 hit 5 released/produced

Unit 78

78.2 1 in; about 2 of 3 for 4 in 5 to

78.3 1 comes 2 daily 3 monthly 4 journalists/reporters 5 headline
6 photographers 7 article/report 8 review 9 advertisements/adverts
10 According

78.4 *Possible answers:*

2 Japan and the US are going to start fresh discussions
3 Germany supports the US plan/has decided to support the …
4 The police have discovered an important witness
5 The government is going to reduce spending on new hospitals
6 (The) bad weather has had a bad effect on the railway service
7 Ministers are in a new argument over tax
8 There will be a new attempt to reduce teenage smoking

Unit 79

79.1 *Possible answers:*

2 Could you turn it up?
3 Could you turn/switch over?
4 Could you turn it down?
5 Could you turn/switch it off?

79.2 Documentary: World in Action and Cutting Edge
Quiz show: Telly Addicts
Game show: Bruce's Price is Right (The Krypton Factor is also a game show)
Drama series: Cracker
Current affairs: World in Action

Comedy series: 2 Point 4 Children
Soap operas: EastEnders and Coronation Street

79.3 1 on; operas 2 highlights 3 on; repeat

Unit 80

80.1 *Possible answers:*

phone card; phone box; phone call; phone directory; answerphone; mobile phone; public phone; on the phone

80.2 1 speak to 2 Speaking 3 My name is 4 message
5 out/not here/in a meeting 6 back 7 (phone) number
8 Is that 9 here/in 10 be 11 leave 12 message
13 give 14 ring/call 15 (phone) number 16 Is that
17 This is/It's 18 through 19 engaged 20 on

Unit 81

81.1 2 floppy disk 3 user-friendly 4 Internet Service Provider 5 keyboard
6 e-mail address 7 laser printer 8 laptop 9 back-up copy 10 websites

81.2 1 save the data in this document 2 cut 3 open a new document 4 copy
5 print 6 open an existing document 7 paste

81.3 1 printed; crashed 2 connect 3 download 4 virus
5 checked; sent 6 browsing 7 search 8 at; dot

Unit 82

82.1 2 science 3 technology 4 art 5 French 6 history
7 English 8 geography 9 music 10 chemistry

82.2 1 3 2 5 3 11 4 16 5 go to university or college/get a job

82.3 1 divided 2 lessons 3 breaks
4 pupils 5 subjects 6 terms

82.4 2 into hospital 3 to bed 4 to university 5 to church 6 to prison

82.5 1 I failed my exam. 2 I did very badly.
3 I'm hopeless/terrible/not very good at English. 4 I got a very low mark.

Unit 83

83.1 2 medicine/biology 3 agriculture/chemistry 4 psychology 5 business studies
6 history of art 7 politics 8 law

83.2 1 a grant 2 a degree 3 undergraduates 4 lecturers
5 graduates 6 postgraduates 7 research 8 lectures

83.3 1 get 2 go to 3 doing 4 get 5 lasts/goes on for

83.4 1 at 2 in 3 doing; in(to)/on 4 postgraduate/Masters 5 department

Unit 84

84.1 1c 2i 3g 4h 5b 6f 7d 8a 9e

84.2 2 the judge 3 prisoners 4 the jury 5 barristers (lawyers) 6 criminals

84.3 1 broken   2 committed   3 against   4 illegal   5 fine
6 prove   7 guilty   8 evidence   9 sentence   10 offence

84.4 *Possible answers (for Britain):*

1 Yes
2 Visit the owner and the house that was broken into and take fingerprints if possible
3 Probably not (less than 50% of burglars are caught)
4 Burglary
5 No, not at 15
6 Probably a suspended sentence (= the boys are free but if they commit another crime in the next year or two years, they will receive a much tougher punishment) unless the boys already have a record for burglary. In this case, they could be sent to a centre for young offenders.

Unit 85

85.1

crime	person
murder	murderer
burglary	burglar
theft	thief
shoplifting	shoplifter

85.2 2 murder   3 with shoplifting   4 charged with manslaughter
5 been charged with theft

85.3 2d   3f   4a   5b   6e

85.5 1 carry/have   2 allowed/able/permitted   3 punishment   4 reduce/prevent

Unit 86

86.1 1 monarchy   2 republic/democracy   3 dictatorship

86.2

general noun	person
democracy	democrat
politics	politician
conservatism	conservative

verb	general noun
elect	election
govern	government
vote	vote

86.3 1 Elections are held every five years.
2 The government is left-wing.
3 I believe in democracy.
4 Who is in power at the moment?

86.4 1 elections   2 Prime   3 vote   4 party
5 votes   6 majority   7 leader   8 policies

Unit 87

87.2 landing card; birth/marriage certificate; driving licence; application/enrolment form

87.3 2 checked   3 fill   4 sign   5 signature
6 runs out/expires; renew   7 surname/family name   8 enrolment/registration

87.5 2 Where do you come from?/Where are you from?
3 Are you single or married?
4 When did you arrive?
5 When are you leaving?/When do you leave?

87.6 *Problems mentioned were:*

- Delays, e.g. in getting a new passport
- Officials putting the wrong information on documents, which then need to be changed, e.g. driving licence
- Officials losing information you have given them
- Being asked to explain the same information over and over again to different officials, especially over the telephone
- Spending a long time getting a document in one country, then discovering that nobody is interested in it when you arrive in another country
- Officials who behave like policemen

Unit 88

88.2

noun	verb
waste	waste
pollution	pollute
damage	damage

noun	verb
protection	protect
destruction	destroy
survival	survive

88.3 1 recycle
2 waste; save/conserve
3 cut down/destroy; protect

88.4 1b   2d   3a   4c

88.5 1 carbon dioxide   2 terrible happens (and people often die)   3 food
4 rain   5 rain   6 fighting between two or more groups   7 the same country
8 kill (a famous person, usually for political reasons)   9 army
10 in the armed forces (army, navy or air force)

88.6 *Possible answers:*

1 plane/bus   2 President/Prime Minister   3 bomb
4 hostages/prisoners   5 killed/injured/wounded   6 settlement

Unit 89

89.1 1 boarding card   2 excess baggage   3 check-in desk
4 flight number   5 overhead locker   6 departure lounge
7 baggage reclaim   8 passport control   9 hand luggage

89.2 1 check-in (desk)   2 boarding card   3 excess baggage   4 hand luggage
5 overhead locker   6 runway   7 cabin crew   8 hire

89.3 1 delay   2 cards   3 lounge
4 customs   5 luggage (also 'bags')   6 board

89.4 1 took off   2 captain/pilot   3 fasten   4 flew
5 crew   6 landed   7 get off   8 flight/journey

Unit 90

90.1 *Hotel:* 1g   2i   3b   4d   5k   6h   7e   8f   9j   10a   11c
Restaurant: 1f   2i   3d   4k   5h   6a   7j   8g   9b   10e   11c

90.2 1 bill   2 board   3 room (or twin-bedded room)   4 available ('free' is possible)
5 lift   6 order   7 wine   8 meal   9 have   10 included

90.3 *Possible answers:*

2 I'd like to book a double room for next weekend. *or* Do you have any double rooms available next weekend?

3 Could you order a taxi for me, please? *or* Could I pay my bill, please?

4 How do I get to the nearest bank from here? *or* Could you tell me the way to the nearest bank, please?

Unit 91

91.1 1 time   2 sightseeing   3 packed   4 look   5 galleries
6 lost   7 market/place   8 go out   9 spent   10 photos/pictures

91.3 *Possible answers:*

1 Yes, it's a great place.
2 Yes, it's very cosmopolitan.
3 Yes, it was (absolutely) packed.
4 Yes, the nightlife is very good.
5 Yes, we had a great time.
6 Yes, Kyoto is definitely worth seeing/worth a visit.

Unit 92

92.1 *Possible answers:*

suntan; sunbathe; sunburn; sunblock

92.2 2d   3e   4a   5f   6c

92.3 1 playing volleyball   2 windsurfing   3 paddling   4 sunbathing

92.4 *Vertical:* cool down, tan, brown, camping
Horizontal: calm, towel, rock(s), cliff, horizon, swim, skin

92.5 1 go   2 spend   3 rent   4 go   5 lying/sitting/being   6 get

Unit 93

93.1 1 at   2 in   3 at   4 in   5 on   6 at
7 On   8 at   9 on   10 at   11 in   12 on

93.2 1 by   2 until   3 since   4 for   5 during   6 for   7 in   8 in

93.3 2 the other day   3 recently/lately   4 for ages   5 for the time being

93.4 1 two   2 19th; 20th   3 1963; 40
4 eight   5 ten

Possible answers:

    1 7; 8   2 the morning   3 Saturdays   4 August   5 two years
    6 1999   7 last Wednesday   8 40 minutes   9 you're 17   10 October

Unit 94

94.1
1 four hundred and sixty-two
2 two and a half
3 two thousand three hundred and forty-five
4 nought point two five
5 one million two hundred and fifty thousand
6 ten point oh four (*or* nought four)
7 forty-seven per cent
8 the tenth of April (*or* April the tenth)
9 the third of July (*or* July the third)
10 six oh two eight four seven seven (*or* double seven)
11 five degrees below zero (*or* minus five degrees centigrade)
12 nineteen seventy-six

94.2
1 **thousand**   2 the **fourth of** August   3 two hundred **and** twenty
4 the **thirty-first of** August   5 seven **two three** six **oh** nine

94.3
1 majority   2 minority   3 calculator   4 work   5 stuck

94.4
1 59   2 192   3 60   4 5   5 8   6 15

94.5
Answers to questions 6 and 7:

    6 thirty seven point six (degrees)   7 approximately one point six kilometres in a mile

Unit 95

95.1
Possible answers:

1 It's about two minutes' walk.
2 It's about a kilometre.
3 No, it isn't.
4 Yes, it's too far to walk.
5 Yes, quite a long way.
6 It's about 20 kilometres.
7 It's about 15 minutes' walk.
8 No, not far.

95.2
Possible questions:

What's the size of the lake?
How deep is it? *or* What's the depth of the lake?
How far is it from one side of the lake to the other?
How high is the mountain? *or* What's the height of the mountain?
How long is the pitch? *or* What's the length of the pitch?
How wide is the pitch? *or* What's the width of the pitch?
How tall is she?

95.3
1 No, he's quite thin.
2 No, it's quite shallow.
3 No, it's quite narrow.

4 No, he's fairly short.
5 No, it's quite big (*or* it's a great big place).
6 No, it's great/really interesting/very lively.

Unit 96

96.1 1 square 2 rectangular 3 round 4 pointed

96.2 1 grey 2 pink 3 beige 4 purple 5 turquoise

96.3 2 a star-shaped ring 3 a round mirror 4 a pointed nose
5 diamond-shaped earrings 6 a striped sofa 7 a light blue shirt
8 a dark blue jumper 9 a tartan tie

96.4 1 a pencil 2 a football/rugby/hockey pitch 3 a carrot 4 the moon
5 the sea 6 an egg 7 a (coat/clothes) hanger 8 prawns

Unit 97

97.1 *Possible answers:*

Please queue other side
Mind the step
Sold out
Out of order
Keep right; Keep off the grass
Beware of pickpockets
Mind your head
Please do not disturb; Please do not feed the animals
No exit; No smoking; No parking

97.2 *Possible answers:*

2 in a Bed & Breakfast (cheap hotel) 6 outside a theatre/cinema/concert hall
3 on the underground 7 on the outside of a parcel/package
4 in a bank or post office 8 in a park
5 by a public telephone

97.3 1 Please do not feed the animals 5 Do not lean out of the window
2 Do not leave bags unattended 6 No smoking
3 Please do not disturb 7 Keep right; No smoking; No exit
4 No parking 8 Mind your head

Unit 98

98.1 *Possible answers:*

2 the key 3 whisky 4 knives and forks 5 flour
6 programme 7 clothes/belongings 8 a type of toy
9 a suitcase 10 shampoo/conditioner

98.2 *Possible answers:*

1 About/Around/Roughly 2 sort of 3 things 4 a bit 5 sort of/a bit
6 and things/stuff like that *or* and that sort of thing 7 more or less/or so 8 a bit

Possible answers:

  2 sort of/blueish   3 more or less/roughly   4 sort of
  5 a bit/sort of   6 any time

Unit 99

99.1

formal	informal
purchase	handy
resume	loo
thus	terrific
commence	quid
apprehend	reckon
	guy
	cheers

99.2 so/thus   buy/purchase   convenient/handy   catch/apprehend
          start/commence   man/guy   start again/resume   pounds/quid
          thanks/cheers   think/reckon   marvellous/terrific   toilet/loo

99.3 1 Where did you buy/get that book?
          2 I'm just going to the loo.
          3 The woman on the desk told us to go to gate 12.
          4 What's up?
          5 Do you fancy going out for a meal?
          6 When are you going to pick up your bike?
          7 My flat is five minutes from where I work, so it's very handy.
          8 The guy in the market wanted 20 quid for this ring.
          9 Most of the kids are very bright.
          10 I reckon it'll start pretty soon.

99.4 We <u>regret to inform you</u> that we <u>are unable to</u> lend you the sum of £500 that you <u>require</u>, but it may be possible to …

          If you would like to contact the branch and <u>speak to</u> Mrs Jenkins, she will <u>arrange</u> an appointment with the assistant manager. He will …

99.5 a drag (*infml*) = boring
          pinched (*infml*) = stolen
          patrons (*fml*) = People who use a hotel/restaurant or shop. The word patron often appears on notices in hotel or restaurant car parks.
          bloke (*infml*) = man
          hassle (*infml*) = trouble or inconvenience
          permitted (*fml*) = allowed

Unit 100

100.1 1 British Broadcasting Corporation   2 Member of Parliament
           3 World Wide Web   4 Compact Disc   5 Prime Minister
           6 United Nations   7 Personal Computer   8 Identification

100.2 Michael,

Peter had a <u>maths exam</u> this afternoon and then he had to take his <u>bike</u> to the repair shop, so he'll probably be a bit late home. You can watch <u>TV/telly</u> while you're waiting for him, and please help yourself to anything in the <u>fridge</u>. If there's a problem (<u>e.g.</u> <u>Dr</u> Brown rings about the <u>flu</u> vaccination), my <u>phone</u> number is next to the <u>photos</u> on the dining room table. I should be home myself by about five.

Margaret (Peter's <u>mum</u>)

100.3 1 e.g. 2 etc. 3 St 4 i.e. 5 Mr 6 Dr

100.4 2 e.g. 3 CV 4 board 5 etc. 6 flu 7 ad(vert)
8 fridge 9 i.e. 10 stand

100.5 PTO stands for 'please turn over' at the bottom of a page.

RSVP means 'please reply' (from the French 'répondez, s'il vous plaît') and is found at the bottom of formal invitations, e.g. to a reception or wedding.

ASAP/asap stands for 'as soon as possible' and is commonly used in e-mails and faxes.

CC/cc stands for 'carbon copy' and is used in business letters and e-mails to show you are sending a copy to someone else. In the past, carbon copies were made using carbon paper. We don't use this any more, but we still use the abbreviation.

Phonemic symbols

Vowel sounds

Symbol	Examples		
/iː/	sleep	me	
/i/	happy	recipe	
/ɪ/	pin	dinner	
/ʊ/	foot	could	pull
/uː/	do	shoe	through
/e/	red	head	said
/ə/	arrive	father	colour
/ɜː/	turn	bird	work
/ɔː/	sort	thought	walk
/æ/	cat	black	
/ʌ/	sun	enough	wonder
/ɒ/	got	watch	sock
/ɑː/	part	heart	laugh
/eɪ/	name	late	aim
/aɪ/	my	idea	time
/ɔɪ/	boy	noise	
/eə/	pair	where	bear
/ɪə/	hear	beer	
/əʊ/	go	home	show
/aʊ/	out	cow	
/ʊə/	pure	fewer	

Consonant sounds

Symbol	Examples		
/p/	put		
/b/	book		
/t/	take		
/d/	dog		
/k/	car	kick	
/g/	go	guarantee	
/tʃ/	catch	church	
/dʒ/	age	lounge	
/f/	for	cough	
/v/	love	vehicle	
/θ/	thick	path	
/ð/	this	mother	
/s/	since	rice	
/z/	zoo	houses	
/ʃ/	shop	sugar	machine
/ʒ/	pleasure	usual	vision
/h/	hear	hotel	
/m/	make		
/n/	name	now	
/ŋ/	bring		
/l/	look	while	
/r/	road		
/j/	young		
/w/	wear		

Pronunciation problems

when 'a' is /eɪ/	when 'u' is /ʌ/	when 'i' is /aɪ/	when 'o' or 'oo' is /ʌ/
patient	punctual	pilot	gloves
Asia	luggage	virus	oven
dangerous	hungry	dial	month
pavement	discuss	hepatitis	front
bacon	function	minus	monkey
phrase	publish	licence	government
engaged	customs	diet	worry
sunbathe	luck	striped	flood
lately	bankrupt	tiny	blood

When ow is /əʊ/, e.g. row (= line), throw, blow, show, know, elbow
When ou or ow is /aʊ/, e.g. lounge, drought, row (= argument), towel, allowed, blouse, shower
When ou is /uː/, e.g. soup, group, through, wound, souvenir, routine
When ou is /ʌ/, e.g. cousin, couple, trouble, tough, rough, enough
When a, au or aw is /ɔː/, e.g. draw, raw, law, stall, fall, cause, audience, launch, exhausted
When a or au is /ɑː/, e.g. vase, calm, laugh, draughty, half
When a or u is /ɪ/, e.g. busy, business, minute, lettuce, purchase, surface, orange, damage
When o is /uː/, e.g. move, prove, improve, lose
When or or ur is /ɜː/, e.g. purple, burn, burglary, worth, work, curtain
When ea is /e/, e.g. dreadful, jealous, health, dead, bread, instead, pleasant, weather, weapon

Silent letters (the underlined letters are silent):
island, knee, knife, know, knock, knowledge, wrong, wrist, muscle, castle, whistle, fasten, listen, bomb, lamb, thumb, comb, scissors, psychology, honest, hour, cupboard, answer, guess, handsome, aisle, half, calm, Christmas, mortgage

Short syllables (the underlined letters often disappear or are only /ə/):
fattening, miserable, comfortable, fashionable, restaurant, strawberry, eventually, parliament, actually, occasionally, prisoner, medicine, favourite, temperature, literature

Problem pairs:
quite /kwaɪt/ and quiet /'kwaɪət/   desert /'dezət/ and dessert /də'zɜːt/   soup /suːp/ and soap /səʊp/

Note:
The pronunciation of these letters at the end of words is often like this:
-ous /əs/, e.g. famous, dangerous, unconscious, ambitious, cautious, jealous
-age /ɪdʒ/, e.g. luggage, baggage, village, damage, cabbage, bandage, message, manage
-able /əbl/, e.g. comfortable, reliable, suitable, unbreakable, vegetable, fashionable, miserable
-are /eə/, e.g. care, spare, square, beware, stare, fare, aware, rare(ly), barely
-ile /aɪl/, e.g. fragile, mobile, file, while
-tory/tary /təri/, e.g. directory, history, secretary, documentary
-ture /tʃə/, e.g. picture, signature, departure, capture, temperature, literature, feature
-ate /eɪt/ at the end of verbs, e.g. educate, operate, communicate
-ate /ət/ at the end of nouns and adjectives, e.g. graduate, approximate, certificate

Index

bureaucrat /'bjʊərəkræt/ 87

burglar /'bɜːglə/ 85

burglar alarm /'bɜːglə əˌlɑːm/ 85

burglary /'bɜːgləri/ 85

burn (n, v) /bɜːn/ 60

burn (v) 57

bus /bʌs/ 68

bus driver /'bʌs ˌdraɪvə/ 7, 10

bus station /'bʌs ˌsteɪʃən/ 68

bus stop /'bʌs ˌstɒp/ 10, 68

business studies /'bɪznɪs ˌstʌdiz/ 83

busy /'bɪzi/ 90

but /bʌt/ 40

butcher /'bʊtʃə/ 62

butterfly /'bʌtəflaɪ/ 45

button /'bʌtən/ 61

buy /baɪ/ 70

by (a book by Dickens, etc.) /baɪ/ 15

by (10%) 73

by (8.15) 93

by accident /baɪ 'æksɪdənt/ 15

by bus/car/taxi, etc. 15, 68

by chance (meet somebody by chance) /baɪ 'tʃɑːns/ 15

by hand (made by hand) /baɪ 'hænd/ 15

by mistake (take something by mistake) /baɪ mɪ'steɪk/ 15

by myself /baɪ maɪ'self/ 15

cabbage /'kæbɪdʒ/ 63

cabin crew /'kæbɪn kruː/ 89

cable TV /'keɪbl ˌtiː'viː/ 79

calculator /'kælkjəleɪtə/ 72, 94

calendar /'kæləndə/ 72

calf /kɑːf/ 63

call (n) (local/international) /kɔːl/ 80

calm (sea) /kɑːm/ 92

camel /'kæməl/ 45

camping (go/do a lot of) /kæmpɪŋ/ 75

can (of cola) /kæn/ 32

cancel /'kænsəl/ 16

can't stand /ˌkɑːnt stænd/ 19

can't stand (+ -ing) 34

capital (city) /'kæpɪtəl/ 46

capital punishment 85

captain (= pilot) /'kæptɪn/ 89

car /kɑː/ 68

car park /'kɑː pɑːk/ 65

career /kə'rɪə/ 71

careful /'keəfəl/ 8, 35

careless /'keələs/ 8

Caribbean (the Caribbean) /ˌkærɪ'biːən/ 46

carpenter /'kɑːpəntə/ 70

carpet /'kɑːpɪt/ 55

carrot /'kærət/ 63

carry a gun /'kæri/ 85

carry on 3, 23

carton (of orange juice) /'kɑːtən/ 32

case (= suitcase) /keɪs/ 100

cash desk /'kæʃ ˌdesk/ 62

cash machine /'kæʃ məˌʃiːn/ 10

cassette /kə'set/ 5

cassette recorder /kə'set rɪkɔːdə/ 5

castle /'kɑːsl/ 91

catch (I didn't catch that) /kætʃ/ 28

catch a ball 28, 74

catch a bus/train 12, 28, 68

catch a cold/flu 28

catch a criminal 28, 84

catch (somebody doing something) 28

cathedral /kə'θiːdrəl/ 91

cauliflower /'kɒlɪˌflaʊə/ 63

CD (compact disc) /ˌsiː'diː/ 100

CD player /ˌsiː'diː ˌpleɪə/ 55

CD-ROM /ˌsiːdiː'rɒm/ 81

celery /'seləri/ 63

cellist /'tʃelɪst/ 77

cello /'tʃeləʊ/ 77

central heating /ˌsentrəl 'hiːtɪŋ/ 54

century /'senʃəri/ 93

certificate (exam/marriage) /sə'tɪfɪkət/ 87

chalk /tʃɔːk/ 5

change (bus/train) /tʃeɪndʒ/ 68

change (into other clothes) 61

change my mind 13

changing room /'tʃeɪndʒɪŋ ruːm/ 62

channel (TV) /'tʃænəl/ 79

charge (money) /tʃɑːdʒ/ 58

charge (somebody with a crime) 84

chat (n, v) /tʃæt/ 9

chat room /'tʃæt ˌruːm/ 10

chat show /'tʃæt ˌʃəʊ/ 79

cheap /tʃiːp/ 58

check (= examine) /tʃek/ 87, 89

check (adj) 96

check in (v) /tʃek 'ɪn/ 90

check out (v) /ˌtʃek 'aʊt/ 90

check (the meaning) 3

check-in (desk) /'tʃekɪn/ 89

cheek /tʃiːk/ 47

cheers /tʃɪəz/ 22, 99

chemist /'kemɪst/ 59, 62

chemistry /'kemɪstri/ 82

cherry /'tʃeri/ 63

chest /tʃest/ 47

chest of drawers /ˌtʃest əv 'drɔːz/ 56

chicken /'tʃɪkɪn/ 63

childhood /'tʃaɪldhʊd/ 52

chilled /tʃɪld/ 64

chilly /'tʃɪli/ 44

chimney /'tʃɪmni/ 54

chin /tʃɪn/ 47

China /'tʃaɪnə/ 46

Chinese /tʃaɪ'niːz/ 46

choice /tʃɔɪs/ 1, 3

choir /kwaɪə/ 77

choose /tʃuːz/ 1, 3

chop (v) /tʃɒp/ 63

circle /'sɜːkl/ 96

circle (theatre) 76

circuit (racing) /'sɜːkɪt/ 75

circulation /ˌsɜːkjə'leɪʃən/ 78

civil war /ˌsɪvəl 'wɔː/ 88

civilian /sɪ'vɪliən/ 88

clap /klæp/ 50

classical music /ˌklæsɪkəl 'mjuːzɪk/ 77

classmate /'klɑːsmeɪt/ 51

clean (v, adj) /kliːn/ 9

clean (v) 5

clean my teeth 53, 56

cleaner /'kliːnə/ 53

clever /'klevə/ 49

client /'klaɪənt/ 69

cliff(s) /klɪfs/ 92

climb /klaɪm/ 54

close down /ˌkləʊz 'daʊn/ 6

close (to the station) /kləʊs/ 54

close (friend/family) 51

cloud /klaʊd/ 44

cloudy /'klaʊdi/ 8, 44

club (football/golf) /klʌb/ 74, 75

coach (type of transport) /kəʊtʃ/ 68

coat /kəʊt/ 61

coffee table /'kɒfi ˌteɪbl/ 55

coin /kɔɪn/ 58

cold (n, adj) /kəʊld/ 9

cold (= illness) 59

collar /'kɒlə/ 61

colleague /'kɒliːg/ 51, 72

colour /'kʌlə/ 96

comb (your hair) /ˌkəʊm/ 47

come across (= seem) /ˌkʌm ə'krɒs/ 49

come from (I come from Argentina) /'kʌm frəm/ 46

depressing/depressed
/dɪ'presɪŋ/dɪ'prest/ 36
depth /depθ/ 95
desert /'dezət/ 43
design /dɪ'zaɪn/ 70, 96
desk /desk/ 72
despite (the fact that) /dɪ'spaɪt/ 40
dessert /dɪ'zɜːt/ 64, 90
destination /ˌdestɪ'neɪʃən/ 89
destroy /dɪ'strɔɪ/ 43, 88
destruction /dɪ'strʌkʃən/ 88
dial /daɪəl/ 80
dialling code /'daɪəlɪŋ ˌkəʊd/ 80
diamond /'daɪəmənd/ 96
diarrhoea /ˌdaɪə'rɪə/ 59
diary /'daɪəri/ 72
dictator /dɪk'teɪtə/ 86
dictatorship /dɪk'teɪtəʃɪp/ 86
diet (n, v) (go on a diet) /daɪət/ 9
different from /'dɪfərənt frɒm/ 14,
    41
dimension /ˌdaɪ'menʃən/ 95
dining room /'daɪnɪŋ ruːm/ 10, 55
director (film/theatre) /dɪ'rektə/ 76
dirty /'dɜːti/ 3, 8, 65
disagree /ˌdɪsə'griː/ 6, 18
disappear /ˌdɪsə'pɪə/ 6
disappointing/disappointed
    /ˌdɪsə'pɔɪntɪŋ/ /ˌdɪsə'pɔɪntɪd/ 36
disaster /dɪ'zɑːstə/ 43, 88
disaster movie /dɪ'zɑːstə ˌmuːvi/ 76
discuss /dɪ'skʌs/ 7, 35
discussion /dɪ'skʌʃən/ 7
disease /dɪ'ziːz/ 59
disgusting /dɪs'gʌstɪŋ/ 18
dishonest /dɪ'sɒnɪst/ 6, 49
dishwasher /'dɪʃˌwɒʃə/ 10, 55
disk (hard/floppy) /dɪsk/ 81
dislike /dɪ'slaɪk/ 6
dismiss somebody /dɪ'smɪs/ 71
distance /'dɪstəns/ 95
divide (arithmetic) /dɪ'vaɪd/ 94
divided (into) 82
diving /'daɪvɪŋ/ 92
division /dɪ'vɪʒən/ 94
do (my) homework /duː
    'həʊmwɜːk/ 3, 26
do (the) housework /duː
    'haʊswɜːk/ 26
do (my) packing /duː 'pækɪŋ/ 6
do a bit/a lot of sightseeing 91
do a course 26
do a degree 83
do a sport 75
do a subject 26, 82, 83

do an exam 82
do an exercise 1
do not lean out of the window 97
do not leave bags unattended 97
do research (in/into) 26
do somebody a favour 26
do something/nothing 26
do the shopping 26, 62
do up (your jacket) 61
do well/badly 26, 82
Do you think you could …? /duː
    juː ˌθɪŋk juː kʊd/ 17
doctor /'dɒktə/ 70
document /'dɒkjəmənt/ 81, 87
documentary /ˌdɒkjə'mentəri/ 79
dollar /'dɒlə/ 58
don't worry /ˌdəʊnt 'wʌri/ 16
doorbell /'dɔːbel/ 54
dope (= drugs) /dəʊp/ 99
double room /'dʌbl ˌruːm/ 90
doubt (I doubt it) /daʊt/ 21
down /daʊn/ 37
down (= not working) 72
download /ˌdaʊn'ləʊd/ 81
Dr /'dɒktə/ 100
drama series /'drɑːmə ˌsɪəriːz/ 79
draughty /'drɑːfti/ 54
draw (n, v) (= the same score)
    /drɔː/ 74
drawer(s) /drɔːz/ 72
dreadful /'dredfəl/ 36, 76
dream (n, v) (have a dream) /driːm/
    9
drive(r) /'draɪvə/ 68
driving licence /draɪvɪŋ ˌlaɪsəns/ 87
drizzle /'drɪzl/ 44
drop (v) /drɒp/ 57, 73
drop (of milk) 32
drop (v) (= stop) 68
drought /draʊt/ 88
drown /draʊn/ 43
drummer /'drʌmə/ 77
drums /drʌmz/ 77
dry weather /ˌdraɪ 'weðə/ 12
dry wine /ˌdraɪ 'waɪn/ 12
dub (dubbed) /dʌb/ 76
due to (arrive) /'djuː tuː/ 68
due to (= because of) 42
during /'djʊərɪŋ/ 93
duty free /ˌdjuːti 'friː/ 89
DVD /ˌdiː ˌviː 'diː/ 81

e-mail /'iːmeɪl/ 72
e-mail (send/check) 81
e-mail address /'iːmeɪl əˌdres/ 81

e.g. /ˌiː 'dʒiː/ 100
eagle /'iːgl/ 45
earache /'ɪəreɪk/ 59
early night /ˌɜːli 'naɪt/ 13
earn /ɜːn/ 69, 71
earrings /'ɪərɪŋz/ 10, 61
earth /ɜːθ/ 43
earthquake /'ɜːθkweɪk/ 43, 88
easy-going /ˌiːzi'gəʊɪŋ/ 11, 49
economic policy /ˌiːkəˌnɒmɪk
    'pɒləsi/ 86
economical /ˌiːkə'nɒmɪkəl/ 8
economist /ɪ'kɒnəmɪst/ 7
editor /'edɪtə/ 78
Egypt /'iːdʒɪpt/ 46
Egyptian /ɪ'dʒɪpʃən/ 46
elbow /'elbəʊ/ 47
elderly /'eldəli/ 52
elect /ɪ'lekt/ 7, 86
election (win the election) /ɪ'lekʃən/
    7, 86
electrical appliances /ɪˌlektrɪkəl
    ə'plaɪənsɪz/ 62
electrician /ɪˌlek'trɪʃən/ 70
elephant /'elɪfənt/ 45
embarrassing/embarrassed
    /ɪm'bærəsɪŋ/ /ɪm'bærəst/ 36
embarrassment /ɪm'bærəsmənt/ 50
emergency services /ɪˌmɜːdʒənsi
    'sɜːvɪsɪz/ 70
emotional /ɪ'məʊʃənəl/ 8
employee /ɪm'plɔɪiː/ 71
employer /ɪm'plɔɪə/ 7, 71
engaged (= busy) /ɪn'geɪdʒd/ 80
engineer /ˌendʒɪ'nɪə/ 70
engineering /ˌendʒɪ'nɪərɪŋ/ 83
enjoy (+ -ing) /ɪn'dʒɔɪ/ 2, 34
enjoy your meal /ɪnˌdʒɔɪ jɔː 'miːl/
    22
enjoyable /ɪn'dʒɔɪəbl/ 8
enormous /ɪ'nɔːməs/ 36, 54
enough (big enough) /ɪ'nʌf/ 61
enrolment form /ɪn'rəʊlmənt ˌfɔːm/
    87
enter (university) /'entə/ 83
enthusiasm /ɪn'θjuːziæzəm/ 21
environment /ɪn'vaɪrənmənt/ 88
equator /ɪ'kweɪtə/ 43
equipment /ɪ'kwɪpmənt/ 33, 74
escape /ɪ'skeɪp/ 85
etc. /et'setrə/ 100
EU (European Union) /ˌiː'juː/ 100
euro /'jʊərəʊ/ 58
Europe /'jʊərəp/ 46
eventually /ɪ'ventʃuəli/ 39

front garden /ˌfrʌnt ˈgɑːdən/ 54
fruit /fruːt/ 63
fry /fraɪ/ 64
frying pan /ˈfraɪɪŋ pæn/ 10, 55
full board /ˌfʊl ˈbɔːd/ 90
full name /ˌfʊl ˈneɪm/ 51
full of (something) 14
full stop /ˌfʊl ˈstɒp/ 4
full up /ˌfʊl ˈʌp/ 68
full-time (end of game) /ˌfʊlˈtaɪm/ 74
full-time job 11
fully booked /ˌfʊli ˈbʊkt/ 90
fun (play for fun) /fʌn/ 75
furniture /ˈfɜːnɪtʃə/ 33

gale /geɪl/ 44
game show /ˈgeɪm ʃəʊ/ 79
gang (of youths/kids) /gæŋ/ 32
garage /ˈgærɑːʒ/ 54
garlic /ˈgɑːlɪk/ 63
gate /geɪt/ 54, 66, 89
generally /ˈdʒenərəli/ 46
generous /ˈdʒenərəs/ 49
geography /dʒiˈɒgrəfi/ 82
German /ˈdʒɜːmən/ 46
Germany /ˈdʒɜːməni/ 46
get (= arrive/reach) /get/ 29, 67, 99
get (= become) 29
get (= fetch) 29
get (= find/buy) 29
get (= receive) 29, 99
get a bus/train 65
get a job 82
get a place (at university) 83
get away (= escape) 85
get back (= return) 80
get by 24
get changed 29
get delayed/held up 16
get divorced 29, 52
get dressed 6, 29, 61
get fit 75
get home 53
get in (a car) 68
get in touch (with somebody) 99
get into (a fight) 60
get into bed 56
get into trouble 85
get lost 29, 91
get married 14, 29, 52
get off (a bus) 2, 12, 68
get on (a plane) 68, 89
get on (with somebody) 21, 23, 29
get on (my) nerves 13, 29

get out (of a car) 68
get over (an illness) 23
get ready 29
get rid of something /ˌget ˈrɪd əv/ 13, 29
get through (= finish) /ˌget ˈθruː/ 23
get through (= make phone contact) 23, 80
get to know somebody 29
get to work 53
get undressed 6, 29
get up (= get out of bed) 29, 53
get whatever/wherever you want 65
getting (hot/cold/better/worse) /ˈgetɪŋ/ 29
getting nowhere 13
giraffe /dʒɪˈrɑːf/ 45
girlfriend /ˈgɜːlfrend/ 52
give somebody a hand 27
give somebody a hug 27
give somebody a kiss 27
give somebody a lift 27
give somebody a message 80
give somebody a push 27
give somebody a ring 9, 27, 80
give up (= stop doing something) /ˌgɪv ˈʌp/ 23, 34, 75
glance (at) (n, v) /glɑːns/ 50
glass (of water) /glɑːs/ 32
global warming /ˌgləʊbəl ˈwɔːmɪŋ/ 88
glove /glʌv/ 2, 61
go (= its usual position) /gəʊ/ 30
go (= leads to/takes you) 30
go ahead 13
go along here 67
go and get ... 30
go back to school 82
go bald /ˌgəʊ ˈbɔːld/ 30
go bankrupt /ˌgəʊ ˈbæŋkrʌpt/ 30
go blind /ˌgəʊ ˈblaɪnd/ 30
go camping/swimming/diving, etc. 92
go deaf /ˌgəʊ ˈdef/ 30
go down 73
go (out) for a walk/drive/drink/meal 30
go grey 30
go into hospital 60, 82
go into the army/navy 70
go into town 65
go mad 30
go off (= ring) /gəʊ ɒf/ 23
go off (= explode) 23

go off (= go bad) 23
go on (= continue) 83
go on a (training) course 71
go on a diet 9
go on a tour of ... 91
go on holiday 92
go out (social activity) 53, 91
go out with somebody 52
go shopping 62
go sightseeing 91
go skiing/swimming 75
go through customs 89
go to bed 53
go to court 84
go to school/university/church 82
go to sleep 53, 56
go to university 52, 83
go to work 56
go together 30
go up (= increase) 23, 73
go wrong 76
goal /gəʊl/ 74
goat /gəʊt/ 45
goldfish /ˈgəʊlfɪʃ/ 45
golf (course) /gɒlf/ 74
golf (club) /gɒlf/ 74
good at something 14, 82
good for you 75
good fun 49, 76
good luck 22
good morning/afternoon/evening night 22
good-looking /ˌgʊdˈlʊkɪŋ/ 11, 48
gorilla /gəˈrɪlə/ 45
govern /ˈgʌvən/ 7
government /ˈgʌvənmənt/ 7, 86
GP /ˌdʒiːˈpiː/ 70
grade /greɪd/ 82
gradual(ly) /ˈgrædʒuəli/ 73
graduate (n) /ˈgrædʒuət/ 83
graduate (v) /ˈgrædʒueɪt/ 83
grandfather/grandmother /ˈgrænˌfɑːðə/ /ˈgrænˌmʌðə/ 51
grant (n) /grɑːnt/ 83
grapes /greɪps/ 63
grass /grɑːs/ 66
great (= fantastic) /greɪt/ 17, 36
great big (dog) 95
great success /ˌgreɪt səkˈses/ 12
great time /ˌgreɪt ˈtaɪm/ 12
Greece /griːs/ 46
Greek /griːk/ 46
green beans /ˌgriːn ˈbiːnz/ 63
greetings /ˈgriːtɪŋz/ 22
grey /greɪ/ 96

grill (v) /grɪl/ 64
grill (n) 55
gripping /ˈɡrɪpɪŋ/ 76
ground floor /ˌɡraʊnd ˈflɔː/ 54
group (rock/pop) /ɡruːp/ 77
group (of people) 32
grow /ɡrəʊ/ 73
grow (apples/wheat/crops) 66
grow up /ˌɡrəʊ ˈʌp/ 24, 52, 66
guess (n, v) (have a guess) /ɡes/ 9
guess the meaning 3
guidebook /ˈɡaɪdbʊk/ 91
guilty /ˈɡɪlti/ 84
guitar /ɡɪˈtɑː/ 77
guitarist 77 /ɡɪˈtɑːrɪst/
guy /ɡaɪ/ 99
gym /dʒɪm/ 75, 100

hair /heə/ 33
hair dryer /ˈheə ˌdraɪə/ 10
haircut /ˈheəkʌt/ 10
half /hɑːf/ 94
half board /ˌhɑːf ˈbɔːd/ 90
hall /hɔːl/ 55
hand /hænd/ 47
hand luggage /ˈhænd ˌlʌɡɪdʒ/ 33, 89
handbag /ˈhænbæɡ/ 61
handle (v) /ˈhændl/ 69
handsome 48 /ˈhænsəm/
handy 99 /ˈhændi/
hang on /ˌhæŋ ˈɒn/ 13
hang something up 61
hangover /ˈhæŋəʊvə/ 59
happiness /ˈhæpɪnəs/ 7, 50
Happy Birthday/Christmas/New Year 22
hard disk /ˈhɑːd ˌdɪsk/ 81
hard question 12
hard work 12
hard-working /ˌhɑːdˈwɜːkɪŋ/ 49
hardly /hɑːdli/ 38
hardly ever 38
hardware /ˈhɑːdweə/ 81
hat /hæt/ 61
hate /heɪt/ 19, 50
have a baby 25
have a break 53
have a dream 9, 25
have a drink 25
have a(n) early/late night 53
have a go 30
have a guess 9
have a lie-in 53
have a look 9, 25

have a look at something 55
have a look round 91
have a nice weekend 22
have a nice/great/terrible time 25, 91
have a party 25
have a problem (-ing/with something) 25
have a rest 9, 25
have a shower/bath/shave/wash 25, 53, 56
have a sleep 25, 53
have a swim/paddle 92
have a think 25
have a try 25
have a word (with somebody) 25, 99
have an argument 25
have breakfast/lunch/a meal 25, 53
have friends for dinner 53
have got 25
have got something left 28
have something/nothing in common 41
have the bill 25
Have you got the time? 20, 25
head (the ball) /hed/ 74
headache /ˈhedeɪk/ 59
headline /ˈhedlaɪn/ 78
headphones /ˈhedfəʊnz/ 33
healthy /ˈhelθi/ 64
healthy economy 73
hear (versus listen to) /hɪə/ 31
hearing /ˈhɪərɪŋ/ 31
heart /hɑːt/ 59
heart attack /ˈhɑːt əˌtæk/ 59
heat (n) /hiːt/ 44
heat (v) 54
heatwave /ˈhiːtweɪv/ 44
heavy rain 12, 44
heavy smoker 12
heavy traffic 12
Hebrew /ˈhiːbruː/ 46
heel /hiːl/ 47
height /haɪt/ 95
height (medium height) 48
held up (be/get held up) /ˌheld ˈʌp/ 16
help yourself /help jɔːˈself/ 17
helpful /ˈhelpfəl/ 8
hemisphere (northern/southern) /ˈhemɪsfɪə/ 43
hepatitis /ˌhepəˈtaɪtɪs/ 59
herd (of cows) /hɜːd/ 32
high /haɪ/ 95

high-rise (building) /ˌhaɪˈraɪz/ 65
highlight (new words) /ˈhaɪlaɪt/ 5
highlighter pen /ˈhaɪˌlaɪtə pen/ 5
highlights (recorded highlights) /ˈhaɪlaɪts/ 79
hijack /ˈhaɪdʒæk/ 88
hiking /haɪkɪŋ/ 75
hip /hɪp/ 47
hire /haɪə/ 89
historic monuments /hɪˌstɒrɪk ˈmɒnjəmənts/ 91
history /ˈhɪstəri/ 82
history of art 83
hit (a ball) /hɪt/ 74
hit (= affect badly) 43, 78
hit (record/single) 77
hit (your head) 60
hob /hɒb/ 55
hockey /ˈhɒki/ 74
hold /həʊld/ 31
hold (an election) 86
homeless /ˈhəʊmləs/ 8
homesick /ˈhəʊmsɪk/ 3
homework /ˈhəʊmwɜːk/ 33
honest /ˈɒnɪst/ 49
hoover (v) /ˈhuːvə/ 56
hoover/vacuum cleaner 56
hope (+ inf) /həʊp/ 34
hopeless /ˈhəʊpləs/ 66
hopeless at something 82
horizon /həˈraɪzən/ 92
horror film /ˈhɒrə ˌfɪlm/ 76
hospital /ˈhɒspɪtəl/ 70
hostage /ˈhɒstɪdʒ/ 88
hot /hɒt/ 44
household (goods) /ˌhaʊsəʊld/ 62
housework /ˈhaʊswɜːk/ 3, 33, 56
How about you? 20, 22
How about (+ -ing)? 17
How are things? 98
How are you getting on? 29
How are you? 20, 22
How do I get to ...? 20, 90
How do you do? 22
How do you feel about ...? 18
How do you pronounce ...? 5
How do you spell ...? 5
How do you use ...? 5
how fantastic/exciting/awful 21
How far is it? 20, 95
How long are you here for? 20
How long are you staying? 20
How long does it take? 26
How long have you been here? 20
How long/wide/high/deep is ...? 95

How much does he/she weigh? *48*
How much is that? *20*
How much longer (are you
  staying)? *20*
How old are you? *20*
How tall is he/she? *48*
How was (the party)? *20*
however /haʊ'evə/ *40*
How's it going? *20, 22, 30*
hug (give somebody a hug) /hʌg/ *27*
huge /hjuːdʒ/ *36, 54*
humid /'hjuːmɪd/ *44*
humidity /hjuː'mɪdəti/ *44*
hundred /'hʌndrəd/ *94*
hungry (be hungry) /'hʌŋgri/ *25*
hurricane /'hʌrɪkən/ *43, 44*
hurry up /ˌhʌri 'ʌp/ *23*
hurt /hɜːt/ *60*
hurt (oneself) *59*
hyphen /'haɪfən/ *4*

I (don't) think so *21*
I beg your pardon *16*
I don't mind *17, 21*
I doubt it *21*
I haven't a clue *13*
I hope not *21*
I hope so *21*
I regret to inform you *99*
I see *21, 27*
I see what you mean *18, 27*
I take your point *18*
I was wondering if …? *17*
I won't be long *16*
i.e. /ˌaɪ 'iː/ *100*
ice /aɪs/ *44*
ice hockey *75*
icy /'aɪsi/ *44*
identity card (ID) /aɪ'dentəti kɑːd/
  87, 100
idiom /'ɪdiəm/ *4*
idiot /'ɪdiət/ *49*
if you like *13, 17, 21*
ill /ɪl/ *1*
illegal /ɪ'liːgəl/ *6, 84, 85*
illegible /ɪ'ledʒəbl/ *6*
illness (serious illness) /'ɪlnəs/ *7, 59*
imagine (+ -ing) /ɪ'mædʒɪn/ *34*
impatient /ɪm'peɪʃənt/ *6*
impolite /ˌɪmpəl'aɪt/ *3, 6*
impossible /ɪm'pɒsəbl/ *6*
impression (make a good
  impression) /ɪm'preʃən/ *49*
improve /ɪm'pruːv/ *7*
improvement /ɪm'pruːvmənt/ *7*

in (Africa) *37*
in (April) *93*
in (ten days') time *93*
in a hurry *15, 65*
in a mess *6*
in a moment *15*
in a newspaper/magazine *15*
in addition *40*
in advance *76, 90*
in business *15*
in charge of *69, 71*
in comparison with *41*
in danger of extinction *45*
in front of *37*
in general *46*
in good condition *54*
in love *15*
in my opinion *18*
in order to *42*
in other words *100*
in power *86*
in practice *13*
in spite of *40*
in the blue jumper/dark glasses *15*
in the centre *54*
in the country/countryside *66*
in the end *15, 39*
in the long term *13*
in the morning/afternoon/evening *15*
in the short term *13*
in the wild *45*
in theory *13*
in time *15*
in your twenties/thirties, etc. *52*
in-house (training) /ˌɪn'haʊs/ *71*
inadequate /ɪ'nædɪkwət/ *6*
included (Is breakfast included?)
  /ɪn'kluːdɪd/ *90*
income /'ɪŋkʌm/ *69*
income tax *10, 69*
incomprehensible
  /ɪnˌkɒmprɪ'hensəbl/ *8*
incorrect /ˌɪnkər'ekt/ *6*
increase (n, v) /'ɪnkriːs/ *73*
incredibly (expensive/cheap)
  /ɪn'kredɪbli/ *38, 58*
indefinite article /ɪnˌdefɪnət 'ɑːtɪkl/
  4
independent school /ˌɪndɪ'pendənt
  ˌskuːl/ *82*
industrial /ɪn'dʌstriəl/ *8*
infinitive /ɪn'fɪnətɪv/ *4*
inflation /ɪn'fleɪʃən/ *73*
inflexible /ɪn'fleksəbl/ *49*
inform /ɪn'fɔːm/ *7*

informal /ɪn'fɔːməl/ *6*
information /ˌɪnfə'meɪʃən/ *7, 33*
information technology *82*
injection /ɪn'dʒekʃən/ *59*
injure /'ɪndʒə/ *60*
injured (badly injured) /'ɪndʒəd/ *67*
injury /'ɪndʒəri/ *60*
innocent /'ɪnəsənt/ *84*
insect /'ɪnsekt/ *45*
insensitive /ɪn'sensətɪv/ *49*
install /ɪn'stɔːl/ *70*
interest (pay interest) /'ɪntrəst/ *73*
interest (v) *1*
interest rate /'ɪntrəst reɪt/ *73*
interested in something /'ɪntrəstɪd
  ɪn/ *14, 19*
(the) Internet (the Net) /'ɪntənet/
  81
into /'ɪntuː/ *37*
intransitive verb /ɪnˌtrænsətɪv
  'vɜːb/ *4*
investigate /ɪn'vestɪgeɪt/ *84*
investment /ɪn'vesmənt/ *73*
invisible /ɪn'vɪzəbl/ *6, 8*
invoice /'ɪnvɔɪs/ *72*
involve /ɪn'vɒlv/ *69, 71*
iron /aɪən/ *56*
ironing (do the ironing) /'aɪənɪŋ/
  53, 56
irregular (verbs) /ɪ'regjələ/ *6*
irresponsible /ˌɪrɪ'spɒnsəbl/ *6*
Is that …? (on the phone) /ɪz ˌðæt/
  80
Is this the first time you've been
  to …? *20*
island /'aɪlənd/ *3, 43*
ISP (Internet Service Provider)
  /ˌaɪes'piː/ *81, 100*
Israel /'ɪzreɪl/ *46*
Israeli /ɪz'reɪli/ *46*
it doesn't matter *16*
It says (in the paper) /ɪt ˌsez/ *78*
Italian /ɪ'tæliən/ *46*
Italy /'ɪtəli/ *46*
it's a bit difficult (actually) … *17*
it's up to you *13*
I'd love to *17*
I'll clear it up *16*
I'll leave it *62*
I'll sort it out *16*
I'll take it/them *62*
I'm (very) sorry *16*
I'm afraid I can't *17*
I'm afraid not *17, 21*
I'm afraid so *21*

pepper (red/green) 63
per cent /pɜː 'sent/ 94
perform /pəˈfɔːm/ 77
performance /pəˈfɔːməns/ 76
perhaps /pəˈhæps/ 18
personally I ... /ˈpɜːsənəli aɪ/ 18
persuade (somebody + inf) /pəˈsweɪd/ 35
pessimistic /ˌpesɪˈmɪstɪk/ 49
pet /pet/ 45
petrol station /ˈpetrəl ˌsteɪʃən/ 67
PhD /ˌpiːeɪtʃˈdiː/ 83
philosophy /fɪˈlɒsəfi/ 83
phone /fəʊn/ 100
phone box/card/number 80
phone somebody back 80
photo (photograph) /ˈfəʊtəʊ/ 26, 100
photocopier /ˈfəʊtəˌkɒpiə/ 5, 72
photocopy /ˈfəʊtəˌkɒpi/ 5
photographer /fəˈtɒgrəfə/ 78
phrasal verb /ˈfreɪzəl ˌvɜːb/ 4
physics /ˈfɪzɪks/ 82
pianist /ˈpiːənɪst/ 77
piano /piˈænəʊ/ 77
pick something up (= take it using one's hands) /ˌpɪk ˈʌp/ 23
pick something/somebody up (= collect) 23, 99
piece (of toast/advice) /piːs/ 32
pig /pɪg/ 45
pillow /ˈpɪləʊ/ 56
pilot /ˈpaɪlət/ 68, 70
pineapple /ˈpaɪnæpl/ 63
pink /pɪŋk/ 96
piss (v) (slang) /pɪs/ 99
pitch /pɪtʃ/ 74
pity (that's a pity) /ˈpɪti/ 21
place /pleɪs/ 91
place of birth 87
plain /pleɪn/ 48
plan (v) /plæn/ 70
plane /pleɪn/ 68, 100
planet /ˈplænɪt/ 88
plant /plɑːnt/ 66
plant bombs 88
plaster /ˈplɑːstə/ 60
plate /pleɪt/ 90
platform /ˈplætfɔːm/ 3, 68
play (n) /pleɪ/ 76
play a game 75
play cards /ˌpleɪ ˈkɑːdz/ 53
pleasant /ˈplezənt/ 49
please accept our apologies 16
please do not disturb 97

please do not feed the animals 97
please queue other side 97
pleased to meet you 22
plenty (there's plenty to do) /ˈplenti/ 65
plug /plʌg/ 5
plug something in /ˌplʌg ˈɪn/ 5, 79
plum /plʌm/ 63
plumber /ˈplʌmə/ 70
plural noun /ˌplʊərəl ˈnaʊn/ 4
plus /plʌs/ 94
PM (Prime Minister) /ˌpiːˈem/ 100
pocket /ˈpɒkɪt/ 61
point /pɔɪnt/ 96
point (at something/somebody) 50
point (decimal) 94
point (I don't see the point of ...) 27
point (I take your point) 18
pointed /ˈpɔɪntɪd/ 96
Poland /ˈpəʊlənd/ 46
pole (north/south) /pəʊl/ 43
police force /pəˈliːs ˌfɔːs/ 70
police officer /pəˈliːs ˌɒfɪsə/ 70
policeman/policewoman /pəˈliːsmən/ /pəˈliːswʊmən/ 70
policy (economic/foreign) /ˈpɒləsi/ 86
Polish /ˈpəʊlɪʃ/ 46
polite /pəˈlaɪt/ 3
political /pəˈlɪtɪkəl/ 8
political party 86
politician /pɒlɪˈtɪʃən/ 86
politics /ˈpɒlətɪks/ 83, 86
pollute /pəˈluːt/ 88
polluted /pəˈluːtɪd/ 65
pollution /pəˈluːʃən/ 88
pond /pɒnd/ 2
pop music /pɒp/ 77
pop singer 7
pop star 10
popular press /ˌpɒpjələ ˈpres/ 78
population /ˌpɒpjəˈleɪʃən/ 46
pork /pɔːk/ 63
porter /ˈpɔːtə/ 90
Portuguese /ˌpɔːtʃəˈgiːz/ 46
possibly /ˈpɒsəbli/ 18
post office /ˈpəʊst ˌɒfɪs/ 10
postbox /ˈpəʊstbɒks/ 10
postgraduate (course/degree) /ˌpəʊsˈgrædʒuət/ 83
postman /ˈpəʊsmən/ 10
potato /pəˈteɪtəʊ/ 63
pour (with rain) /pɔː/ 44
prawn /prɔːn/ 63

prefer (I'd prefer to ...) /prɪˈfɜː/ 17, 19
prefer (+ -ing or inf) 34
prefer (Which do/would you prefer?) 19
prefer (I prefer X to Y) 19
prefix /ˈpriːfɪks/ 4
pregnant /ˈpregnənt/ 52
preposition /ˌprepəˈzɪʃən/ 4
prescription /prɪˈskrɪpʃən/ 59
press (a button) /pres/ 31, 50
pretty (adv) /ˈprɪti/ 38
pretty (adj) /ˈprɪti/ 48
prevent /prɪˈvent/ 67, 85
price /praɪs/ 58
pride /praɪd/ 50
primary school /ˈpraɪməri ˌskuːl/ 82
Prime Minister /ˌpraɪm ˈmɪnɪstə/ 86
print /prɪnt/ 81, 87
print something out /ˌprɪnt ˈaʊt/ 81
printer /ˈprɪntə/ 81
prison (in prison) /ˈprɪzən/ 84
prisoner /ˈprɪzənə/ 84
privacy /ˈprɪvəsi/ 66
private school /ˌpraɪvɪt ˈskuːl/ 82
prize /praɪz/ 79
proceed to ... /prəˌsiːd ˈtuː/ 99
produce (= manufacture) /ˈprɒdˈjuːs/ 72
produce an album 77
profession /prəˈfeʃən/ 70
professional (footballer) /prəˈfeʃənəl/ 7
professor /prəˈfesə/ 83
profit (make a profit) /ˈprɒfɪt/ 73
program (computer) /ˈprəʊgræm/ 81
programme (TV) 79
progress (make progress) /ˈprəʊgres/ 26, 33
promise (+ inf) /ˈprɒmɪs/ 34
promote /prəˈməʊt/ 71
pronounce /prəˈnaʊns/ 1
properly (it isn't working properly) /ˈprɒpəli/ 57
property /ˈprɒpəti/ 85
prospects /ˈprɒspekts/ 71
protect /prəˈtekt/ 45, 88
protect (oneself) 85
protect your skin /prəˌtekt jɔ ˈskɪn/ 92
protection /prəˈtekʃən/ 88
proud (of) /praʊd/ 50

rural (area) /ˈrʊərəl/ 66
rush hour /ˈrʌʃ ˌaʊə/ 65
rushed (to hospital) /rʌʃt/ 60
Russia /ˈrʌʃə/ 46
Russian /ˈrʌʃən/ 46

sack (v) /sæk/ 71
sadness /ˈsædnəs/ 50
safe (adj) /seɪf/ 65
safe (n) 85
sailor /ˈseɪlə/ 70
salad /ˈsæləd/ 63
salad dressing /ˈsæləd dresɪŋ/ 63
salary /ˈsæləri/ 69, 71
sales rep /ˈseɪlz ˌrep/ 100
salmon /ˈsæmən/ 63
salt /sɔːlt/ 64
salty /ˈsɔːlti/ 64
same to you /ˌseɪm tu: ˈjuː/ 22
sand /sænd/ 92
sandy (beach) /ˈsændi/ 92
satellite TV/dish /ˈsætəlaɪt
    ti:ˈviː/ˈdɪʃ/ 79
satisfied (with something)
    /ˈsætɪsfaɪd/ 14
saucepan /ˈsɔːspən/ 2, 55
saucer /ˈsɔːsə/ 55
Saudi Arabia /ˌsaʊdi əˈreɪbiə/ 46
Saudi Arabian /ˌsaʊdi əˈreɪbiən/ 46
save (= conserve) /seɪv/ 88
save (up) 23, 58
save (data) 81
saxophone/saxophonist
    /ˈsæksəfəʊn/ˈsækˈsɒfənɪst/ 77
say (the paper/TV says that …)
    /seɪ/ 18
say (that + clause) 35
say the word aloud 1
scales /skeɪlz/ 33
scar /skɑː/ 48
scarf /skɑːf/ 61
science /ˈsaɪəns/ 82
science fiction /ˌsaɪəns ˈfɪkʃən/ 10
scissors /ˈsɪzəz/ 33
score /skɔː/ 74
screen (cinema) /skriːn/ 76
screen (computer) 81
sea /siː/ 43
seafood /ˈsiːfuːd/ 63
search engine /ˈsɜːtʃ ˌendʒɪn/ 81
seaside resort /ˈsiːsaɪd rɪˌzɔːt/ 92
seat /siːt/ 3
seats (in parliament) 86
second(ly) /ˈsekəndli/ 39
second(s) (n) /ˈsekəndz/ 93

second-hand /ˌsekənˈhænd/ 11
secondary school /ˈsekəndəri
    ˌskuːl/ 82
see (= understand) /siː/ 27
see (= find out) 3, 27
see versus watch versus look at 31
see you later/tomorrow/soon 22
seem (+ inf) /siːm/ 34
seldom /ˈseldəm/ 38
self-confident /ˌselfˈkɒnfɪdənt/ 49
self-employed /ˌselfɪmˈplɔɪd/ 69
self-service /ˌselfˈsɜːvɪs/ 67
self-study /ˌselfˈstʌdi/ 1
sell /sel/ 70
semi-circle /ˈsemiˌsɜːkl/ 96
send (e-mail) /send/ 72
sense of humour /ˌsens əv ˈhjuːmə/
    49
senses /ˈsensɪz/ 31
sensitive /ˈsensɪtɪv/ 49
sentence (prison) /ˈsentəns/ 84
separated /ˈsepəreɪtɪd/ 51
series (comedy/drama) /ˈsɪəriːz/ 79
serious injury /ˌsɪəriəs ˈɪndʒəri/ 12
seriously injured /ˌsɪəriəsli ˈɪndʒəd/
    60
set (be set in …) /set/ 76
set off /ˌset ˈɒf/ 24
set the alarm 56
shade /ʃeɪd/ 96
shake (hands) /ʃeɪk/ 47
shake your head 47
Shall we …? /ˈʃæl wiː/ 17
shallow (lake) /ˈʃæləʊ/ 95
shame (what a shame) /ʃeɪm/ 21
shape /ʃeɪp/ 96
share /ʃeə/ 5
shark /ʃɑːk/ 45
sharp(ly) /ˈʃɑːpli/ 73
sheep /ʃiːp/ 45
sheet /ʃiːt/ 56
sheet (of paper) 32
shiftwork /ˈʃɪftwɜːk/ 69
shirt /ʃɜːt/ 61
shoe /ʃuː/ 61
shoot /ʃuːt/ 60
shop around /ʃɒp əˈraʊnd/ 62
shop manager 7
shop window 62
shop/sales assistant 62
shoplift(er) /ˈʃɒpˌlɪftə/ 85
shoplifting /ˈʃɒplɪftɪŋ/ 85
shopping (do the shopping) /ˈʃɒpɪŋ/
    53
shopping centre 62, 65

shopping list 62
short /ʃɔːt/ 48, 95
short-sleeved /ˌʃɔːtˈsliːvd/ 11
shorts /ʃɔːts/ 33, 75
shoulder /ˈʃəʊldə/ 47
shout (at somebody/to somebody)
    /ʃaʊt/ 14, 50
show (somebody + wh- word) /ʃəʊ/
    35
show (= for people to see) 76
show one's feelings 49
show somebody (a)round 72
shower (in the bathroom) /ˈʃaʊə/
    56
shower (of rain) 44
shower curtain 56
showery /ˈʃaʊəri/ 44
shy /ʃaɪ/ 49
sick (be sick/feel sick) /sɪk/ 59
sick pay 69
sight /saɪt/ 31
sightseeing /ˈsaɪtsiːɪŋ/ 91
sightseeing tour 91
sign (your name) /saɪn/ 87
signature /ˈsɪgnətʃə/ 87
silence (silence: exam in progress)
    /ˈsaɪləns/ 97
silent(ly) /ˈsaɪləntli/ 1
similar /ˈsɪmɪlə/ 41
similar (to) 7, 14
similar taste 41
similarity (a similarity between X
    and Y) /ˈsɪmɪˈlærəti/ 7, 41
since (+ a point in time) /sɪns/ 93
single (not married) /ˈsɪŋgl/ 20
single (hit single) 77
single (n) (single to Edinburgh) 68
single room 90
single-parent (family)
    /ˌsɪŋglˈpeərənt/ 51
sink /sɪŋk/ 55
sister-in-law /ˈsɪstərɪnlɔː/ 51
sit down /ˌsɪt ˈdaʊn/ 23
size /saɪz/ 61, 62
skiing /ˈskiːɪŋ/ 75
skilled /skɪld/ 70
skin (dark/pale) /skɪn/ 47, 48
skirt /skɜːt/ 61
skis /skiːz/ 75
skyscraper /ˈskaɪˌskreɪpə/ 65
slang /slæŋ/ 99
sleeves /sliːvz/ 61
slice (of bread) /slaɪs/ 32
slight (accent) /slaɪt/ 12
slightly /ˈslaɪtli/ 38

surrounded (by) /sə'raʊndɪd/ 66
survival /sə'vaɪvəl/ 88
survive /sə'vaɪv/ 88
swap places /,swɒp 'pleɪsɪz/ 5
sweet /swiːt/ 64
sweet wine 12
swimming (costume/trunks) /'swɪmɪŋ/ 75
swimming pool 75
Swiss /swɪs/ 46
switch off (the light) /swɪtʃ ɒf/ 56
switch something on/off/over 79
Switzerland /'swɪtsələnd/ 46
swollen /'swəʊlən/ 60
syllable /'sɪləbl/ 4
sympathetic /,sɪmpə'θetɪk/ 49
symptom /'sɪmtəm/ 59
synonym /'sɪnənɪm/ 4

T-shirt /'tiːʃɜːt/ 10
table tennis /'teɪbl ,tenɪs/ 74
tabloid /'tæblɔɪd/ 78
tailback /'teɪlbæk/ 67
take (= steal) /teɪk/ 85
take a break 26
take a bus/taxi 26, 65, 68
take a decision 2, 26
take a photo 2, 26, 91
take a seat 26
take a shower 2, 26
take after somebody 51
take an exam 26, 82
take it in turns 13
take off (= leave the ground) /'teɪk ɒf/ 23, 24
take-off (n) /'teɪkɒf/ 89
take over (= take control) 71
take place 86
take something back (= return it) 23
take something off (= remove clothes) 23, 24
take something seriously 75
take something up (= start a sport/hobby) 75
take the first/second turning on the left/right 67
take time (e.g. it takes 20 minutes) 2, 26, 93
take time off 26
talks /tɔːks/ 78
tall /tɔːl/ 48, 95
tan /tæn/ 92
tap /tæp/ 55
tape /teɪp/ 5

tape recorder /'teɪp rɪ,kɔːdə/ 5
tartan /'tɑːtən/ 96
taste (n, v) /teɪst/ 9, 64
taste (in music) 77
taste (v) (it tastes strange) 31
taste (n) (the taste of olives) 31
taste like (it tastes like chicken) 31
tasty /'teɪsti/ 64
tax cut /'tæks kʌt/ 73
taxi /'tæksi/ 68
taxi rank 68
teacher /'tiːtʃə/ 83
team /tiːm/ 75
teenager /'tiːn,eɪdʒə/ 52
telephone directory /'telɪfəʊn dɪ,rektəri/ 80
television commercial /'telɪvɪʒən kə'mɜːʃəl/ 79
television/TV /'telɪvɪʒən/ /,tiː'viː/ 79
tell (somebody + inf) /tel/ 35
tell (somebody + wh- word) 35
tell a joke 12, 47
tell a story 12
tell the truth 12
telly/TV /'teli/ /,tiː'viː/ 100
temperature (weather) /'temprətʃə/ 44
temperature (body) 59
temple /'templ/ 91
ten-minute walk /,tenmɪnɪt 'wɔːk/ 11
ten-pound note /,tenpaʊnd 'nəʊt/ 58
ten-year-old (boy/girl) /'tenjɪərəʊld/ 11
tend to /tend tuː/ 46
tennis /'tenɪs/ 74
tense /tens/ 49
tent /tent/ 92
term /tɜːm/ 82
terminal building /'tɜːmɪnəl bɪldɪŋ/ 89
terrible pain /'terəbl peɪn/ 59
terribly (sorry) (to bother you) /'terəbli/ 12
terrific /tə'rɪfɪk/ 36, 99
terrifying/terrified /'terəfaɪŋ/ /'terəfaɪd/ 36
terrorism /'terərɪzəm/ 88
terrorist /'terərɪst/ 88
text message /'tekst ,mesɪdʒ/ 80
thank you /'θæŋk juː/ 22
thank you very much 16
thanks (a lot) /θæŋks/ 16

that sort of thing 19, 98
that sounds interesting/wonderful/terrible 17, 21
that's a good idea 17
that's great/brilliant/dreadful 21
that's OK 16
that's to say (i.e.) 100
that's very kind of you 16
the other day 93
the press 78
theft /θeft/ 85
then /ðen/ 39
therefore /'ðeəfɔː/ 42
there's something wrong with ... 57, 90
these days /'ðiːz deɪz/ 93
thick (= stupid) /θɪk/ 99
thick fog 44
thief /θiːf/ 85
thigh /θaɪ/ 47
thin /θɪn/ 48
thing(s) /θɪŋz/ 98
thing (best/worst thing about ...) /θɪŋ/ 65, 66
things (are going well) 98
things got worse 57
things like that 19, 98
think (I think .../I don't think ...) /θɪŋk/ 18
thinking (of going/doing) /,θɪŋkɪŋ/ 14
third(ly) /'θɜːdli/ 39
thirsty (be thirsty) /'θɜːsti/ 25
though /ðəʊ/ 40
thoughtful /'θɔːtfəl/ 8
thousand /'θaʊzənd/ 94
three-quarters /,θriː'kwɔːtəz/ 94
thriller /'θrɪlə/ 76
through /θruː/ 37
throw (something at somebody/to somebody) /θrəʊ/ 14, 74
throw something away 24, 88
thumb /θʌm/ 2, 47
thunder and lightning /,θʌndə ən 'laɪtnɪŋ/ 44
thunderstorm /'θʌndəstɔːm/ 44
thus /ðʌs/ 99
tick /tɪk/ 3
tidy /'taɪdi/ 56
tie /taɪ/ 61
tiger /'taɪgə/ 45
tights /taɪts/ 61
till /tɪl/ 62
time difference /'taɪm ,dɪfərəns/ 43
(It's) time to go 30

wake up /ˌweɪk ˈʌp/ 23, 24, 53
want (somebody + inf) /wɒnt/ 35
want (+ inf) 34
war /wɔː/ 88
war film 76
wardrobe /ˈwɔːdrəʊb/ 56
warn (somebody + inf) /wɔːn/ 35
warning /ˈwɔːnɪŋ/ 97
wash (my hair) /wɒʃ/ 53
washable /ˈwɒʃəbl/ 8
washbasin /ˈwɒʃˌbeɪsən/ 56
washing (do the washing) /ˈwɒʃɪŋ/ 53, 56
washing machine /ˈwɒʃɪŋ məˌʃiːn/ 10, 55, 56
washing-up (do the washing-up) /ˌwɒʃɪŋˈʌp/ 53, 56
waste (v) /weɪst/ 58
waste (n, v) 88
waste time/money 12
wastepaper basket /ˌweɪsˈpeɪpə ˌbɑːskɪt/ 72
watch (versus see versus look at) /wɒtʃ/ 31
wave (goodbye) /weɪv/ 50
waves /weɪvz/ 92
wavy hair /ˈweɪvi heə/ 48
we could … /wiː ˌkʊd/ 17
weak (opp strong) /wiːk/ 7
weak coffee 12
weakness (the main weakness) /ˈwiːknəs/ 7
weapon /ˈwepən/ 60
weather /ˈweðə/ 2
website /ˈwebsaɪt/ 81
weekly /ˈwiːkli/ 78
weigh (your luggage) /weɪ/ 89
weigh oneself 33
weight /weɪt/ 48
well aware of the problem 12
well done /ˌwel ˈdʌn/ 22
well-behaved /ˌwelbɪˈheɪvd/ 11
well-done (meat) /ˌwelˈdʌn/ 64
well-equipped /ˌwelɪˈkwɪpt/ 11
well-known /ˌwelˈnəʊn/ 11
well-off /ˌwelˈɒf/ 11, 58
well-organised /ˌwelˈɔːgənaɪzd/ 11

well-paid /ˌwelˈpeɪd/ 11
well-written /ˌwelˈrɪtən/ 11
wet weather /wet ˈweðə/ 12
whale /weɪl/ 45
What about …? 17
What are you doing at the moment? 20
What are you doing this evening? 20
What do you do for a living? 69
What do you do? 20, 69
What do you think about …? 18
What do you think of …? 18
What does (it) stand for? 100
What does he/she look like? 48
What does X mean? 5
What sort/kind of …? 20
What time do you have breakfast? 25
What time's (the film) on? 79
whatever you like 21
What's (the flat) like? 20
what's more 40
What's on? 79
What's the difference between X and Y? 5
What's the length/width of …? 95
What's the matter? 20
What's up? 13, 99
What's your address/phone number? 20
What's your job? 69
when /wen/ 39
whenever you like 21
Where are you from? 20
Where do you come from? 20
Whereabouts? 20
whereas /weəˈræz/ 40
wherever you like 21
while /ˈwaɪl/ 39
whisper (n, v) /ˈwɪspə/ 50
whistle (n) /ˈwɪsl/ 74
(the) whole page/book 1
Who's calling? (on the phone) 80
Why don't we …? 17
wide /waɪd/ 95
wide awake /ˌwaɪd əˈweɪk/ 12

wide range /ˌwaɪd ˈreɪndʒ/ 65
widow /ˈwɪdəʊ/ 51
widower /ˈwɪdəʊə/ 51
width /wɪtθ/ 95
win /wɪn/ 74
wind /wɪnd/ 44
window shopping /ˈwɪndəʊ ˌʃɒpɪŋ/ 62
windsurfing /ˈwɪnsɜːfɪŋ/ 92
windy /ˈwɪndi/ 44
wine glass /ˈwaɪn glɑːs/ 90
wine list 90
winner /ˈwɪnə/ 74
witness (n) /ˈwɪtnəs/ 84, 85
woods /wʊdz/ 66
work (in a bank) /wɜːk/ 69
work (for a company) 69
work (= function) (it isn't working) 57, 72
work at a computer 72
work something out (= calculate) 94
working hours /ˈwɜːkɪŋ ˌaʊəz/ 69
world /wɜːld/ 43, 86
worldwide /ˌwɜːldˈwaɪd/ 81
worry about something/somebody /ˈwʌri əˌbaʊt/ 14
worth (+ -ing) /wɜːθ/ 58, 91
worth a visit 91
would rather (I'd rather …) /wʊd ˈrɑːðə/ 17, 19
Would you like to …? 17
wound (n, v) /wuːnd/ 60
wrist /rɪst/ 2, 47
write something down 5
writing paper /ˈraɪtɪŋ ˌpeɪpə/ 10
wrong number /ˌrɒŋ ˈnʌmbə/ 80
WWW (World Wide Web) /ˌdʌbljuːdʌbljuːˈdʌbljuː/ 100

yacht /jɒt/ 92
yawn /jɔːn/ 47
you get (= it exists) 66

zebra /ˈzebrə/ 45
zero /ˈzɪərəʊ/ 44, 94
zoo /zuː/ 45

Acknowledgements

For this new edition I am particularly grateful to lexicographer Julie Moore. Working with the *Cambridge International Corpus* of written and spoken English, she has provided information and insights which have been invaluable in guiding lexical selection and example sentences in the book.

A number of people have reviewed different parts of the manuscript and given me extremely useful feedback. My thanks to the following reviewers:

Miles Craven, Cambridge, UK
Eryl Griffiths, Cambridge, UK
Agnieska Lenko-Szymanska, Milanowek, Poland
Chris Nicol, Cannes, France
Jeanine Saelens, Heule, Belgium
Olga Vinogradova, Moscow, Russia

My editor Alison Silver has been wonderful. She has worked with great professionalism on a long and intricate manuscript, and the final product is immeasurably improved as a result of her contribution. My thanks to Ruth Carim for her proof-reading and comments on the final manuscript.

Finally, I would like to thank Oxford Designers & Illustrators for their elegant design of this new edition, and Nóirín Burke at Cambridge University Press. Nóirín has guided the project from its infancy, and coordinated the various stages of both editions with calm efficiency.

Stuart Redman

London, 2002

The author and publishers would like to thank the following for permission to reproduce photographs and other illustrative material:

p. 158 newspaper mast heads: Daily Mirror © Mirror Syndication International, The Guardian © Guardian Newspapers Limited 2002, The Sun © N I Syndication Limited, London, 3 December 2002, The Independent © Independent Newspapers (UK) Limited, The Times © N I Syndication Limited, London, 3 December 2002, Daily Mail by permission of Atlantic Syndication; p. 182 Corbis (©Macduff Everton); p. 184 Objectif Photos.

Illustrations by Sophie Joyce, Nick Davies, David Mostyn and Oxford Designers & Illustrators.